Communications
in Computer and Information Science 247

Costantino Grana Rita Cucchiara (Eds.)

Multimedia for Cultural Heritage

First International Workshop, MM4CH 2011
Modena, Italy, May 3, 2011
Revised Selected Papers

Springer

Volume Editors

Costantino Grana
Rita Cucchiara
Università degli Studi di Modena e Reggio Emilia
Dipartimento di Ingegneria dell'Informazione
Via Vignolese 905/b, 41125 Modena, Italy
E-mail: costantino.grana@unimore.it, rita.cucchiara@unimore.it

ISSN 1865-0929 e-ISSN 1865-0937
ISBN 978-3-642-27977-5 ISBN 978-3-642-27978-2 (eBook)
DOI 10.1007/978-3-642-27978-2
Springer Heidelberg Dordrecht London New York

Library of Congress Control Number: 2011945108

CR Subject Classification (1998): H.5, H.4, I.2, H.3, I.4, I.5

Typesetting: Camera-ready by author, data conversion by Scientific Publishing Services, Chennai, India

Printed on acid-free paper

Springer is part of Springer Science+Business Media (www.springer.com)

Preface

Multimedia technologies have recently created the conditions for a true revolution in the cultural heritage area, with reference to the study, valorization, and fruition of artistic works. The use of these technologies allows the creation of new digital cultural experiences by means of personalized and engaging interaction. New multimedia technologies could be used to design new approaches to the comprehension and fruition of the artistic heritage, for example, through smart, context-aware artifacts and enhanced interfaces with the support of features like story-telling, gaming and learning. To these aims, open and flexible platforms are needed, to allow building of services that support the use of cultural resources for research and education. A likely expectation is the involvement of a wider range of users of cultural resources in diverse contexts and considerably altered ways to experience and share cultural knowledge between participants.

The First International Workshop on Multimedia for Cultural Heritage (MM4CH 2011) was held in Modena, Italy on May 3, 2011, with the aim of creating a profitable informal working day to discuss hot topics in multimedia, with specific application to cultural heritage. The workshop was particularly successful in bringing together people from different countries (Czech Republic, Greece, Germany, Italy, The Netherlands, Spain, Switzerland, USA), who shared their opinions during the two oral sessions and the poster/demo session also extended during lunch. The afternoon discussion was an important venue in which to present and compare researchers' opinions related to different topics, partially inspired by the EU work program topics.

Of the 25 papers received for reviewing, 17 were accepted (68% acceptance rate), of which 8 for oral presentations and 9 for poster presentation. This volume collects the 17 presented papers, revised according to the reviewers' suggestions, and another one which resumes the outcome of the discussion session, with proper reference to the literature.

We wish to thank all people in the Scientific Committee, who provided tremendous help during the reviewing process, perfectly respecting the deadlines and giving effective advice for manuscript preparation. We also thank everyone at ImageLab who contributed to the success of the workshop.

October 2011

Costantino Grana
Rita Cucchiara

Organization

Workshop Chairs

Costantino Grana	Università di Modena e Reggio Emilia, Italy
Rita Cucchiara	Università di Modena e Reggio Emilia, Italy

Local Chair

Daniele Borghesani	Università di Modena e Reggio Emilia, Italy

Scientific Committee

Maristella Agosti	Università di Padova, Italy
Giuseppe Amato	ISTI-CNR, Pisa, Italy
Giovanni Attolico	ISSIA-CNR, Bari, Italy
Sebastiano Battiato	Università di Catania, Italy
Olga Regina Pereira Bellon	Universidade Federal do Paraná, Brazil
Alberto Del Bimbo	Università di Firenze, Italy
Antonio Gentile	Università di Palermo, Italy
Martin Kampel	Vienna University of Technology, Austria
Eamonn Keogh	University of California - Riverside, USA
Martha Larson	Delft University of Technology, The Netherlands
Frank Le Bourgeois	Institut National des Sciences Appliquées de Lyon, France
Josep Lladós	Centre de Visió per Computador, Spain
Giuseppe Maino	Università di Bologna, Italy
Roberto Scopigno	ISTI-CNR, Pisa, Italy
Arnold Smeulders	University of Amsterdam, The Netherlands
Enrique Vidal	Istituto Tecnologico de Informatica, Valencia, Spain

Sponsoring Institutions

Fondazione Cassa di Risparmio di Modena
Accademia Nazionale di Scienze Lettere e Arti di Modena
Gruppo Italiano Ricercatori in Pattern Recogntition
Università degli Studi di Modena e Reggio Emilia
Facoltà di Ingegneria "Enzo Ferrari"
Biblioteca Estense Universitaria
Franco Cosimo Panini Editore

Table of Contents

Oral Session: Interaction

Oral Session: Analysis and Management

Poster and Demo Session

Discussion Session

Landmark Recognition in VISITO Tuscany*

Giuseppe Amato, Fabrizio Falchi, and Fausto Rabitti

ISTI-CNR, Pisa, Italy
{giuseppe.amato,fabrizio.falchi,fausto.rabitti}@isti.cnr.it

Abstract. This paper discusses and compares various approach to automatic landmark recognition in pictures, based upon image content analysis and classification. The paper first compares various visual features and image similarity functions based on local features. Finally it discusses and compares a new classification technique to decide the landmark contained in an image that first classifies the local features of the image and then uses this result in order to take a final decision on the entire image. Experiments demonstrate this last approach is the most effective one. The discussed techniques were used and tested in the project VISITO Tuscany.

Categories and Subject Descriptors: H.3 [Information Storage and Retrieval]: H.3.3 Information Search and Retrieval;

Keywords: Image classification, Content Based Retrieval.

1 Introduction

An emerging challenge that is recently attracting attention in the field of multimedia information retrieval is that of landmark recognition [15]. It consists in automatically recognizing the landmark (a building, a square, a statue, a monument, etc.) appearing in a non annotated picture. Landmark recognition is particularly appealing for instance in applications for mobile devices, where one wants to obtain information on monuments by simply taking a picture, or automatic annotation of media published on social network services.

The project VISITO Tuscany (VIsual Support to Interactive TOurism in Tuscany[1]) aims at addressing this interesting issue with the purpose of investigating and realizing technologies able to offer an interactive and customized advanced tour guide service to visit the cities of art in Tuscany. More specifically, it focuses on offering services to be used (see Figure 1):

During the tour – through the use of mobile devices of new generation, in order to improve the quality of the experience. The mobile device is used by the user to get detailed information about what he's watching, or about the context he's placed in. While taking pictures of monuments, places and other close-up objects, the user points out what, according to him, seems to be more interesting. When a picture is taken it

* This work was partially supported by the VISITO Tuscany project, funded by the Regione Toscana, Italy within the POR CREO FESR program.

[1] http://www.visito-tuscany.it/

C. Grana and R. Cucchiara (Eds.): MM4CH 2011, CCIS 247, pp. 1–13, 2012.

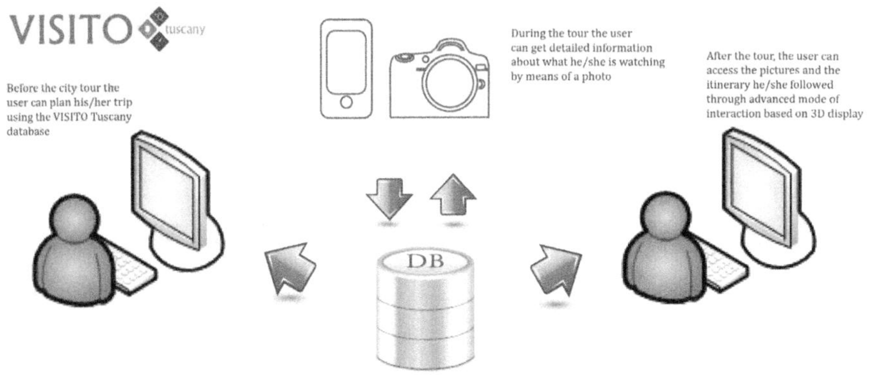

Fig. 1. The VISITO Tuscany project services

is processed by the system to infer which are the user's interests and to provide him relevant and customized information. For example, if a user takes a picture of the bell tower of Giotto, he can get detailed information describing the bell tower, its structural techniques, etc.

Before the tour – to plan the visit in a better way. Both the information sent by other users and their experiences, can be employed by the user to better plan his own visit, together with the information already included in the database system and, more generally, on the web. The interaction will take place through advanced methods based on 3D graphics.

After the tour – to keep the memory alive and share it with other people. The user can access the pictures and the itinerary he followed through advanced mode of interaction based on 3D graphics. Moreover, he might share his information and experiences with other users by creating social networks.

Even if the general objective of the VISITO Tuscany project is broader, in this paper we will just focus on the aspect of automatic landmark recognition in images. In particular after a description of the idea of landmark recognition given in Section 2, Section 3 we first compare the performance of various visual features, considering both global and local features. Then we compare various similarity functions based on local features in Section 4. Finally in Section 5 we discuss a technique for landmark recognition that classifies an image by first classifying its local features.

2 Landmark Recognition

In the last few years, the problem of recognizing landmarks has received growing attention by the research community. As an example, Google presented its approach to building a web-scale landmark recognition engine [15] that was also used to implement the Google Goggles service [10].

The problem of landmark recognition is typically addressed by leveraging on techniques of automatic classification, as for instances kNN Classification [9], applied to image features.

More in details, given a set of documents D and a predefined set of *classes* (also known as *labels*, or *categories*) $C = \{c_1, \ldots, c_m\}$, *single-label document classification* (SLC) is the task of automatically approximating, or estimating, an unknown *target function* $\Phi : D \to C$, that describes how documents ought to be classified, by means of a function $\hat{\Phi} : D \to C$, called the *classifier*, such that $\hat{\Phi}$ is an approximation of Φ.

A well-known classification technique, which we have used for landmark recognition tests, is the *single-label distance-weighted k-NN*. It decides about the class of a document in two steps. First it executes a k-NN search between the objects of the *training set*. The result of such operation is a list of labeled documents d_i belonging to the *training set* ordered with respect to the decreasing values of the similarity $s(d_x, d_i)$ between d_x and d_i. The label $\Phi_s(d_x)$ assigned to the document d_x by the classifier is the class $c_j \in C$ that maximizes the sum of the similarity between d_x and the documents d_i in the k-NN results list $\chi^k(d_x)$ labeled c_j.

Therefore, first a score $z(d_x, c_i)$ for each label is computed for any label $c_i \in C$:

$$z(d_x, c_j) = \sum_{d_i \in \chi^k(d_x)\,:\,\Phi(d_i) = c_j} s(d_x, d_i) \,.$$

Then, the class that obtains the maximum score is chosen:

$$\hat{\Phi}^s(d_x) = \arg\max_{c_j \in C} z(d_x, c_j) \,.$$

It is also convenient to express a degree of confidence on the answer of the classifier. For the *Single-label distance-weighted kNN* classifier described here we defined the confidence as 1 minus the ratio between the *score* obtained by the second-best label and the best label, i.e,

$$\nu_{doc}(\hat{\Phi}^s, d_x) = 1 - \frac{\max\limits_{c_j \in C - \hat{\Phi}^s(d_x)} z(d_x, c_j)}{\max\limits_{c_j \in C} z(d_x, c_j)} \,.$$

This classification confidence can be used to decide whether or not the predicted label has an high probability to be correct.

The similarity function s between two documents plays a strategic role for the effectiveness of the image classification algorithm. In fact images can be compared on the basis of different visual features and even once fixed a visual feature various similarity functions can be defined. In the following we will first test the effectiveness of various visual features for the landmark recognition task, then we compare various similarity measures.

2.1 Landmark Recognition Test Settings

The landmark recognition task was executed using the above mentioned single-label distance-weighted k-NN classification strategy employing specific similarity functions between images depending on the tested visual features.

To compare the various visual features we identified 12 landmarks, and we manually built the training sets for them by identifying a congruous number of pictures representing them. The dataset that we used for our tests is publically available and composed of 1,227 photos of 12 landmarks located in Pisa and was used also in [5,3,4]. The photos have been crawled from Flickr, the well known on-line photo service. The IDs of the photos used for these experiments together with the assigned label and extracted features can be downloaded from [1].

In order to build and evaluating a classifier for these classes, we divided the dataset in a *training set* (Tr) consisting of 226 photos (approximately 20% of the dataset) and a *test set* (Te) consisting of 921 (approximately 80% of the dataset). The image resolution used for feature extraction is the standard resolution used by Flickr i.e., maximum between width and height equal to 500 pixels.

The total number of local features extracted by the SIFT and SURF detectors were about 1,000,000 and 500,000 respectively.

3 Comparisons of Visual Features

Content based retrieval and content based classification techniques typically are not directly applied to images content. Rather, matching and comparisons between low level mathematical descriptions of the images visual appearance, in terms of color histograms, textures, shapes, point of interests, etc., are used. Different visual features represent different visual aspects of an image. All together, different visual features, contribute, not exhaustively, to represent the complete information contained in an image. A single feature is generally able to carry out just a limited amount of this information. Therefore, its performance varies in dependence of the specific dataset used and the type of conceptual information one wants to recognize.

The goal of this section is to compare various visual features or combination of visual features that provides us with the best performance with the landmark recognition task.

In order to perform our evaluation we choose various global and local visual features. Specifically, we evaluated the performance of the 5 MPEG-7 [11] visual features (Color Layout, Color Structure, Edge Hystogram, Homogeneous Textures, Scalable Colour), the Scale invariant Feature Transform (SIFT) [13], the ColorSIFT [8], and the Speeded Up Robust Features (SURF) [7]. In the following we give a brief description of their principles.

3.1 MPEG-7

MPEG-7 visual descriptors consist of a set of 5 different global descriptors of the low level visual content of an image [11]. These 5 descriptors are mathematical representations of different statistical measures that can be computed analyzing the structure and placement of the colored pixel in an image. In particular:

- Scalable Color is an histogram of the colors of the pixel in an image, when colors are represented in the Hue Saturation Value (HSV) space
- Color Structure expresses local color structure in an image by use of a structuring element that is comprised of several image samples
- Color Layout is a compact description of the spatial distribution of colors in an image

- Edge Histogram descriptor describes edge distribution with a histogram based on local edge distribution in an image, using five types of edges
- Homogeneous Texture descriptor characterizes the properties of the texture in an image.

For extracting the MPEG-7 visual descriptors we made use of the MPEG-7 eXperimental Model (XM) Reference Software [12].

3.2 SIFT

The Scale Invariant Feature Transformation (SIFT) [13] is a representation of the low level image content that is based on a transformation of the image data into scale-invariant coordinates relative to local features. Local feature are low level descriptions of keypoints in an image. Keypoints are interest points in an image that are invariant to scale and orientation. Keypoints are selected byf choosing the most stable points from a set of candidate location. Each keypoint in an image is associated with one or more orientations, based on local image gradients. Image matching is performed by comparing the description of the keypoints in images.

3.3 ColorSIFT

ColorSIFT local features [8] are an extension of the original SIFT definition to also take color into account. Basically, the original SIFT definition describes the local edge distribution around keypoints. The ColorSIFT extends the description of a keypoint also to colors around it. This is obtained by considering color gradients, rather than just intensity gradients. Between the various proposals they made, we tested the colour-based SIFT invariant to shadow and shading effects which performed best in the experiments reported in [8].

3.4 SURF

The basic idea of Speeded Up Robust Features (SURF) [7] is quite similar to SIFT. SURF detects some keypoints in an image and describes these keypoints using orientation information. However, the SURF definition uses a new method for both detection of keypoints and their description that is much faster still guaranteeing a performance comparable or even better than SIFT. Specifically, keypoint detection relies on a technique based on a approximation of the Hessian Matrix. The descriptor of a keypoint is built considering the distortion of Haar-wavelet responses around the keypoint itself.

3.5 Similarity Measures

For each feature used in the experiments we need a measure that evaluates the similarity between two photos. For the MPEG-7 visual descriptors we used the distances suggested by the MPEG Group in [12]. Let $d(d_x, d_y)$ be the distance, we defined the similarity between to objects as:

$$s(d_x, d_y) = 1 - w * d(d_x, d_y) \tag{1}$$

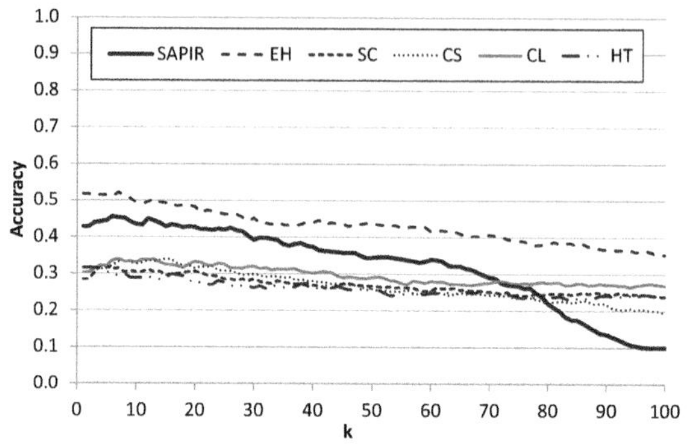

Fig. 2. Micro-averaged accuracy of the classifier for various *k* and various global features (MPEG-7 Visual Descriptors and the combination used in the SAPIR project)

where w is a fixed number that guarantees that $w * d(x, y) < 1$ for any d_x and d_y.

In the experiments we also tested the weighted sum distance of these 5 MPEG-7 Visual Descriptors used in the *Search in Audiovisual using Peer-to-Peer Information Retrieval (SAPIR) FP6 European research project* [2]. More information about this combination can be found in [6].

A common strategy to compare two images d_x and d_y using local features (e.g., SIFT, ColorSIFT and SURF) is typically the number of keypoints in d_x that have a match in d_y. We translate this information in a similarity function dividing the number of matches by the number of keypoints in d_x. In other words we used the ratio of keypoints in d_x that do have a match in d_y as the similarity between d_x and d_y for all the local features used for the experiments (i.e., SIFT, ColorSIFT and SURF). Later on, in the paper, we will also propose and compare alternative strategies to define local feature based similarity functions.

The algorithms used for matching the keypoints for the various local features are the ones suggested by the features authors and that are also used in their public available implementations. In particular both SIFT and ColorSIFT performs a 2-NN search between the keypoints in d_y for any keypoint in d_x. A match is identified if the 1st result in the 2-NN has a distance from the query keypoint less than 0.6 times the distance of the 2nd result. SURF matching algorithm is very similar except that the distance of the 1st nearest neighbor must be less than $1/\sqrt{2}$. More information can be found in [13,8,7].

3.6 Results

In Figure 2 we report the micro-averaged *accuracies* obtained for some MPEG-7 Visual Descriptors and their weighted sum combination used in the SAPIR Project (see 3.5). The best performance is obtained using the EdgeHistogram visual descriptor. The color-based features (i.e., ColorLayout, ColorStructure, ScalableColor) have very similar performance while HomogenousTexture obtained the worst values of *accuracy*. The weighted-sum combination of these visual descriptor performs slightly worst than

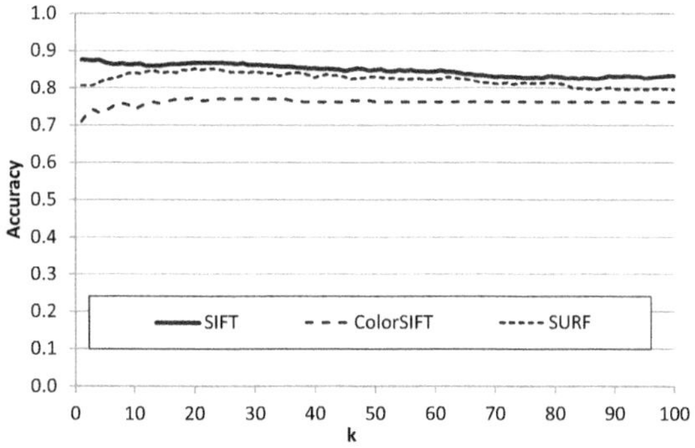

Fig. 3. Micro-averaged accuracy of the classifier for various k and various local features (SIFT, Color-SIFT, SURF)

EdgeHistogram alone. Even if for big values of k the SAPIR metric is preferable, the best *accuracy* for the various k is higher for EdgeHistogram alone.

The *accuracy* obtained for the local features are reported in Figure 3. As expected, all of them perform significantly better than the global features. In fact, the dataset used is specific for landmarks recognition and they are supposed to work well for general recognition tasks. What was not obvious is that SIFT (the oldest) perform better than the others. Both SURF and ColorSIFT are basically extensions of the SIFT but for this specific task they are less effective than SIFT.

4 Comparisons of Various Local Feature Based Image Similarity Functions for Landmark Recognition

In previous section we compared various visual features with a kNN classifier and results proved that the best performance was achieved using local features In particular the best performance was obtained the SIFT local descriptor. The similarity function used with local features was defined as the ratio between the matching keypoints and the total number of keypoints in the compered image. However, additional improvement can be obtained by varying the definition of the similarity function.

In order to define image similarity functions based on local features we first need to define the notion of similarity between local features themselves. The Computer Vision literature related to local features, generally uses the notion of distance, rather than that of similarity. However in most cases a similarity function $s()$ can be easily derived from a distance function $d()$. For both SIFT and SURF the Euclidean distance is typically used as measure of dissimilarity between two features [13,7].

Let $d(p_1, p_2) \in [0, 1]$ be the normalized distance between two local features p_1 and p_2. We can define the similarity between local features as:

$$s(p_1, p_2) = 1 - d(p_1, p_2)$$

Obviously $0 \leq s(p_1, p_2) \leq 1$ for any p_1 and p_2.

Another useful aspect that is often used when dealing with local features is the concept of local feature matching, that is deciding if a given local feature of an image matches a some local feature of another image. In [13], a distance ratio matching scheme was proposed that has also been adopted by [7] and many others. Let's consider a local feature p_x belonging to an image d_x (i.e. $p_x \in d_x$) and an image d_y. First, the point $p_y \in d_y$ closest to p_x (in the remainder $NN_1(p_x, d_y)$) is selected as candidate match. Then, the distance ratio $\sigma(p_x, d_y) \in [0, 1]$ of closest to second-closest neighbors of p_x in d_y is considered. The distance ratio is defined as:

$$\sigma(p_x, d_y) = \frac{d(p_x, NN_1(p_x, d_y))}{d(p_x, NN_2(p_x, d_y))}$$

Finally, p_x and $NN_1(p_x, d_y)$ are considered matching if the distance ratio $\sigma(p_x, d_y)$ is smaller than a given threshold. Thus, a function of matching between $p_x \in d_x$ and an image d_y is defined as:

$$m(p_x, d_y) = \begin{cases} 1 \text{ if } \sigma(p_x, d_y) < c \\ 0 \text{ otherwise} \end{cases}$$

In [13], $c = 0.8$ was proposed reporting that this threshold allows to eliminate 90% of the false matches while discarding less than 5% of the correct matches. Please note, that this parameter will be used in defining the image similarity measure used as a baseline and in one of our proposed local feature based classifiers.

In the following, we finally define 5 different approaches to compute image similarity measures relying on local features.

1-NN Similarity Average – s^1. The simplest similarity measure only consider the closest neighbor for each $p_x \in d_x$ and its distance from the query point p_x. The similarity between two documents d_x and d_y can be defined as the average similarity between the local features in d_x and their closest neighbors in d_y. Thus, we define the *1-NN Similarity Average* as (for simplicity, we indicate the number of local features in an image d_x as $|d_x|$):

$$s^1(d_x, d_y) = \frac{1}{|d_x|} \sum_{p_x \in d_x} \max_{p_y \in d_y} (s(p_x, p_y))$$

Percentage of Matches – s^m. A reasonable measure of similarity between two image d_x and d_y is the percentage of local features in d_x that have a match in d_y. Using the distance ratio criterion described above for individuating matches, we define the *Percentage of Matches* similarity function s^m as follows:

$$s^m(d_x, d_y) = \frac{1}{|d_x|} \sum_{p_x \in d_x} m(p_x, d_y)$$

where $m(p_x, d_y)$ is 1 if p_x has a match in d_y and 0 otherwise.

Distance Ratio Average – s^{σ}. The matching function $m(p_x, d_y)$ used in the *Percentage of Matches* similarity function is based on the ratio between closest to second-closest neighbors for filtering candidate matches as proposed in [13]. However, this distance ratio value can be used directly to define a *Distance Ratio Average* function between two images d_x and d_y as follows:

$$s^{\sigma}(d_x, d_y) = \frac{1}{|d_x|} \sum_{p_x \in d_x} \sigma(p_x, d_y)$$

Please note that function does not require a distance ratio c threshold.

Hough Transform Matches Percentage – s^{h}. An Hough transform is often used to search for keys that agree upon a particular model pose. The Hough transform can be used to define a *Hough Transform Matches Percentage*:

$$s^{h}(d_x, d_y) = \frac{|M_h(d_x, d_y)|}{|d_x|}$$

where $M_h(d_x, d_y)$ is the subset of matches voting for the most voted pose. For the experiments, we used the same parameters proposed in [13], i.e. bin size of 30 degrees for orientation, a factor of 2 for scale, and 0.25 times the maximum model dimension for location.

4.1 Results

In Table 1, *Accuracy* and macro averaged F_1 of the image similarity based classifiers for the 4 similarity functions are reported. Note that the *single-label distance-weighted kNN* technique has a parameter k that determines the number of closest neighbors retrieved in order to classify a given image. This parameter should be set during the training phase and is kept fixed during the test phase. However, in our experiments we decided to report the result obtained ranging k between 1 and 100. For simplicity, in the Table, we report the best performance obtained and the k for which it was obtained. Moreover, we report the performance obtained for $k = 1$ which is a particular case in which the kNN classifier simply consider the closest image.

The *Hough Transform Matches Percentage* (s^{h}) similarity function is the best choice for both SIFT and SURF. The second best is *Distance Ratio Average* (s^{σ}) which only considers the distance ratio as matching criterion. Please note that s^{σ} does not require a distance ratio threshold (c) because it weights every match considering the distance ratio value. Moreover, s^{σ} performs sightly better than *Percentage of Matches* (s^{m}) which requires the threshold c to be set. The results obtained by the *1-NN Similarity Average* (s^{1}) function show that considering just the distance between a local features and its closest neighbors gives worse performance than considering the distance ratio s^{σ}. In other words, the similarity between a local feature and its closest neighbor is meaningful only if compared to the other nearest neighbors, which is exactly what the distance ratio does.

Regarding the parameter k it is interesting to note that the k value for which the best performance was obtained for each similarity measure is typically much higher for SURF than SIFT. In other words, the closest neighbors in the training set are more relevant using SIFT than using SURF.

Table 1. Comparisons of the performance of the various image similarity functions based on local features

similarity function			s^1 Avg 1-NN	s^m Perc. of Matches	s^σ Avg Sim. Ratio	s^h Hough Transf.
Best	Acc	**SIFT**	0.75	0.88	0.89	**0.92**
		SURF	0.79	0.85	0.82	**0.89**
	F_1	**SIFT**	0.72	0.86	0.87	**0.90**
		SURF	0.76	0.83	0.81	**0.87**
k =1	Acc	**SIFT**	0.73	0.88	0.89	**0.91**
		SURF	0.79	0.81	0.81	**0.87**
	F_1	**SIFT**	0.72	0.86	0.87	**0.90**
		SURF	0.76	0.79	0.80	**0.85**
Best k	Acc	**SIFT**	*9*	*1*	*1*	*2*
		SURF	*3*	*20*	*8*	*21*
	F_1	**SIFT**	*1*	*1*	*1*	*2*
		SURF	*1*	*18*	*8*	*21*

5 kNN Based on Local Feature Similarity

In the previous section, we considered the classification of an image d_x as a process of retrieving the most similar ones in the *training set* Tr and then applying a kNN classification technique in order to predict the class of d_x.

In this section, we discuss a new approach that first assigns a label to each local feature of an image. The label of the image is then assigned by analyzing the labels and confidences of its local features.

This approach has the advantage that any access method for similarity search in metric spaces (see [14]) can be used to speed-up classification.

The proposed *Local Feature Based Classifiers* classify an image d_x in two steps:

1. first each local feature p_x belonging to d_x is classified considering the local features of images in Tr;
2. second the whole image is classified considering the class assigned to each local feature and the confidence of the classification.

Note that classifying individually the local features, before assigning the label to an image, we might loose the implicit dependency between interest points of an image. However, surprisingly, we will see that this method offers better effectiveness than the other approaches presented before. In other words we are able to improve at the same time both efficiency and effectiveness.

In the following, we assume that the label of each local feature p_x, belonging to images in the training set Tr, is the label assigned to the image it belongs to (i.e., d_x):

$$\forall p_x \in d_x,\ \forall d_x \in Tr\ , \Phi(p_x) = \Phi(d_x).$$

In other words, we assume that the local features generated over interest points of images in the training set can be labeled as the image they belong to. Note that the noise introduced by this label propagation from the whole image to the local features can be managed by the local features classifier. In fact, we will see that when very similar training local features are assigned to different classes, a local feature close to them is classified with a low confidence.

Given $p_x \in d_x$, a local feature classifier $\hat{\Phi}_l$ returns both a class $\hat{\Phi}_l(p_x) = c_i \in C$ to which it believes p_x to belong *and* a numerical value $\nu(\hat{\Phi}_l, p_x)$ that represents the confidence that $\hat{\Phi}$ has in its decision. High values of ν correspond to high confidence. These are defined as follows:

$$\begin{cases} \hat{\Phi}^l(p_x) = \Phi(NN_1(p_x, Tr)) \\ \nu(\hat{\Phi}^l, p_x) = (1 - \dot{\sigma}(p_x, T_r))^2 \end{cases}$$

Where $NN_1(p_x, Tr)$ is the local feature of Tr most similar to p_x and $\dot{\sigma}$ is defined as

$$\dot{\sigma}(p_x, T_r) = \frac{d(p_x, NN_1(p_x, Tr))}{d(p_x, NN_2^*(p_x, Tr))}$$

where $NN_2^*(p_x, Tr)$ is the closest neighbor that is known to be labelled differently than the first as suggested in [13].

The intuition is that we use use $1 - \dot{\sigma}(p_x, t_r)$ that basically is a distance ratio, as a measure of confidence to be used during the classification of the whole image. The value is squared to emphasize the relative importance of greater distance ratios.

Please note that for this classifier we do not have to specify any parameter at all.

As we said before, the local feature based feature classification is composed of two steps . We have just dealt with the issue of classifying every local feature of an image. Now we discuss the second phase of the local feature based classification of images. In particular we consider the classification of the whole image given the label $\hat{\Phi}(p_x)$ and the confidence $\nu(\hat{\Phi}, p_x)$ assigned to its local features $p_x \in d_x$ during the first phase.

To this aim, we use a confidence-rated majority vote approach. We first compute a score $z(p_x, c_i)$ for each label $c_i \in C$. The score is the sum of the confidence obtained for the local features predicted as c_i. Formally,

$$z(d_x, c_i) = \sum_{p_x \in d_x, \hat{\Phi}(p_x) = c_i} \nu(\hat{\Phi}_l, p_x)\ .$$

Then, the label that obtains the maximum score is chosen:

$$\hat{\Phi}(d_x) = \arg\max_{c_j \in C} z(d_x, c_j)\ .$$

As measure of confidence for the classification of the whole image we use ratio between the predicted and the second best class:

$$\nu_{img}(\hat{\Phi}, d_x) = 1 - \frac{\max\limits_{c_j \in C - \hat{\Phi}(p_x)} z(d_x, c_j)}{\max\limits_{c_j \in C} z(d_x, c_j)}\ .$$

This whole image classification confidence can be used to decide whether or not the predicted label has an high probability to be correct.

5.1 Results

Also in this case we report the *Accuracy* and macro averaged F_1 of the classifier. Results are shown in Table 2. Comparing these results with those reported in Table 1 it is evident that the local feature based kNN classifier is better than the single-label distance weighted kNN classifier applied to the best similarity function both using SIFT and SURF. In fact, best accuracy was 0.92 for SIFT and 0.89 for SURF, while the new classifier offers an accuracy of 0.95 for SIFT and 0.93 for SURF. Similar considerations can be done for the F_1 measure.

Table 2. Performance of the local feature classifier

		$\hat{\Phi}$
Accuracy	**SIFT**	**0.95**
	SURF	**0.93**
F_1 Macro	**SIFT**	**0.95**
	SURF	**0.92**

6 Conclusions and Future Work

This paper presented the techniques for landmark recognition that were used in the project VISITO Tuscany. An extensive evaluation was performed to compare the various techniques and to asses the most effective method. In particular the paper performed a comparisons of various image visual features and various similarity functions used to build the classifier. In addition we also proposed a new classification method based on the idea of first classifying the local feature of images and to use this result to classify an entire image. Our experiments proved that this was the most effective method and that it also opens up new opportunities for efficient implementation of the landmark recognition approach on a large scale.

References

1. Pisa landmarks dataset, `http://www.fabriziofalchi.it/pisaDataset/`
2. Search in Audiovisual using Peer-to-Peer Information Retrieval (SAPIR) FP6 European research project, `http://www.sapir.eu`
3. Amato, G., Falchi, F.: kNN based image classification relying on local feature similarity. In: SISAP 2010: Proceedings of the Third International Conference on Similarity Search and Applications, pp. 101–108. ACM, New York (2010)

4. Amato, G., Falchi, F.: Local feature based image similarity functions for kNN classfication. In: Proceedings of the 3rd International Conference on Agents and Artificial Intelligence (ICAART 2011), vol. 1, pp. 157–166. SciTePress (2011)
5. Amato, G., Falchi, F., Bolettieri, P.: Recognizing landmarks using automated classification techniques: an evaluation of various visual features. In: Proceeding of The Second Interantional Conference on Advances in Multimedia (MMEDIA 2010), pp. 78–83. IEEE Computer Society (2010)
6. Batko, M., Falchi, F., Novak, D., Perego, R., Rabitti, F., Sedmidubsky, J., Zezula, P.: Building a web-scale image similarity search system. In: Multimedia Tools and Applications (to appear)
7. Bay, H., Tuytelaars, T., Van Gool, L.: SURF: Speeded Up Robust Features. In: Leonardis, A., Bischof, H., Pinz, A. (eds.) ECCV 2006, Part I. LNCS, vol. 3951, pp. 404–417. Springer, Heidelberg (2006)
8. Burghouts, G.J., Geusebroek, J.M.: Performance evaluation of local colour invariants. Computer Vision and Image Understanding 113, 48–62 (2009)
9. Dudani, S.: The distance-weighted k-nearest-neighbour rule. IEEE Transactions on Systems, Man and Cybernetics SMC-6(4), 325–327 (1975)
10. Google. Goggles (2011), `http://www.google.com/mobile/goggles/`
11. ISO/IEC. Information technology - Multimedia content description interfaces (2003), 15938
12. ISO/IEC. Information technology - Multimedia content description interfaces. Part 6: Reference Software (2003), 15938-6:2003
13. Lowe, D.G.: Distinctive image features from scale-invariant keypoints. International Journal of Computer Vision 60(2), 91–110 (2004)
14. Zezula, P., Amato, G., Dohnal, V., Batko, M.: Similarity Search: The Metric Space Approach. Advances in Database Systems, vol. 32. Springer, Heidelberg (2006)
15. Zheng, Y., Zhao, M., Song, Y., Adam, H., Buddemeier, U., Bissacco, A., Brucher, F., Chua, T.-S., Neven, H.: Tour the world: Building a web-scale landmark recognition engine. In: Proceedings of IEEE Conference on Computer Vision and Pattern Recognition (CVPR 2009), pp. 1085–1092 (2009)

Automatic Texturing without Illumination Artifacts from In-Hand Scanning Data Flow

Frédéric Larue[1], Matteo Dellepiane[1], Henning Hamer[2], and Roberto Scopigno[1]

[1] ISTI-CNR, Pisa, Italy
[2] ETH, Zürich, Switzerland

Abstract. This paper shows how to improve the results of a 3D scanning system to allow to better fit the requirements of the Multi-Media and Cultural Heritage domains. A real-time in-hand scanning system is enhanced by further processing its intermediate data, with the goal of producing a digital 3D model with a high quality color texture and an improved representation of the high-frequency shape detail. The proposed solution starts from the usual output of the scanner, a 3D model and a video sequence gathered by the scanner sensor, for which the rigid motion is known at each frame. The produced color texture is deprived of the typical artifacts that generally appear while creating textures from several pictures: ghosting, shadows and specular highlights. In the case of objects made of diffuse materials, the system is also able to compute a normal map, thus improving the geometry acquired by the scanner. Results demonstrate that our texturing procedure is quite fast (a few minutes to process more than a thousand images). Moreover, the method is highly automatic, since only a few intuitive parameters must be tuned by the user, and all required computations are particularly suited to GPU programming, making the method convenient and scalable to graphics hardware.

Keywords: 3D Scanning, Texturing, Bump Map fitting, Video analysis.

1 Introduction

Thanks to the fact that scanning technologies are nowadays quite affordable and reliable, the acquisition of digital 3D models from real objects is becoming more and more common for many application fields of Computer Graphics, such as video games, cinema, edutaining and/or entertaining software. Despite this fact, the whole pipeline enabling to pass from real to virtual still remains a complex process. Moreover, providing a good representation of the geometry is not sufficient for many applications, such as for example the Multimedia or the Cultural Heritage domains. In these applications, we need to pair the geometry model with an accurate representation of the surface appearance (color, small shape details, reflection characteristics); interactive visualization requires to be able to provide synthetic images as near as possible to the real appearance of the depicted object. Commercial scanning systems have mostly focused

C. Grana and R. Cucchiara (Eds.): MM4CH 2011, CCIS 247, pp. 14–26, 2012.

on shape measurement, putting aside until recently the problem of recovering quality textures from real objects. This has led to a lack of efficient and automatic processing tools for color acquisition and reconstruction: in the Computer Graphics industry, even while working with meshes coming from 3D scanning, the texturing phase is still mainly performed by hand and consists in one of the most tedious tasks to be done in order to produce multimedia content.

In fact, creating quality textures for 3D models by using real pictures is a process that is prone to many problems. Among them, there are the calibration of the pictures with respect to the 3D model, and the significant artifacts that may appear in the reconstructed color, due to the presence of shadows, specular highlights, lighting inconsistencies, or small reprojection misalignment because of calibration inaccuracies.

In this paper, we present a complete system performing in an intuitive and highly automatic manner the simultaneous acquisition of shape and color, as well as the texturing of the recovered mesh. During a first step, the acquisition is made by an in-hand digitization device performing 3D scanning in real-time, which captures at the same time a color video flow of the measured object. This flow is used during the texturing step to produce over the object surface a diffuse color texture deprived of the aforementioned artifacts. Moreover, our system is also able to estimate a normal map starting from the video flow, in order to extract the finest geometric features that cannot be properly acquired by the scanning device.

The integration of the proposed method with the in-hand scanning system permits to obtain accurate 3D models of small objects within minutes. In the field of Cultural Heritage, this permits to digitize a big number of artifacts in a short time, for the purposes of archival, knowledge sharing, monitoring, restoration.

The remainder of this paper is organized as follows. The Section 2 reviews related work on software approaches or complete systems for color acquisition and texture reconstruction. The Section 3 presents our texturing method, as well as the real-time in-hand scanning system it is based on, and our approaches for hole filling and normal map extraction. Finally, Section 4, shows some results and Section 5 draws the conclusions.

2 Related Work

2.1 Color Acquisition and Visualization on 3D Models

Adding color information to an acquired 3D model is a complex task. The most flexible approach starts from a set of images acquired either in a second stage with respect to the geometry acquisition, or simultaneously but using different devices. Image-to-geometry registration, which can be solved by automatic [15,21,7] or semi-automatic [12] approaches, is then necessary. In the method proposed here, this registration step is not required, because the in-hand scanning system provides images which are already aligned to the 3D model.

Once alignment is performed, it's necessary to extract information about the surface material appearance and transfer it on the geometry. The most correct way to represent the material properties of an object is to describe them through a reflection function (e.g. BRDF), which attempts to model the observed scattering behavior of a class of real surfaces. A detailed presentation of its theory and applications can be found in Dorsey [10]. Unfortunately, state-of-the-art BRDF acquisition approaches rely on complex and controlled illumination setups, making them difficult to apply in more general cases, or when fast or unconstrained acquisition is needed.

A less accurate but more robust solution is the direct use of images to transfer the color to the 3D model. In this case, the apparent color value is mapped onto the digital object's surface by applying an inverse projection. In addition to other important issues, there are numerous difficulties in selecting the correct color when multiple candidates come from different images.

To solve these problems, a first group of methods selects, for each surface part, a portion of a representative image following a specific criterion - in most cases, the orthogonality between the surface and the view direction [5,1]. However, due to the lack of consistency from on image to the other, artifacts are visible at the junctions between surface areas receiving color from different images. These can be partially removed by working on these junctions [5,1,6].

Another group "blends" all image contributions by assigning a weight to each one or to each input pixel, and selecting the final surface color as the weighted average of the input data, as in Pulli et al. [17]. The weight is usually a combination of various quality metrics [3,2,18]. In particular, Callieri et al. [4] presented a flexible weighting system that can be extended in order to accommodate additional criteria. These methods provide better visual results and their implementation permits very complex datasets to be used, i.e. hundreds of images and very dense 3D models. Nevertheless, undesirable ghosting effects may be produced when the starting set of calibrated images is not perfectly aligned. This problem can be solved, for example, by applying a local warping using optical flow [11,9].

Another issue, which is common to all the cited methods, is the projection of lighting artifacts on the model, i.e. shadows, highlights, and peculiar BRDF effects, since the lighting environment is usually not known in advance. In order to correct (or to avoid to project) lighting artifacts, two possible approaches include the estimation of the lighting environment [22] and the use of easily controllable lighting setups [8].

2.2 Real-Time 3D Scanning

An overview of the 3D Scanning and Stereo reconstruction goes well beyond the scope of this paper. We will mainly focus on systems for real-time, in-hand acquisition of geometry and/or color. Their main issues are the availability of technology and the problem of aligning data in a very fast way.

3D acquisition can be based on stereo techniques or on active optical scanning solutions. Among the latter, the most robust approach is based on the use of fast structured-light scanners [14], where a high speed camera and a projector are

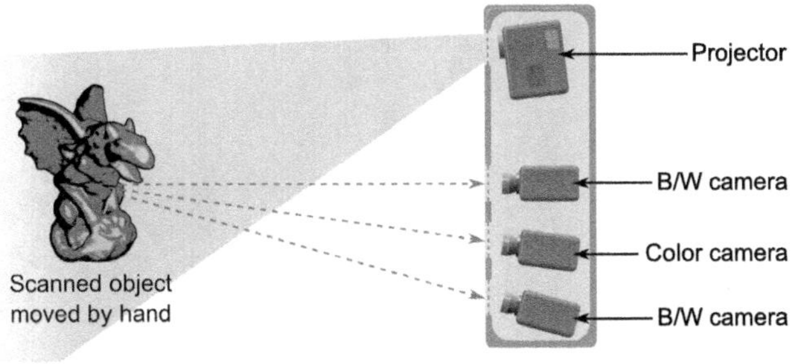

Fig. 1. The in-hand scanning device producing the data flow used as input for the methods described in this paper

used to recover the range maps in real-time. The alignment problem is usually solved with smart implementations of the ICP algorithm [20,24], where the most difficult aspect to solve is related to the loop closure during registration.

In the last few years, some in-hand scanning solutions have been proposed [20,25,23]: they essentially differ on the way projection patterns are handled, and in the implementation of ICP. None of the proposed systems take into account the color, although the one proposed by Weise et al [23] contains also a color camera (see next section for a detailed description). This is essentially due to the low resolution of the cameras, and to the difficulty of handling the peculiar illumination provided by the projector. Other systems have been proposed which take into account also the color, but they are not able to achieve real-time performances [16] or to reconstruct the geometry in an accurate way [13].

3 Texturing from In-Hand Scanning Data Flow

The scanning device which produces the data flow used by our texturing approach [23] is shown in Figure 1. Shape measurement is performed by phase-shifting, using three different sinusoidal patterns to establish correspondences (and then to perform optical triangulation) between the projector and the two black and white video cameras. The phase unwrapping, namely how the different signal periods are demodulated, is achieved by a GPU stereo matching between both cameras. The whole process produces one range map every $14ms$. Simultaneously, a color video flow is captured by the third camera. During an acquisition, the only light source in the scene is the scanner projector itself, for which the position is always perfectly known.

The scanning can be performed in two different ways. If the object color is neither red nor brown, it can be done by holding the object directly by hand. In this case, occlusions are detected by a hue analysis which produces, for each video frame, a map of skin presence probability. Otherwise, a black glove must be used. Although much less convenient for the scanning itself, it makes the occlusion detection trivial by simply ignoring dark regions in the input pictures.

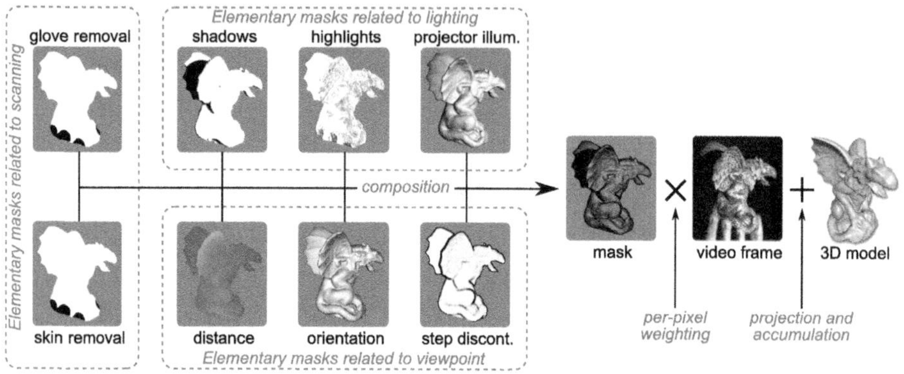

Fig. 2. The texture is computed as the weighted average of all video frames. Weights are obtained by the composition of multiple elementary masks, each one corresponding to a particular criterion related to viewing, lighting or scanning conditions.

Each scanning session then produces a 3D mesh and a color video flow. For each video frame, the viewpoint and the position of the light are given, as well as the skin probability map in the case of a digitization performed by hand.

3.1 Artifacts-Free Color Texture Recovery

Our texturing method extends the work proposed in [4] so as to adapt it to the data flow produced by the scanning system presented above. The idea, summarized in Figure 2, is to weight each input picture by a mask (typically a gray scale image) which represents a per-pixel confidence value. The final color of a given surface point is then computed as the weighted average of all color contributions coming from the pictures into which this point is visible. Masks are built by the composition of multiple elementary masks, which are themselves computed by image processing applied either on the input image or on a rendering of the mesh performed from the same viewpoint. In the original paper, the approach has been designed for the general case, meaning that absolutely no information is available about the lighting environment or about how the geometry has been acquired. For this reason, only the following criteria related to viewing conditions have been initially considered, defined to deal with data redundancy in a way that ensures seamless color transitions:

- *Distance to the camera.* When a part of the object surface is visible in two different pictures, the one for which the viewpoint is the closest obviously contains a more accurate sampling of the color information. This elementary mask assigns to a pixel a confidence value which decreases when the distance to the camera of the corresponding surface point increases.
- *Orientation wrt. the camera.* Similarly, the more grazing the angle between the line of sight and the surface, the lower the quality of the sampling. This mask is computed as the dot product of the normal vector by the viewing direction, giving more importance to surface parts facing the camera.

- *Step discontinuities.* Due to inaccuracies during calibration, slight misalignment may be observed while collecting color contributions by reprojecting the mesh onto the picture. The most noticeable reprojection errors obviously occur near the object silhouette and the step discontinuities. A lower weight is then assigned to these regions so as to avoid misalignment artifacts.

Although these masks are sufficient to avoid texture cracks, they obviously cannot handle self projected shadows or specular highlights, since knowledge about lighting environment is necessary. In our case, as explained before, both the positions of the viewpoint and the light (the projector lamp) are always exactly known. Moreover, the light moves with the scanner, which means that highlights and shadows are different for each frame, but also that the incident illumination angle changes. So, by setting appropriate masks, we can make prevailing image parts deprived of illumination effects. We then define the three following masks to account for illumination:

- *Shadows.* Since the complete geometric configuration of the scene is known, we can use a simple shadow mapping algorithm to estimate shadowed areas, to which a null weight is assigned.
- *Specular highlights.* Conversely to shadows, highlights partially depend on the object material, which is unknown. For this reason, we use a multi-pass algorithm to detect them. The first pass computes the object texture without accounting for highlights. Due to the data redundancy, the averaging tends to reduce their visual impact. During the subsequent passes, highlights are identified by computing the luminosity difference between the texture obtained at the previous pass and the input picture. This difference corresponds to our highlight removal mask. In practice, only two passes are sufficient.
- *Projector illumination.* This mask aims at avoiding luminosity loss during the averaging by giving more influence to surface parts facing the light source. The mask values correspond to the dot product between the surface normal and the line of sight.

We also introduce two other elementary masks to cope with the occlusions that are inherent to in-hand scanning. Indeed, if they are ignored, picture regions that do not correspond to the real object color might be introduced in the computation, leading to visible artifacts in the final texture. Thus, when digitization is performed with the dark glove, an occlusion mask is simply computed by thresholding pixel intensities, so as to discard the darkest picture regions. In the case of a digitization made by hand, we use the skin probability map produced by the scanner to generate the mask values.

Each elementary mask contains values in the range $]0,1]$. They are multiplied all together to produce the final mask that selectively weights the pixels of the corresponding picture. During this operation, each elementary mask can obviously be applied more than once. The influence of each criterion can then be tuned independently, although we empirically determined default values that work quite well for most cases.

All operations consist in local computations, making the process suitable for a GPU support. Moreover, pictures are processed sequentially, which makes the memory consumption independent to the length of the video flow.

3.2 Assisted Selection for Texture Hole Filling

If each independent weighting mask represents the confidence of a given video frame, the total weight sum at a given surface point can be seen as a quality measurement of the color sampling at this point. Indeed, a low sum value may represent either a sparse picture coverage or the fact that the point always projects onto picture areas of low confidence. In both cases, the reconstructed texture can be considered as less reliable at this point than on the rest of the surface. In practice, regions for which the sum is relatively small mostly correspond to concavities or surface parts acquired only at grazing angles, where color defects arise due to the lack of quality in the input sampling.

This information can then be exploited advisedly to rectify holes and poorly sampled texture regions. While computing the texturing, we keep track of the total weight sum at each surface point, as well as of its minimum and maximum bounds for the whole surface. The user is then asked to choose a threshold in this range. All surface points for which the total weight sum is lower than this threshold are considered as belonging to a hole. In the current implementation, filling is finally performed by diffusing inside holes the colors of the valid points located on their boundaries. More sophisticated approaches based on texture inpainting can also be designed.

3.3 Normal Map Recovery

Since the light position is known for each video frame, shape-from-shading can be used to extract a bump map, similarly to [19]. Let p be a point on the object surface and F_i a video frame into which this point is visible. We then denote by the column vector l_i the unit incident light direction at p, by d_i the distance of p to the light, and by c_i the color intensity observed at p. If we assume that the surface is purely Lambertian, the following equation can be written:

$$\rho_d \, (n^T \, l_i) = d_i^2 \, c_i \tag{1}$$

where the column vector n is the normal at p and ρ_d is a constant depending on the light intensity, the surface diffuse albedo and the camera transfer function. If p is visible in several frames $\{F_i\}_{1 \leq i \leq N}$, the normal n that fits the best the N measurements can be found by solving the following equation:

$$\rho_d \; n = \arg\min \xi(X) \tag{2}$$

where ξ is a quadratic form defined as:

$$\xi(X) = (LX - C)^2 \quad \text{with } L = \begin{bmatrix} w_1 \, l_1^T \\ \vdots \\ w_N \, l_N^T \end{bmatrix} \quad \text{and } C = \begin{bmatrix} w_1 \, c_1 \, d_1^2 \\ \vdots \\ w_N \, c_N \, d_N^2 \end{bmatrix} \tag{3}$$

Fig. 3. Comparison of texturing obtained by a naive averaging of all input frames (*top row*) and the proposed approach using weighting masks (*bottom row*)

where w_i is a confidence factor for the ith measurement F_i, corresponding to the weighting masks in our case. Solving equation 2 is equivalent to finding the value of X for which the derivative of ξ is null, which leads to the following solution:

$$\xi'(X) = 0 \iff X = (L^T L)^{-1} (L^T C) \tag{4}$$

If we constrain the normal vector to be unitized, n is finally obtained by normalizing X. Since both matrices $(L^T L)$ and $(L^T C)$ can be constructed incrementally, normal extraction can be performed similarly to color reconstruction, by processing input pictures one by one on GPU. Both processings are then performed simultaneously, without introducing noticeable additional cost.

4 Results

Our texturing results are shown in the bottom row of Figure 3. The top row proposes a comparison to the results obtained by a naive approach that performs a direct averaging of color contributions, ignoring weighting masks. The most obvious difference that can be noticed is clearly the drastic loss of luminosity that occurs in the case of the naive approach. As expected, the *projector illumination*

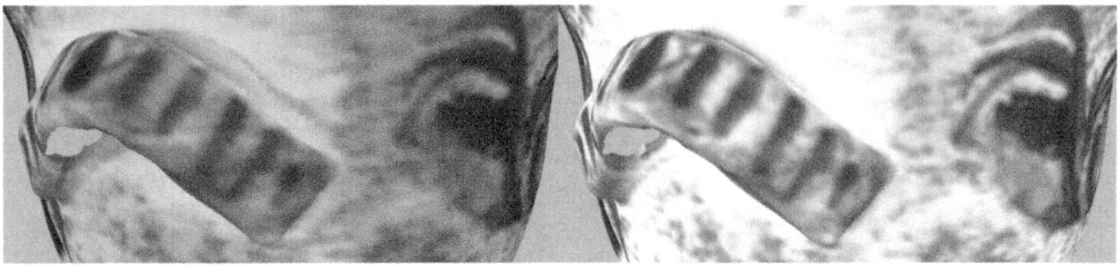

Fig. 4. Example of artifacts appearing due to misalignment errors

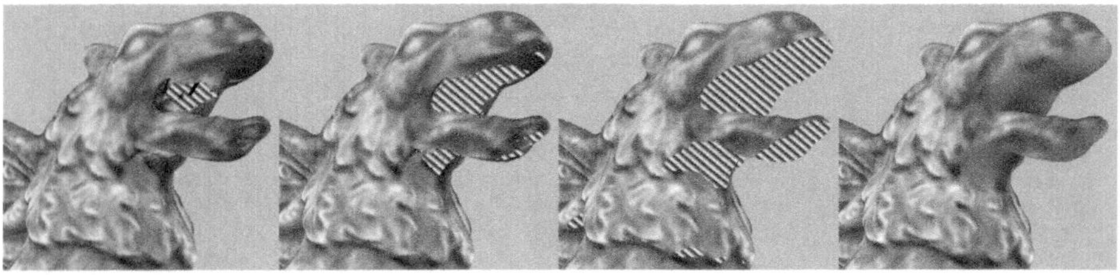

Fig. 5. Hole filling. Regions to process (indicated by yellow/black stripes) are selected by manually setting a threshold on the weight sum that results from the texturing.

mask tends to increase the influence of image regions that corresponds to the most illuminated surface parts, which leads to a conservation of luminosity. Other improvements can be observed. For the Gargoyle model (*left*), we can see that fine details on the wings are much less blurry when the weights are introduced in the computations, thanks to the fact that the surface orientation with respect to the viewpoint is considered. For the Pot model (*middle*), the big vertical crack in the white rectangle results from the fact that one portion of the surface was depicted by a much greater number of frames with respect to the adjacent one: this produces an imbalance among the number of summed color contributions, and the consequent abrupt change of color. Thanks to masks related to visibility and illumination criteria, with our approach the big crack completely disappears. For the Strawberry model (*right*), some regions are slightly brighter in the case of the naive texturing. They arise from strong specular highlights in the input pictures and are highly reduced in the case of our method. Figure 4 shows the typical artifact appearing at step discontinuities when misalignment errors are neglected. Once again, the use of the adequate mask permits to remove it.

Figure 5 illustrates the hole filling. The left image shows a region left empty by the texturing process. Around this hole, artifacts can be seen due to the fact that the surface was captured at grazing angle during the whole video, then leading to a color sampling of bad quality. The second and third images show how the selection based on the total weight sum adapts its shape when the threshold is changed. The right image finally shows the model once the selected region has been filled.

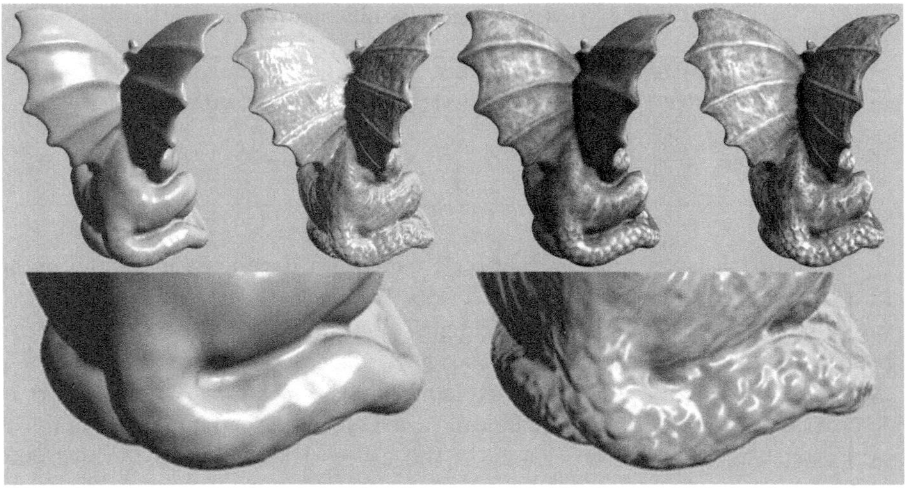

Fig. 6. The Gargoyle model rendered with and without the extracted normal map

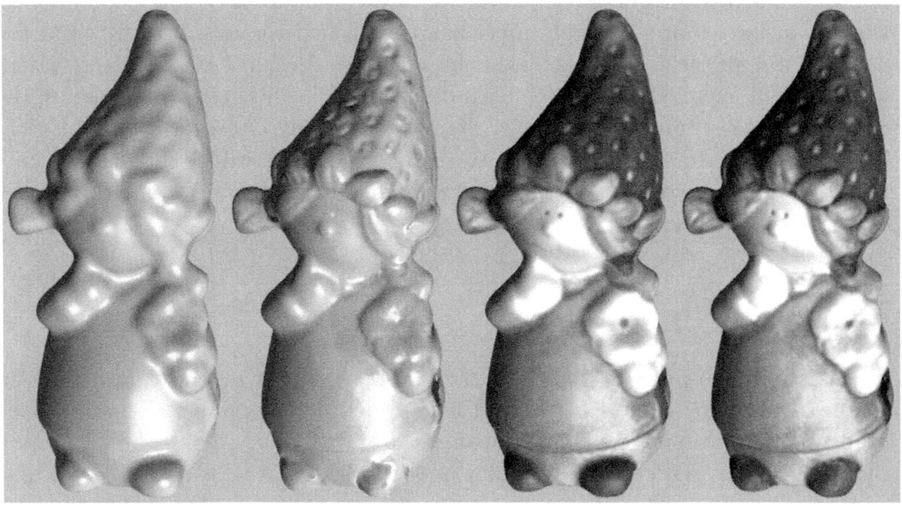

Fig. 7. The Strawberry model rendered with and without the extracted normal map

Figures 6 and 7 shows different renderings of the Gargoyle and the Strawberry models, with and without the normal map extracted by our system. As it can be seen, high-frequency shape details are clearly missing in the rough geometry acquired by the in-hand scanner. Thanks to our shape-from-shading approach, these details can be accurately captured and rendered afterward by bump mapping.

Table 1. Texturing times for different data sets

Model	*No. of pictures*	*No. of highlight detection passes*	*Total texturing time (in seconds)*	
			without normal map	*with normal map*
Gargoyle	1070	2	194	198
Strawberry	2110	2	266	277
Pot	330	2	27.5	29

Computation times are reported on Table 1 and have been measured on an Intel i7 2.8GHz and a GeForce GTX 480. Recorded times correspond to two texturing passes, since specular highlight removal has been activated. It can be noted that the additional computation cost introduced by the normal map extraction is negligible. It can be explained by the fact that color and normal reconstructions are performed simultaneously: the data loading on the graphics card (which is the main bottleneck of the process) has to be performed only once.

The parameters that must be set by the user are the followings: the hole filling selection threshold, for which a visual feedback similar to what is shown in Figure 5 is provided in real time, the iteration number for the diffusion process, which can be set progressively until having reached the desire result, and the number of applications for each elementary mask. As said before, default values working well for most cases have been determined. Nonetheless, considering the aforementioned computation times, the user can easily try several combinations by relaunching the texturing so as to see how different values impact the final result. The set of parameters is then really small and can be tuned in an easy and intuitive manner.

5 Conclusion

In this paper, we presented an automatic approach that produces an enhanced textured mesh for a model acquired using an in-hand scanner. The approach proposed is quite general, since it can be applied to any 3D scanning system that is based on structured light, and uses a video-camera as sensing unit. The advantages of the enhanced digital model are extremely important for all those applications where knowledge of the pure shape is not enough; pairing the overall shape model with data on color, surface reflection and high-frequency scale geometry detail is of paramount importance to produce high quality digital replicas of real objects. An advantage of our proposal is that it does not require to modify the scanning hardware design, since it is based only on an automatic, improved processing of the input data.

Some possible future work is as follows. In the current implementation, texturing is performed as a post-processing task; but we could also study a solution to perform the texturing online, while the measurement is performed, to present immediate feedback to the user during the scanning session. The current bump map estimation tends to produce inconsistent normals when the sampling is too sparse; one possible idea to improve robustness is to perform a constrained computation by analyzing the dispersion of the cone defined by the sampling directions. Finally, displacement mapping can be added on the base of the information contained in the normal map, to enrich the rough geometry given by the scanner with a better visualization.

Acknowledgment. This work has been performed in the frame of the ERCIM fellowship program.

The research leading to these results has received funding from the EU 7th Framework Programme (FP7/2007-2013), through the 3D-COFORM project, under grant agreement n. 231809.

References

1. Bannai, N., Agathos, A., Fisher, R.B.: Fusing multiple color images for texturing models. In: 3DPVT 2004, pp. 558–565 (2004)
2. Baumberg, A.: Blending images for texturing 3d models. In: BMVC 2002. Canon Research Center Europe (2002)
3. Bernardini, F., Martin, I.M., Rushmeier, H.: High-quality texture reconstruction from multiple scans. IEEE Tr. on Visual. and Comp. Graph. 7(4), 318–332 (2001)
4. Callieri, M., Cignoni, P., Corsini, M., Scopigno, R.: Masked photo blending: mapping dense photographic dataset on high-resolution 3d models. Computer & Graphics 32(4), 464–473 (2008)
5. Callieri, M., Cignoni, P., Scopigno, R.: Reconstructing textured meshes from multiple range rgb maps. In: 7th Intl. Fall Workshop on Vision, Modeling, and Visualization 2002, Erlangen (D), November 20-22, pp. 419–426 (2002)
6. Chuang, M., Luo, L., Brown, B.J., Rusinkiewicz, S., Kazhdan, M.: Estimating the laplace-beltrami operator by restricting 3d functions. In: Proceedings of the Symposium on Geometry Processing, pp. 1475–1484 (July 2009)
7. Corsini, M., Dellepiane, M., Ponchio, F., Scopigno, R.: Image-to-geometry registration: a mutual information method exploiting illumination-related geometric properties. Computer Graphics Forum 28(7), 1755–1764 (2009)
8. Dellepiane, M., Callieri, M., Corsini, M., Cignoni, P., Scopigno, R.: Improved color acquisition and mapping on 3d models via flash-based photography. ACM Journ. on Computers and Cultural heritage 2(4), 1–20 (2010)
9. Dellepiane, M., Callieri, M., Marroquim, R., Cignoni, P., Scopigno, R.: Flow-based local optimization for image-to-geometry projection. IEEE Transaction on Visualization and Computer Graphics (in press, 2011)
10. Dorsey, J., Rushmeier, H., Sillion, F.: Digital modeling of material appearance. Morgan Kauf./Elsevier (2007)
11. Eisemann, M., De Decker, B., Magnor, M., Bekaert, P., de Aguiar, E., Ahmed, N., Theobalt, C., Sellent, A.: Floating textures. Computer Graphics Forum (Proc. Eurographics EG 2008) 27(2), 409–418 (2008)
12. Franken, T., Dellepiane, M., Ganovelli, F., Cignoni, P., Montani, C., Scopigno, R.: Minimizing user intervention in registering 2D images to 3D models. The Visual Computer 21(8-10), 619–628 (2005)
13. Gal, R., Wexler, Y., Ofek, E., Hoppe, H., Cohen-Or, D.: Seamless montage for texturing models. Comput. Graph. Forum 29(2), 479–486 (2010)

14. Hall-Holt, O., Rusinkiewicz, S.: Stripe boundary codes for real-time structured-light range scanning of moving objects. In: ICCV 2001, vol. 2, pp. 359–366 (2001)
15. Ikeuchi, K., Oishi, T., Takamatsu, J., Sagawa, R., Nakazawa, A., Kurazume, R., Nishino, K., Kamakura, M., Okamoto, Y.: The great buddha project: digitally archiving, restoring, and analyzing cultural heritage objects. Int. J. Comput. Vision 75(1), 189–208 (2007)
16. Larue, F., Dischler, J.-M.: Automatic registration and calibration for efficient surface light field acquisition. In: 7th VAST International Symposium on Virtual Reality, Archeology and Cultural Heritage, Eurographics, pp. 171–178 (2006)
17. Pulli, K., Abi-Rached, H., Duchamp, T., Shapiro, L., Stuetzle, W.: Acquisition and visualization of colored 3d objects. In: Proc. of ICPR 1998, pp. 11–15 (1998)
18. Rankov, V., Locke, R., Edens, R., Barber, P., Vojnovic, B.: An algorithm for image stitching and blending. In: SPIE, vol. 5701, pp. 190–199 (2005)
19. Rushmeier, H.E., Taubin, G., Guéziec, A.: Appying shape from lighting variation to bump map capture. In: Proc. of the Eurographics Workshop on Rendering Techniques 1997, London, UK, pp. 35–44 (1997)
20. Rusinkiewicz, S., Hall-Holt, O., Levoy, M.: Real-time 3d model acquisition. ACM Trans. Graph. 21, 438–446 (2002)
21. Stamos, I., Liu, L., Chen, C., Wolberg, G., Yu, G., Zokai, S.: Integrating automated range registration with multiview geometry for the photorealistic modeling of large-scale scenes. Int. J. Comput. Vision 78, 237–260 (2008)
22. Unger, J., Wenger, A., Hawkins, T., Gardner, A., Debevec, P.: Capturing and rendering with incident light fields. In: EGRW 2003, pp. 141–149 (2003)
23. Weise, T., Leibe, B., Van Gool, L.: Fast 3d scanning with automatic motion compensation. In: IEEE CVPR 2007 (June 2007)
24. Weise, T., Wismer, T., Leibe, B., Van Gool, L.: In-hand scanning with online loop closure. In: 3DIM 2009 (October 2009)
25. Zhang, L., Curless, B., Seitz, S.M.: Spacetime stereo: shape recovery for dynamic scenes. In: Proceedings of IEEE Computer Society Conference on Computer Vision and Pattern Recognition, vol. 2, pp. II-367–II-374 (June 2003)

Voice Technology to Enable Sophisticated Access to Historical Audio Archive of the Czech Radio

Jan Nouza, Karel Blavka, Marek Bohac, Petr Cerva, Jindrich Zdansky, Jan Silovsky, and Jan Prazak

Institute of Information Technology and Electronics, Technical Univesity of Liberec
Studentska 2, 461 17 Liberec, Czech Republic
{jan.nouza,karel.blavka,marek.bohac,petr.cerva,jindrich.zdansky,
jan.silovsky,jan.prazak}@tul.cz

Abstract. The Czech Radio archive of spoken documents is considered one of the gems of the Czech cultural heritage. It contains the largest collection (more than 100.000 hours) of spoken documents recorded during the last 90 years. We are developing a complex platform that should automatically transcribe a significant portion of the archive, index it and eventually prepare it for full-text search. The four-year project supported by the Czech Ministry of culture is challenging in the way that it copes with huge volumes of data, with historical as well as contemporary language, a rather low signal quality in case of old recordings, and also with documents spoken not only in Czech but also in Slovak. The technology used includes speech, speaker and language recognition modules, speaker and channel adaptation components, tools for data indexation and retrieval, and a web interface that allows for public access to the archive. Recently, a demo version of the platform is available for testing and searching in some 10.000 hours of already processed data.

Keywords: audio archive processing, speech-to-text, audio search.

1 Introduction

One of the prospective application areas for modern voice technology is automatic processing of audio archives containing speech. The ultimate goal is to transcribe them and store the transcriptions in the database, in which one can search and retrieve a piece of information he or she is interested in. The search needs not to be focused only on the content, but also on linguistic issues such as the speaking style, pronunciation, spoken language evolution, etc.

The systems developed for audio archive processing are very complex. They include speech and speaker recognition modules as well as tools for indexation, full-text search and audio play. They have been designed namely for broadcast documents [1], for national archives of spoken language [2,3] or for special-purpose collections such as, e.g. MALACH [4]. We have been working on this topic since 2005 [5] and some of the developed tools have been already deployed in broadcast data mining [6].

C. Grana and R. Cucchiara (Eds.): MM4CH 2011, CCIS 247, pp. 27–38, 2012.

This paper presents a large applied-research project supported by the Czech Ministry of culture. The project aims at processing the archive of historical and contemporary recordings of the Czech Radio and making its content available for public access. The archive covers almost 90 years of broadcasting and contains hundreds of thousands spoken documents, from which a large portion should be transcribed by a speech-to-text system developed specially for this purpose in our lab. The project started in 2011 and will run for 4 years. During that period we are going to build the complete archive processing and accessing platform and employ it for transcribing about 100.000 hours of audio data. The project offers several major challenges: a) working with huge volumes of data, b) managing Czech language with its highly inflective nature and very large lexical inventory with more than one million word-forms, c) identifying and processing documents spoken also in Slovak, which was the second official language in former Czechoslovakia, d) dealing with the language and lexicon evolving during the 90-year period and influenced by different political regimes, and last but not least e) coping with rather poor quality of most historical recordings.

In 2000s, a large part of the Czech Radio data has been digitized but the individual recordings are stored on tapes, on CDs, or on hard disks. If one wants to search for any particular piece of information, he or she must browse the catalogue where each document is described by its name, the date of recording or broadcasting and several tags or key-words. Then, it is necessary to retrieve the media from the archive and listen to them in hope that the required information will be found, eventually.

The primary goal of the project is to make this search automated and more comfortable. The user should be able to get answers not only to simple queries made of words or phrases, but he or she could search also for e.g. utterances spoken by a selected person, for historically first occurrence of a given word, or for a particular pronunciation of a word. Moreover, the queries can combine various search criteria to answer, for example, a question like: What did person A say about person B within time period T? Hence, the potential users of the system will be not only the people from the Czech Radio itself, but anybody who is interested in media data mining as well as historians, linguists, phoneticians, communication specialists, students, etc.

Though the project is running its first year, now, the concept of the system has been already set up and some of the essential modules already exist as functional prototypes. We have used them to build a preliminary version of the system to test different techniques and approaches, and to demonstrate it to prospective users. At the moment, the system allows for access to some 10.000 hours of transcribed recordings.

2 Audio Archive Processing Platform

Let us present the archive processing and accessing platform (APAP) from the user's point view, first. Its general overview is depicted in Fig. 1.

Anybody who wants to search in the archive needs to have an access to internet. On the dedicated web page, he or she enters the word(s) or phrase(s), he or she is interested in, optionally sets some search constraints (e.g. time period, program name, speaker name, etc) and clicks the Search button. Immediately after that, the documents meeting the given criteria occur on the screen, being ordered according to the chosen relevancy rate. By clicking on the selected document, the part containing the searched term starts to be played. The user can easily navigate within the text, read it and listen to any part of it.

The associated audio data are streamed from the server located in the premises of the Czech Radio. The link between the audio and the text is provided by the database server. It contains rich text transcriptions created during the process of speech-to-text conversion and indexation. This is the core function of the whole platform as it includes complex audio data processing procedures mentioned below. These procedures are time consuming and they are performed off-line by a computer cluster.

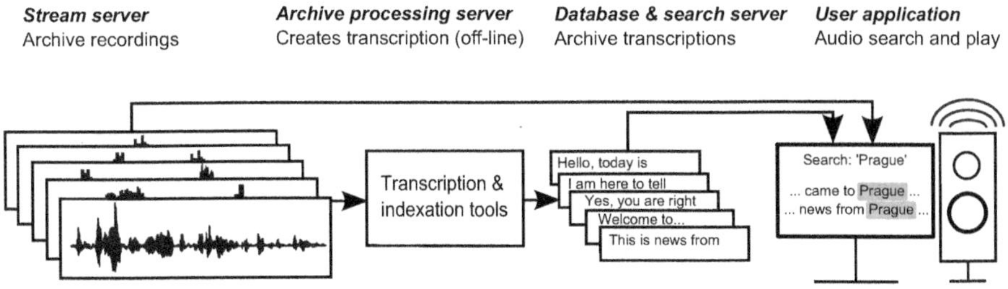

Fig. 1. Data flow in APAP (Archive Processing and Accessing Platform)

The technology behind the platform is much more complex. Its aim is a) to create text documents from the audio ones, b) to establish detailed links between them, c) to store them in the database and d) to allow for their later retrieval. The platform's core is made of several modules as shown in Fig. 2.

The standard procedure for transcribing and indexing an audio document runs as follows: The document passes through an audio processing module where signal samples are converted into feature vectors that are later used in identification, classification and decoding tasks. The next step consists in segmentation of the running signal into speech and non-speech parts (e.g. long silence, noise or music). The speech segments pass into the module that searches for significant changes in signal character, which can be either speaker turns or changes in the signal band-with (usually a part containing telephone talk). These change points are used to split the speech into individual utterances. For each utterance, we try to determine some relevant characteristics such as broad/narrow band signal, clean/noisy speech and male/female speaker. Optionally, we may employ also a speaker identification module operating with a database of a priori known voices. All this kind of information is used to set up the speech recognition module so that it can benefit from employing the proper acoustic model, e.g. the gender or speaker dependent one. The recognition module performs speech decoding using the given (general or topic oriented) lexicon and the corresponding language model. The output from the decoder is the best sequence of recognized words with their pronunciations and time markers. The latter represent beginning and ending times (measured in milliseconds from the start of the document) for each word and each identified non-speech event, and they serve for aligning the audio signal with its text version. Eventually, the raw output from the recognizer undergoes a post-processing stage where, for example, the sequences of numerals are replaced by digits, capital letters and punctuation are added, etc. The final transcription together with the time markers and complementary information, such as speaker's identity, is indexed and stored in the database. More technical details on the modules and procedures can be found in section 4.

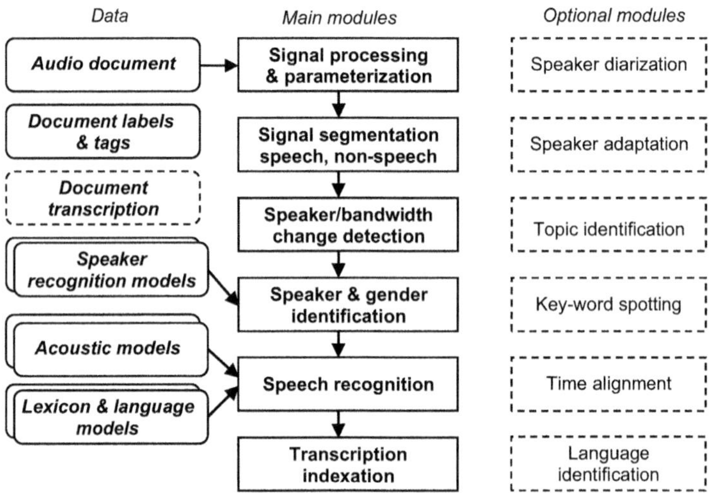

Fig. 2. Data and document processing modules in APAP

Besides this main line of modules, there are also several optional components in the system. The speaker diarization module searches for all segments in the document that belong to the same speakers. This is useful, for example, in the transcription of debate programs where speech segments belonging to speakers unknown to the system can be at least identified as of person A, person B, etc. The speaker adaptation module allows for fitting the available acoustic model to the currently speaking person, which can be employed to improve the accuracy in an optional two-pass decoding procedure. The system performance can be further enhanced if the topic of the document is known and hence a topic dependent lexicon and language model can be employed. The topic can be determined either a priori, from the document tags, or a posteriori during the first-pass speech decoding. For the same purpose we can utilize also a fast performing key-word spotting module. In special situations, where for some documents their transcriptions already exist, the slower speech recognition procedure can be replaced by a much faster signal-to-text alignment routine whose aim is to generate the missing time markers [7]. This technique is very helpful as many recently broadcast programs already have their text forms. It not only saves computing time, but also allows us to index the already existing human-made transcriptions, which are almost 100 % accurate and which can serve also for feed-back training of the recognition modules. At the end of this brief overview, let us mention also a module that must be developed specifically for this project. Its goal is to identify the language of the currently processed utterance, in our case, Czech or Slovak. The two languages are linguistically similar but with significantly different lexicon and grammar.

3 Archive Data

The data in the archive represent almost 90 years of broadcasting in Czechoslovakia and in the Czech Republic. When founded in 1923, the Czech Radiojournal company was only one year younger than the premier world broadcaster, the BBC. Later, the company was transformed into the Czechoslovak Radio and with the split of Czechoslovakia (in 1993) the Czech Radio took over the service and the historical archive. The Czech Radio is the public broadcaster and recently it runs 8 nation-wide channels and 10 regional programs. Two channels are mainly news oriented, another focuses on science programs, and the others offer a mix of spoken word, music and leisure. The three word-oriented channels produce about 8000 hours of unique documents a year.

The oldest preserved recordings date to late 1920s and since 1945 there is an (almost) un-interrupted series of daily news programs recorded originally on tapes and recently digitized. The archive contains more than 100.000 hours of spoken documents, most of them being news programs, daily commentaries, debates, talk-shows. This is the domain the project focuses on.

The audio data that are to be processed and made available for public search differ in technical as well as social aspects, which makes the project really challenging. The documents (or their parts) may vary with respect to:

- *original storage media:* analog (film, tape) or digital memory,
- *audio band-width:* narrow band (AM or telephone), or wide band signal,
- *digital quality:* CD quality as well as highly compressed loss formats,
- *background noise:* from negligible one in case of studio recordings to large-noise in field records; music or another speech may occur in background,
- *speaking style:* read speech, planned talk, spontaneous conversation,
- *historical and social issues:* contemporary language as well as archaic language from 1930s and 1940s, lexicon of communist era (1945-1989), etc.
- *national language:* mainly Czech, but also Slovak (in particular before 1993).

After a closer survey of the archive data, we have classified them into several historical epochs. Because our strategy is to process the archive from the present time towards the history, we denote the contemporary epoch with index 0 and the previous ones with negative indexes. (The positive indexes will be reserved for future epochs if necessary.)

Epoch E0 (2000 – present). The documents from this epoch are usually in good digital quality and when compressed, the distortion is not severe. The amount of recordings is very high (thousands of hours a year). Moreover, literal transcriptions are available for some of them. This will allow us to perform the automatic alignment procedure to speed up the initial feeding of the database and at the same time to re-train the existing acoustic model on the target data. The official transcriptions will also give us enough information to make a large database of voices for the speaker identification module. The lexicon and language model can be further enhanced by analyzing additional text resources, mainly electronic versions of newspapers. Czech is the major language used in the documents and rarely occurring Slovak can be skipped or neglected – at least in the initial stage of the project.

Epoch E-1 (1990 – 2000). The audio data from this epoch were digitized mostly in times where the available storage capacity was strictly limited and therefore most data is compressed using loss formats (mp3, mp2, etc). There exist no literal transcriptions for the documents, only brief summaries and tags. For lexicon and language model building only a limited amount of newspaper texts is available in electronic form. In early 1990s, Slovak frequently occurs as the second language in the spoken documents.

Epoch E-2 (1968 – 1989). The data from this period were originally stored on analog tapes and later converted into loss audio format. No transcriptions neither electronic texts are available to adjust the lexicon, which was significantly influenced by the ruling communist regime. Here, we hope to get access to at least some amount of scanned and OCRed newspapers from that period. The major type of the processed documents will be the daily recordings of main evening news where Czech and Slovak are mixed regularly.

Epoch E-3 (1945 – 1967). The audio archive contains only one major program per day (evening news). Most data is still stored on analog tapes and it will have to be digitized on demand. The signal has very low quality, partly because of AM broadcasting in those days and partly because of the storage media. For adapting the acoustic model to the given signal quality and for building the proper lexicon and language model, some parts of the archive will have to be manually transcribed. We expect that the language (Czech and Slovak) of this period will be also influenced by Russian, as Czechoslovakia was part of the Soviet political sphere that time.

Epoch E-4 (before 1945). From this epoch, there is only a limited amount of spoken documents. However, they have a great historical value because they include, for example, addresses and talks of the first Czechoslovak presidents, speeches from the parliament, programs broadcasted during WWII and the German occupation, etc. It is almost sure that these documents will require individual care to get them transcribed and indexed in the database.

As mentioned earlier, the archive processing work will go against the flow of time, from the present towards the past. The reason is rational. The transcription system has been developed for contemporary language using a large amount of audio and text data collected during the last decade. When moving backwards we have to adjust the lexicon, the language model as well as the acoustic one towards the character of the data of the previous epochs. In other words, we will have to adapt the speech processing front-end and the acoustic model to the gradually decreasing signal quality. At the same time, it will be necessary to modify the lexicon by adding the words specific to the given period. The language model will be forced to forget continually the contemporary phrases and collocations and learn those typical for the target period. The further to the past we go, the harder this tasks will be for automation, as the amount of data available for training the statistical models will be smaller and smaller. Yet, our preliminary experiments have proved that this way back was feasible.

4 Technical Solutions

All the speech processing modules for the APAP are being developed in our lab. The core components, such as the large-vocabulary continuous-speech recognition (LVCSR) system for Czech, or the speaker identification (SID) tool, already exist and the main task in the project is to adapt them for the target application. In case of the LVCSR, the main focus is put on increasing the size of the operating vocabularies (up to 1 million entries) and on eliminating the impact of lower signal quality. Moreover, the Slovak version of the recognizer must be built. The other components, such as the language identification (LID) module, the speaker diarization module, or the speaker adaptation module are still under development. In the following text, we shall briefly describe the main technical parameters of the platform.

4.1 Audio Processing and Acoustic Modeling Part

Because the data in the audio archive are stored in various formats, it is necessary to convert them into a standard one before they enter the signal processing routines. This standard has been set to 16 kHz, 16 bit, PCM WAV format and we use the popular FFmpeg tool [8] for the conversion. After that, the audio signal is parameterized into a stream of feature vectors. These are 39-dimensional mel-frequency cepstral coefficients (MFCCs) computed every 10 ms. The vector includes 13 static, 13 delta and 13 delta-delta coefficients. Using a 2-second long sliding window, the MFCC features are normalized by the cepstral mean subtraction technique.

The acoustic-phonetic inventory of spoken Czech includes 40 phonemes and 8 noise types. They are represented by continuous-density hidden Markov models (HMM) trained on the database of spoken Czech. Recently, it contains 120 hours of annotated speech from more than 1000 speakers. Approximately one half of that amount is made of read speech recordings containing phonetically balanced utterances, the other half comes from broadcasting. This second part is continuously growing, being fed by the already processed archive data. Two types of HMMs have been trained on this database: the context-independent units (monophones) and the context-dependent ones (triphones). The latter (currently represented by 75 thousand gaussians) are employed in the main transcription task, while the former (with some 45 thousand gaussians) find use in situations where higher speed and lower memory requirements are important, namely in the word-spotting and text alignment routines. There are separate models for each gender, and for wide-band and telephone signal. The proper type of model is determined in the speaker and channel recognition modules that employ the same feature vectors and gaussian mixture model (GMM) based classifiers.

4.2 Linguistic Part and Speech Decoding

The linguistic part of the LVCSR system is made of a lexicon and a language model (LM). Recently, the universal lexicon used for the transcription of contemporary archive documents contains 340k words and word-forms. These are the most frequent lexical units that occurred in the 40 GB large corpus of texts covering national media since 1990. The number of all distinctive Czech words found in the corpus is higher than 2 millions and we have chosen those that appeared at least 50 times. The lexicon is gradually growing as new words get over the threshold. For most documents, this size of lexicon can assure the out-of-vocabulary (OOV) rate lower than 2 %. If we wished to get below 1 % for the majority of spoken documents, the lexicon should contain at least 800k entries. At the moment, this is not feasible because it would slow down the transcription process significantly. Yet, we plan to reach that size in near future. It should be also noted that more than one tenth of the words in the lexicon have multiple alternative pronunciations. Their total number is 390k, currently. The language model is based on bigrams. In the above mentioned 40 GB corpus of contemporary Czech texts we found 130 million different word-pairs. The unseen ones have been backed-off by the Witten-Bell smoothing technique, which optimally fits to our implementation of the speech decoder.

The decoder has been designed to manage vocabularies up to 1 million distinct words. When it operates with the current set of 390k pronunciation forms, it is able to do it in real time, at least for clean speech. For larger vocabularies, more spontaneous and noisy utterances, the processing time may be doubled, or in an extreme case, even tripled. When required, speech transcription runs in a two-pass mode. In the first one, a smaller vocabulary with approx. 50k words is utilized with the aim to obtain a good estimate of the phonetic transcription of the utterance. Unsupervised adaptation based on the MLLR technique is performed on this data and immediately applied in the second pass, in which the full lexicon is employed. In the two-pass case, the total transcription time is about 1.5 times longer. Some figures illustrating the system performance can be found in section 5.

4.3 Database and Search Part

The modules mentioned above generate results in form similar to that displayed in Table 1. For each document, this data is stored in the database. We decided for the MySQL [9] solution as it optimally fits to the type and size of data. Every word and every speaker occurrence is indexed using the Sphinx [10] platform, which proved to be fast and flexible enough both for the indexation as well as the search tasks.

Table 1. Data generated by transcription system and stored & indexed in archive database. (The presented data are real and they correspond to the document shown in Fig. 3. The start and end times are in milliseconds.)

Document identification
Channel: CRo1 Program: 20 minut Broadcast: 2009-09-23 17:33

Segment/speaker	***Start***	***End***	***Text***	***Phonetic***
Non-speech	000000	004520	-	/jingle/
Helena Šulcová	004520	005140	Lisabonská	lisabonská
	005140	005560	smlouva	smlouva
	...	...	...	...
Václav Klaus	054740	055070	Tak	tak
	055070	055320	jedna	jedna
	055320	055640	věc	vjec
	...	...	...	...
	073230	073480	Bruselu	bruselu

4.4 User Interface Part

The ultimate goal of the project is to allow for public search in the transcribed archive documents. A user just needs to be connected to internet and have a properly set up web browser that supports audio playback. Currently, he or she can use the demo version of the search interface displayed in Fig. 3 and available at [11].

The user has a lot of choices to formulate a query. He or she can search for a word (or its part using the * convention), a phrase or multiple words. Furthermore, the user can specify the speaker, the broadcast channel, the program name or the time period. After the Search button is pressed, the number of found documents is shown and their list is available for reading and playing with the searched terms being highlighted. The user can click on any word in the selected document and the replay starts from that point. During the playback, the words corresponding to the running audio signal are shown in red color. A picture associated with the speaker or the topic of the document can be retrieved from the archive, too.

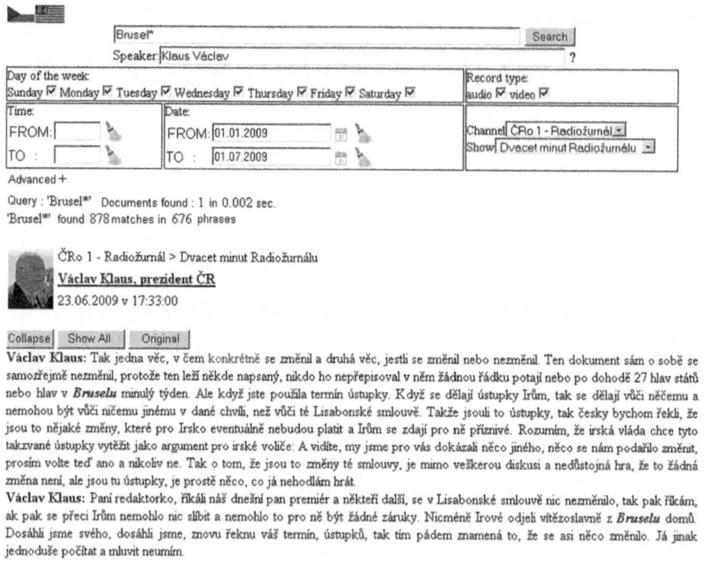

Fig. 3. Web interface for archive search. (The screenshot shows one of the documents containing searched word Brusel* and spoken by Václav Klaus in the given year. The searched word occurs in 73230th millisecond of the talk – compare to Table 1.)

5 Performance Evaluation

In 2011, we have been focusing mainly on setting up the first version of the audio archive platform and on processing the documents from Epoch E0. As explained in section 3, the data from this time period are well covered by the lexicon and language model created previously in our lab [6]. Moreover, for a significant number of documents we have already had their official transcriptions. These can be easily and reliably indexed via the time-alignment procedure mentioned in section 2. An additional benefit is that we can evaluate the performance of the recognition system by comparing its output to the official transcriptions. We do it regularly to investigate the impact of different system settings and the effect of continuously updated acoustic and language model. Some figures illustrating the performance of the current version are summarized in Table 2.

Table 2. Transcription system performance. (The results were obtained with 340k lexicon, bigram LM, 1-pass mode and 10 hours of test recordings from epoch E0 in broadcast quality.)

Document type	Accuracy [%]	OOV [%]	Real-time factor
News from studio	94.67	1.23	1.04
Complete news shows	86.86	1.36	1.26
Talk programs - politics	83.53	1.12	1.43
Talk programs - science	81.61	2.38	1.52

Table 2 shows the basic performance figures for four different types of audio documents. We can see that the transcription accuracy is quite high for news read in studio – 94.67 %. It should be further noted that in this case many recognition errors are deletions of short words (namely one-phoneme prepositions, as 'v', 's', 'z') or minor substitutions in acoustically similar word suffixes due to complex Czech morphology. The results are obviously worse for complete news shows because of their parts recorded out of studio or those with background noise and music. The transcription of discussions and debates suffers mainly due to spontaneous and overlapping speech. We can also see that the debates dealing with more general topics, such as daily politics, are better covered by the lexicon and the language model (which was trained mainly on newspaper texts) than those broadcasted by the science-oriented channel.

Unfortunately, the results get worse if we have to work with loss audio format, such as mp3. This is the real situation because most data in the Czech Radio archive is highly compressed and stored in mp3 files. In that case, the transcription accuracy may decrease by 3 to 5 %. We try to compensate this type of signal degradation in two different ways: The first one utilizes the acoustic models trained on the data that passed through an mp3 decoder and hence better match the compressed audio files. The other approach consists in applying the speaker and channel adaptation technique to each utterance and running the second recognition pass as described in section 4.2.

It should be also noted that the lower recognition accuracy obtained for some parts of the archive does not necessarily mean critical malfunction of the search task. In practice, most queries focus on words or phrases that are more than one syllable long and these have significantly larger chance to be recognized well. So, even though the utterance is transcribed with some errors, most key-words are still searchable and the user usually gets the access to the piece of information he or she is interested in.

6 Conclusions and Future Work

National archives of spoken documents represent a very specific area of cultural heritage. So far they could not be accessed by wide public because their virtual and rather abstract form, together with their specific way of storage, did not allow it. Our project shows that it will be possible soon, thanks to modern information and multimedia technology. At the moment, almost 10.000 documents from the Czech Radio archive have been already transcribed and made accessible. These documents come mainly from the last decade and their processing and publishing was easier compared to what we may expect when moving back towards the historical part of the archive. In order to accomplish the future challenges, we have already started complementary research works, such as scanning historical newspapers and converting them into electronic texts, collecting Czech words and phrases that were typical for specific periods of the Czech and Czechoslovak history and, last but not least, we have begun the development of a module that will be able to process also the Slovak language. The results seem to be promising so far [12].

Although the current project is focused on audio data, the platform is being designed to manage the video broadcast archives as well. This additional feature has been already demonstrated on a small part of the Czech TV archive of news programs [6].

Acknowledgments. This work was supported by project no. DF11P01OVV013 provided by Czech Ministry of culture in research program NAKI.

References

1. Hayashi, Y., et al.: Speech-based and video-supported indexing multimedia broadcast news. In: Proc. ACM SIGIR (2003)
2. Ordelman, R., de Jong, F., Huijbregts, M., van Leeuwen, D.: Robust audio indexing for Dutch spoken word collections. In 16th Int. Conference of the Association for History and Computing, Humanities, Computers and Cultural Heritage, Amsterdam, pp. 215–223 (2005)
3. Hansen, J.H.L., Huang, R., Zhou, B., Seadle, M., Deller, J.R., Gurijala, A.R., Kurimo, M., Angkititrakul, P.: SpeechFind: Advances in Spoken Document Retrieval for a National Gallery of the Spoken Word. IEEE Trans. on Speech and Audio Processing 13(5), 712–730 (2005)
4. Byrne, W., et al.: Automatic recognition of spontaneous speech for access to multilingual oral history archives. IEEE Trans. Speech Audio Process. 12(4), 420–435 (2004)
5. Nouza, J., Zdansky, J., Cerva, P., Kolorenc, J.: A System for Information Retrieval from Large Records of Czech Spoken Data. In: Sojka, P., Kopeček, I., Pala, K. (eds.) TSD 2006. LNCS (LNAI), vol. 4188, pp. 485–492. Springer, Heidelberg (2006)
6. Nouza, J., Zdansky, J., Cerva, P.: System for automatic collection, annotation and indexing of Czech broadcast speech with full-text search. In: 15th IEEE Mediterranean Electrotechnical Conference (MELECON 2010), Malta, pp. 202–205 (2010)
7. Nouza, J., Zdansky, J.: Automatic Alignment between Speech Records and Their Text Transcriptions for Audio Archive Indexing and Searching. In: 6th IEEE Conference on Informatics and Systems, pp. MM6–MM12. IEEE, Egypt (2008)
8. FFmpeg converter program, `http://www.ffmpeg.org/`
9. MySQL platform, `http://www.mysql.com/`
10. SPHINX platform, `http://sphinxsearch.com/`
11. Demo of APAP platform, `http://ahmed.ite.tul.cz/demo/`
12. Nouza, J., Silovsky, J., Zdansky, J., Cerva, P., Kroul, M., Chaloupka, J.: Czech-to-Slovak Adapted Broadcast News Transcription System. In: Proc. of Interspeech 2008, Australia, pp. 2683–2686 (2008)

MNEMOSYNE: Enhancing the Museum Experience through Interactive Media and Visual Profiling

Andrew D. Bagdanov, Alberto Del Bimbo, Lea Landucci, and Federico Pernici

University of Florence,
Media Integration and Communication Center (MICC)
Florence, Italy
{bagdanov,delbimbo,landucci,pernici}@dsi.unifi.it
http://www.micc.unifi.it/

Abstract. MNEMOSYNE is a three year project whose primary goal is to deliver a personalized, interactive multimedia experience to museum visitors through the novel application of personalization driven by computer vision-based profiling. A combination of passive, wall-mounted cameras and sensors carried by guests acquiring active and passive imagery will be used to create a general profile of a museum visitor's interests in order to customize the presentation at interactive tabletop surfaces placed in the museum environment. In this article we discuss the general context in which MNEMOSYNE is defined, as well as the main technical directions the project will follow over the next three years. Some very preliminary results are given for the vision-based techniques to be used for visual profiling of museum visitors.

Keywords: Multimedia interactive museums, personalization, natural interaction, computer vision.

1 Introduction

Museums are traditionally spaces which have, by their very nature, an abundance of information available for dissemination to visitors. This information, however, is also traditionally extremely expensive to place at the disposition of museum visitors due to a number of factors ranging from need for highly qualified curators and exhibit designers to the need to safeguard one-of-a-kind pieces. Because of this, visitor access to museum collections can be limited and at times awkward.

The museum experience can be greatly improved by applying modern techniques of multimedia organization, presentation and interaction and offering different interaction modalities to visitors [24]. Doing this effectively requires a reorganization of the physical and informational space of the museum. A museum must be transformed into an intelligent information space which is, in some sense, aware of the behavior and desires of its visitors, and is able to subsequently provide modes of interaction appropriate to each user. We must in some way unify the physical and virtual museum experiences.

C. Grana and R. Cucchiara (Eds.): MM4CH 2011, CCIS 247, pp. 39–50, 2012.

Access to multimedia information about exhibits can be made highly accessible to non-expert users through the technology of natural interaction [5,6]. However, without appropriate *personalization* of such multimedia information displays, these multimedia stations become little more than fancy Internet kiosks that visitors are uncertain how to access in order to gain more information about aspects of the exhibit of interest to them. Personalization of multimedia museum content is one answer to this problem [1,17]. Personalization offers visitors a customized presentation of appropriate information related to the visitor's tastes and preferences.

In order for personalization to be effective, however, an accurate *profile* of each visitor is necessary, and these profiles should be collected as passively and non-intrusively as possible. Some early approaches to user profiling used sensors attached to, worn or carried by museum visitors. These approaches used first-generation tools and sensors which were very intrusive, such as wearable devices [21]. One of the first attempts was the *Museum Wearable* [20], a wearable computer which orchestrates an audiovisual narration as a function of the visitors interests gathered from his/her physical path in the museum and length of stops. The museum wearable was made by a mobile PC hosted inside a shoulder pack which users had to carry around the museum and a private-eye display that they must wear. Since, according to Donald Norman, the best technology is the one that you just cant see, so easy to use that is becomes "transparent" to the user [16], new less-intrusive solutions have been exploited in recent years. Computer vision technologies have multiple advantages:

- **They are non-intrusive and seamless**
  They are not seen by users, they integrate seamlessly with the architecture, and in many scenarios existing video surveillance infrastructure can be exploited;
- **They are highly scalable**
  The size of deployment can be personal or very large, they can cover a single room of a museum interior, an entire exhibit, or even network multiple museums and multiple exhibits; and
- **They are evolutive and future proof**
  As they rely on cameras, new features and capabilities usually imply software upgrades only.

In a nutshell, the goal of the MNEMOSYNE project is to create an intelligent visual information system capable of constructing a "visual profile" of museum visitors in order to customize interactive multimedia information displays. MNEMOSYNE is a three-year project funded by the Region of Tuscany and the European Commission whose primary goal is to research and develop techniques for delivering a personalized, interactive multimedia experience to museum visitors. The project is challenging as it brings together a number of state-of-the-art and emerging technologies in one application domain. The first main area of expertise is Natural Interaction, which is concerned with providing natural and tangible interfaces to multimedia information systems. In the context of

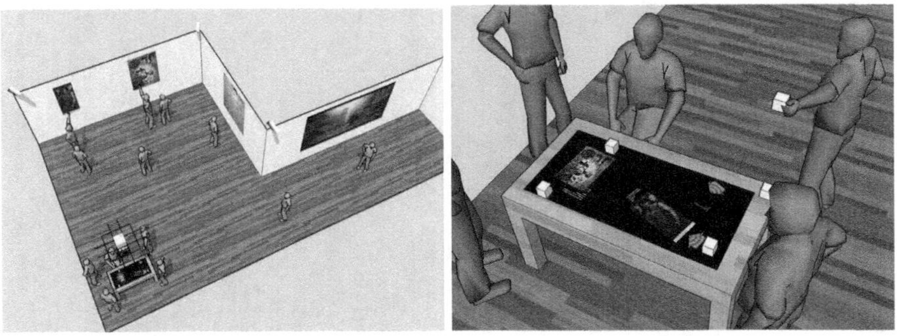

(a) (b)

Fig. 1. (a) Intelligent visual information systems, via a combination of fixed and wearable sensors, will analyze and reason about the interactions of visitors in the physical space. (b) At interactive tabletops placed throughout the museum environment, visitors will be presented with personalized, interactive suggestions about other possible exhibits.

MNEMOSYNE, figure 1b illustrates a scene in which museum visitors are provided with a customizable, personalized interaction surface with which they can interact with museum assets.

The other area of technical expertise key to the MNEMOSYNE project is Computer Vision. In figure 1a is shown a broader view of a museum interior. Using a combination of fixed and worn sensors, intelligent visual information systems will be built to interpret and profile visitors to the museum. In addition to providing a secure environment for physical museum assets, these visual systems will provide the information necessary for profiling the user and customizing the interactive terminals placed throughout the museum environment.

The MNEMOSYNE project is in its initial planning phase in which we have begun consolidating our existing work in related fields. In this article we describe some of the decisions we have made and the direction we will take MNEMOSYNE over the next three years. In the next section we discuss the state-of-the-art in interactive multimedia museums. In section 3 we discuss issues related to personalization in multimedia museum displays. Section 4 contains a discussion of the computer vision techniques we will bring to bear on the problem of visual profiling of museum guests. We conclude with a discussion in section 5 and indications of the trajectory the MNEMOSYNE will follow in the years to come.

2 Multimedia Interactive Museums

The presence of videos, interactive applications and detailed websites not only help visitors to manage the complexity of exhibited content, but also improves the persistence in memory of concepts through the use of different senses. While visitors are becoming acquainted with the presence of computers displaying various media in an exhibition or museum, these devices are usually placed in hidden

Fig. 2. Interactive surfaces engage museum visitors in ways traditional museum exhibits cannot

corners and rarely provide an interface designed for maximizing knowledge transfer and taking account of user experience: when it comes to multimedia, the offer is often limited to variants of common web sites.

Our perspective is centered on user interaction with digital devices specifically designed to reduce cognitive effort: this means that the interface design allows users to interact and to actually concentrate on content rather than thinking about how to use the interface. Focusing on content means that a wider point of view can be conveyed through the use of senses rarely used in a common PC environment, such as a proactive combination of touch, hearing and sight. Having this paradigm in mind, the cognitive load usually carried by the interface can be shifted to data, thus raising the level of complexity of transmitted information and achieving the goal of a technical and scientific communication of exhibit details.

The User Interface (UI) is the main contact point between users and computers: it is what users see, hear and touch; it is the perceptive representation of the communication channel which users use to communicate to the system and vice-versa. The research of new kinds of Natural Human-Computer Interaction systems is a growing field in computer science which aims to develop more intuitive, efficient, easy-to-use and satisfactory interfaces [6]. At the same time, researchers and companies (Microsoft with Surface, Nintendo, etc.) are trying to design and develop new devices to aid this process. In [22], Turk and Robertson divide User Interfaces into 3 different categories:

- **Perceptive user interfaces** which provide computers with human-like perceptual capabilities, so that implicit and explicit information about users and their environment can be conveniently acquired. The machine is able to see, hear or sense;
- **Multimodal user interfaces** which exploit multiple forms of input and/or output. In multimodal UI, various modalities can be used independently or simultaneously; and
- **Multimedia user interfaces** which are focused on media, such as text, graphics, video and/or sound.

Natural Human-Computer Interaction (NHCI) can be seen as a fusion of these kind of interfaces: its task is to make user interfaces more natural by taking into account the ways in which people naturally interact with each other and with the world. Among such systems, interactive surfaces that allow multiple users' touch are suitable for collaborative applications, especially in educational, professional and entertainment environments [13].

In MNEMOSYNE we have chosen the Natural Interaction paradigm because it allows us to design multimedia displays that require no user familiarity or training in order to use. They can begin interacting with their personalized, interactive multimedia presentation by simply walking up to one of the MNEMOSYNE multitouch tables present in the museum exhibit. The challenge will be in designing interfaces, multimedia content and user profiling primitives that interoperate in a seamless and natural way.

3 Personalizing the Multimedia Museum Experience

In recent years, the purpose of museums has shifted from merely providing static information to delivery of personalized interactive contents: before, it was very difficult for museum visitors to find the right information at the right time and at the right level of detail. The idea is then to turn the museum monologue into a user-centred dialog between the museum and its visitors [8]. This solution is what we call personalized multimedia tours. What distinguishes these from the traditional "static" ones is the exploitation of a user-model that represents the characteristics of each user [9]. The information stored in the user-model is exploited in the process of content generation to describe or recommend objects potentially relevant to users.

Personalized applications have exploited recent research results in recommender systems, information retrieval and data mining which provide important solutions for a user-centered interactive information exchange between museums and their visitors. The user information can be inferred implicitly by observing visitor behaviour or during their interactions with the multimedia device; it can also be provided explicitly by the users [8]. The main challenge is to analyse interests and preferences without demanding them to express them explicitly: it is more desirable to start offering recommendations to visitors as soon as possible, hence minimizing intrusiveness to the users [17]. These types of solutions are quite complex and have been developed in the context of academic research. For example, the Wearable Computer (MIT Media Lab) provides audio and visual narration adapting to the users interest from him/her physical path in the museum and length of stops [20]. The PEACH project [18] developed a PDA-based museum tour application, whose content is adapted to the visitor, is location-aware and only available in certain locations in the museum. In CHIP [24] there is an automatic user-model that collects user interests from his or her interactions. Content-based recommendations are then exploited to recommend both artwork and art concepts that might be of interest.

Personalization methods are often classified into main categories such as collaborative filtering, content-based filtering, and hybrid approaches [1]. Collaborative methods divide visitors into groups that have similar known preferences and then recommend to a new visitor those items that were most liked by the group to which he or she belongs. The problem is that new works in the collection will not be recommended until a substantial number of users have rated them.

Content-based methods analyze the common features among the items a visitor liked and recommends those items that have similar features. The main problem of applying content-based techniques for museum tour personalization is that both automatic feature extraction from graphical images and manual assignment of these features are difficult so that a recommender system usually has a rather limited set of features, which may not tell about some qualities of some artwork. An additional problem here is that two different pieces with the same set of features (with similar values), can not be distinguished by the recommender system.

For MNEMOSYNE, we have chosen a Hybrid approach that combines collaborative and content-based methods: we combine recommendations produced separately by content-based and collaborative techniques to develop a generic model that includes elements of both types of techniques.

4 Active Vision for Visitor Profiling

Several application domains, including museum security and surveillance, rely on large number of video sequences captured using a combination of cameras of various types: fixed-lens, steerable pan-tilt-zoom, thermals, omnidirectional, and handheld sensors [11]. Recent progress in camera hardware and communication technologies has led to an evolution of camera networks into networks of smart cameras and highly capable mobile imaging systems. These open up novel opportunities for scientific discovery in image analysis, especially in wide area scene analysis. Wide area scene analysis builds upon multi-view image analysis, which is an active sub-area of computer vision which use visual data captured via camera networks and has its own unique challenges, including:

- The ability to integrate information over a wide area;
- Cooperation between camera;
- Active control of the network; and
- Scalability.

These advances in recent years have created a unique opportunity for the MNEMOSYNE project: to exploit state-of-the-art computer vision techniques in heterogeneous sensor networks as well as the installed video surveillance infrastructure in modern museum environments in order to perform remote visitor profiling in terms of what museum pieces they exhibit interest in, how long they linger before a particular display, and what course they follow through the museum environment. In MNEMOSYNE we will leverage our existing work in computer vision and video surveillance to perform this "visual profiling" of museum guests. In this section we describe some of the architectural aspects of the camera network and systems that we will use to implement museum visitor profiling in the MNEMOSYNE project.

4.1 Building Blocks

In order to profile visitors, the system will use a network of fixed (master) cameras, and a number of active PTZ (slave) cameras. We have described in previous work several components to:

- **Accurately detect and track visitors [3]**
  This module will be responsible for keeping track of visitors and their route as then move through the museum. Our sensor network will incorporate a combination of fixed and active sensors, which complicates this aspect of the system.
- **Capture high-quality face imagery [12]**
  This component will allow us to associate an "identity" in the form of a face with each tracked visitor.
- **Recognize actions of visitors [4]**
  Simple actions like pointing or grouping, when accurately detected, are reasonable indicators of visitor interest.

The first component is one of the most investigated in the literature on computer vision and video surveillance. In the heterogeneous sensor case, however, there is significantly less work to build on. In this case two cameras are typically associated in a master-slave relationship: the master camera is kept stationary and set to have a global view of the scene so as to permit it to track several entities simultaneously. The slave camera is used to follow the target trajectory and generate close-up imagery of the entities driven by the transformed trajectory coordinates, moving from target to target and zooming in and out as necessary. The solutions proposed in [2] [25] do not require direct calibration but impose some restrictions in the setup of the cameras. The viewpoints between the master and slave camera are assumed to be nearly identical so as to ease feature matching. In [25], a linear mapping is used that is computed from a look-up table of manually established pan and tilt correspondences. In [2], a look-up table is employed that also takes into account camera zooming. In [19], it is proposed a method to link the foot position of a moving person in the master camera sequence with the same position in the slave camera view. The methods proposed by [14], [15] require instead direct camera calibration, with a moving person and calibration marks.

4.2 Preliminary Results: Scene Learning and Visitor Tracking

In this preliminary phase of the project the focus is on establishing at frame-rate the time variant mapping between PTZ cameras present in a network as they redirect the gaze and zoom to acquire high resolution images of moving targets

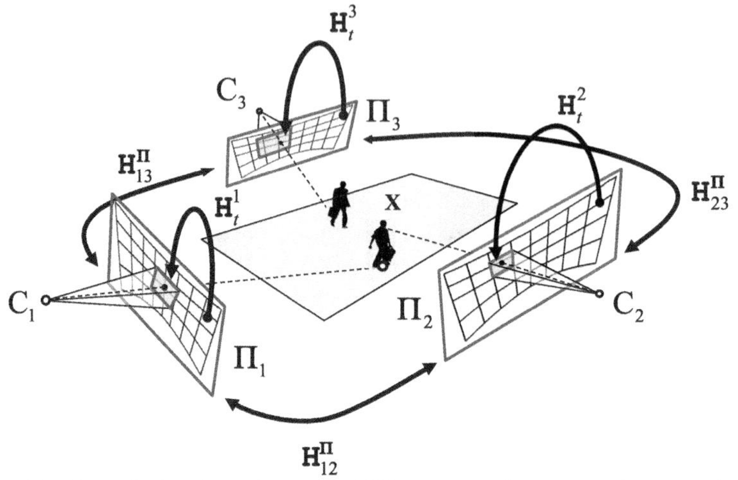

Fig. 3. Pairwise relationships between PTZ cameras for a sample network of three cameras

for profiling purposes. This is critical in the MNEMOSYNE scenario because any system must be easily re-deployable in new environments, and should also work in semi-stable environments in general (exhibits change).

We build upon the work [7] which exploits a prebuilt map of visual 2D landmarks of the wide area to support multi-view image matching. The landmarks are extracted from a finite number of images taken from a non calibrated PTZ camera. At run-time, landmarks that are detected in the current PTZ camera view are matched to those of the base set in the map. The matches are used to localize the camera with respect to the scene and hence estimate the position of the target body parts.

According to [7], cameras with an overlapping field of view can be set in a master-slave relationship pairwise. According to this, given a network of M PTZ cameras $\mathbf{C}_i$ viewing a planar scene, $\mathcal{N} = \{\mathbf{C}_i^s\}_{i=1}^M$, at any given time instant each camera can be in one of two states $s \in \{\text{MASTER}, \text{SLAVE}\}$.

As shown in Fig. 3 the three reference planes Π_1, Π_2, Π_3 observed respectively by the cameras $\mathbf{C}_1$, $\mathbf{C}_2$ and $\mathbf{C}_3$ are related to each other through the three homographies $\mathtt{H}_{12}^{\Pi}$, $\mathtt{H}_{13}^{\Pi}$, $\mathtt{H}_{23}^{\Pi}$. Instead, at time t the current image plane is related to the reference plane through the homographies $\mathtt{H}_t^1$, $\mathtt{H}_t^2$ and $\mathtt{H}_t^3$. If the target $\mathbf{X}$ is tracked by $\mathbf{C}_1$ (acting as MASTER) and followed in high resolution by $\mathbf{C}_2$ (acting as zooming SLAVE), the imaged coordinates of the target are first transferred from Π_1 to Π_2 through $\mathtt{H}_{12}^{\Pi}$ and hence from Π_2 to the current zoomed view of $\mathbf{C}_2$ through $\mathtt{H}_t^2$. Referring to the general case of M distinct cameras, once $\mathtt{H}_t^k$ and $\mathtt{H}_{kl}^{\Pi}$, $k \in 1..M$, $l \in 1..M$ with $l \neq k$ are known, the imaged location of a moving target tracked by a master camera $\mathbf{C}_k$ can be transferred to the zoomed view of a slave camera $\mathbf{C}_l$ according to:

$$\mathtt{T}_t^{kl} = \mathtt{H}_t^l \cdot \mathtt{H}_{kl}^{\Pi} \qquad (1)$$

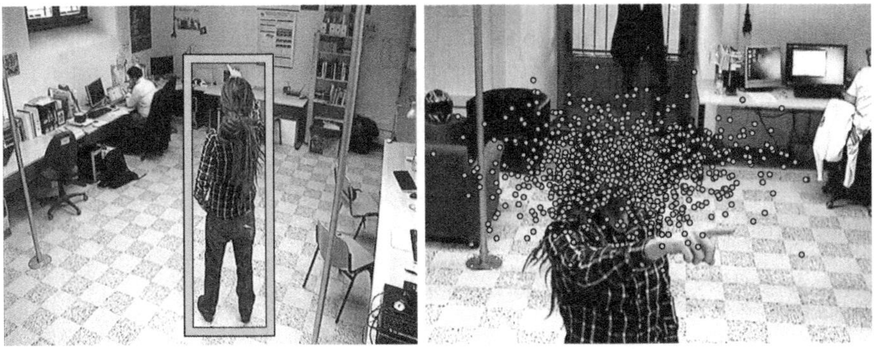

(a) (b)

Fig. 4. Example of a frame analyzed with the proposed technique. (a): Master camera view: the target is detected by background subtraction. (b): Slave camera view: the particles show the uncertainty of the head position of the target.

Under the assumption of vertical stick–like targets moving on a planar scene the target head can be estimated directly by a planar homology [23,10] as shown in Fig. 4.

In our preliminary experiments we have seen that in indoor environments we are able to quickly learn a map of visual landmarks that allow our cameras to orient themselves in the environment. These maps can then be used to accurately locate and track humans in the 3D environment.

4.3 Preliminary Results: Head Localization

In order to extract more information more meaningful to the task of visitor profiling, we have also concentrated on extracting head positions from the views of the slave-camera. In MNEMOSYNE this will be used for focusing higher-level analysis modules on heads in order to estimate, for example, *where* the visitor is looking.

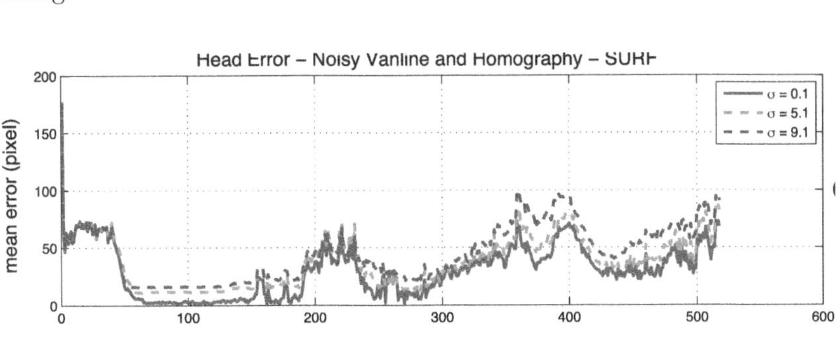

Fig. 5. Head localization accuracy for the test sequence shown in Fig. 4

To evaluate the head localization error in the slave camera we corrupt the two pairs of parallel lines needed to estimate the vanishing line and the four points needed to estimate the homography $\mathtt{H}_{12}^{\Pi}$, with a white, zero mean, Gaussian noise with standard deviation between 0.1 and 9 pixels. This procedure was repeated 1000 times and averaged over trials. Plots of the mean error in head localization are reported in Fig. 5. As it can be seen, after a brief transient (necessary to estimate the initial camera pose), the mean error falls to small values and grows almost linearly as the focal length increases.

5 Discussion

MNEMOSYNE is a three-year project funded by the Region of Tuscany and the European Commission whose main goal is to find new solutions for adaptive user-profiling in interactive museum contexts. The unique and novel aspect of the MNEMOSYNE project is that it exists precisely at the point where interactive museums and computer vision intersect. The tools of computer vision will give us complete coverage of each visitor's pattern of visitation. With this dense flow of information about each visitor, we will be able to build a more accurate profile and customize the experience for them on-the-fly. This type of profiling also opens up the door to suggest other exhibits, other museums, or to create networks of MNEMOSYNE exhibits which are interlinked to create a web of interactive, multimedia museums.

Preliminary experiments with existing computer vision systems have only just begun in a laboratory setting. Ongoing work is concentrating primarily on (i) generalizing the visual landmark mapping system to work in indoor, crowded environments; and (ii) incorporating mobile, worn and/or carried sensors (e.g. smartphones) into our sensor network model, fusing information with these streams in order to accurately associate visitor observations without the need for accurate tracking.

Acknowledgment. This work is supported by a grant from *La Regione Toscana* and the European Commission.

References

1. Adomavicius, G., Tuzhilin, A.: Toward the next generation of recommender systems: A survey of the state-of-the-art and possible extensions. IEEE Transactions on Knowledge and Data Engineering 17 (2005)
2. Badri, J., Tilmant, C., Lavest, J.-M., Pham, Q.-C., Sayd, P.: Camera-to-Camera Mapping for Hybrid Pan-Tilt-Zoom Sensors Calibration. In: Ersbøll, B.K., Pedersen, K.S. (eds.) SCIA 2007. LNCS, vol. 4522, pp. 132–141. Springer, Heidelberg (2007)
3. Bagdanov, A.D., Dini, F., Del Bimbo, A., Nunziati, W.: Improving the robustness of particle filter-based visual trackers using online parameter adaptation. In: Proc. of IEEE International Conference on Advanced Video and Signal based Surveillance (AVSS). IEEE Computer Society, London (2007), http://www.micc.unifi.it/publications/2007/BDDN07a

4. Ballan, L., Bertini, M., Del Bimbo, A., Seidenari, L., Serra, G.: Effective codebooks for human action categorization. In: Proc. of ICCV Int'l Workshop on Video-oriented Object and Event Classification (VOEC), Kyoto, Japan (September 2009), `http://www.micc.unifi.it/publications/2009/BBDSS09a`
5. Baraldi, S., Bimbo, A.D., Landucci, L.: Natural interaction on the tabletop. Multimedia Tools and Applications (2008)
6. Baraldi, S., Bimbo, A.D., Landucci, L., Torpei, N.: Entry: Natural interaction. In: Szsu, M.T., Liu, L. (eds.) Encyclopedia of Database Systems. Springer, Heidelberg (2008)
7. Bimbo, A.D., Dini, F., Lisanti, G., Pernici, F.: Exploiting distinctive visual landmark maps in pan-tilt-zoom camera networks. Computer Vision and Image Understanding 114(6), 611–623 (2010), special Issue on Multi-Camera and Multi-Modal Sensor Fusion
8. Bowen, J., Filippini-Fantoni, S.: Personalization and the web from a museum perspective. In: Proceedings of the 2004 Museums and the Web Conference (2004)
9. Brusilovsky, P., Maybury, M.T.: From adaptive hypermedia to the adaptive web. Communications of the ACM 45(5) (2002)
10. Criminisi, A., Reid, I., Zisserman, A.: Single view metrology. International Journal of Computer Vision 40(2), 123–148 (2000)
11. Del Bimbo, A., Dini, F., Grifoni, A., Pernici, F.: Pan-tilt-zoom camera networks. In: Aghajan, H., Cavallaro, A. (eds.) Multi-Camera Networks: Principles and Applications, Academic Press (2009)
12. Del Bimbo, A., Dini, F., Lisanti, G.: A real time solution for face logging. In: Proc. of International Conference on Imaging for Crime Detection and Prevention, ICDP (2009), `http://www.micc.unifi.it/publications/2009/DDL09`
13. Fikkert, F.W., Hakvoort, M., van der Vet, P.E., Nijholt, A.: Experiences with interactive multi-touch tables. In: Proceedings of INTETAIN (2009)
14. Horaud, R., Knossow, D., Michaelis, M.: Camera cooperation for achieving visual attention. Mach. Vis. Appl. 16(6), 1–2 (2006)
15. Jain, A., Kopell, D., Kakligian, K., Wang, Y.F.: Using stationary-dynamic camera assemblies for wide-area video surveillance and selective attention. In: CVPR 2006: Proceedings of the 2006 IEEE Computer Society Conference on Computer Vision and Pattern Recognition, pp. 537–544. IEEE Computer Society, Washington, DC, USA (2006)
16. Norman, D.: The Invisible Computer. The MIT Press (1998)
17. Pechenizkiy, M., Calders, T.: A framework for guiding the museum tour personalization. In: Proceedings of PEACH 2007 (2007)
18. Rocchi, C., Stock, O., Zancanaro, M., Kruppa, M., Kruger, A.: The museum visit: Generating seamless personalized presentations on multiple devices. In: Proceedings of the 2004 Conference on Intelligent User Interfaces (2004)
19. Senior, A., Hampapur, A., Lu, M.: Acquiring multi-scale images by pan-tilt-zoom control and automatic multi-camera calibration. In: IEEE Workshop on Applications on Computer Vision (2005)
20. Sparacino, F.: The museum wearable: real-time sensor-driven understanding of visitors' interests for personalized visually-augmented museum experiences. In: Proceedings of Museums and the Web, MW 2002 (2002)
21. Starner, T., Mann, S., Rhodes, B., Levine, J., Healey, J., Kirsch, D., Picard, R., Pentland, A.: Augmented reality through wearable computing. Presence 6(4) (1997)
22. Turk, M., Robertson, G.: Perceptual user interfaces. Communications of the ACM (2000)

23. Van Gool, L., Proesmans, M., Zisserman, A.: Grouping and invariants using planar homologies. In: Workshop on Geometrical Modeling and Invariants for Computer Vision. Xidian University Press (1995)
24. Wang, Y., Aroyo, L., Stash, N., Sambeek, R., Schuurmans, Y., Schreiber, G., Gorgels, P.: Cultivating personalized museum tours online and on-site. Interdisciplinary Science Reviews 34(2) (2009)
25. Zhou, X., Collins, R., Kanade, T., Metes, P.: A master-slave system to acquire biometric imagery of humans at a distance. In: ACM SIGMM 2003 Workshop on Video Surveillance, pp. 113–120 (2003)

Computer Tools for Archaeological Reference Collections: The Case of the Ceramics of the Iberian Period from Andalusia (Spain)

A.L. Martínez-Carrillo[1], A. Ruiz[1], M.J. Lucena[2], and J.M. Fuertes[2]

[1] Centro Andaluz de Arqueología Ibérica
[2] Departamento de Informática, Escuela Politécnica Superior
Universidad de Jaén
Campus de las Lagunillas, 23071. Jaén, Spain

Abstract. The use of new media in the service of cultural heritage is a fast growing field. The development of dynamic web has changed the concept for sharing information, allowing quick access to data and enabling the contents update through the active participation of users. Building digital heritage requires substantial resources in materials, expertise, tools and cost. Also there is a necessity of reflection to promote forms of electronic publication adapted to the needs of archaeologists. This contribution describes an approach and it main strategic choices followed in the construction of an open system through Internet to access and share archaeological information concerning to pottery shapes.

Keywords: Archaeological pottery, integrated technologies, web system.

1 Introduction

The study and analysis of archaeological ceramics constitutes one of the most frequent activities of the archaeological work, which consists habitually of classifying the thousands of ceramic fragments gathered in the interventions and selecting those that contribute to deduce forms, functions and chronology [7].

The different criteria used in the elaboration of classifications do not contribute to homogenize the analysis of the pottery shapes, since the election of criteria depends on each researcher and moment [9]. Shepard saw three phases in the election of criteria: the study of whole vessels as culture objects; the study of sherds as dating evidence for stratigraphic sequences; the study of pottery technology as a way of relating more closely to the potter, but she did not try to put dates to them.

Chronologically, the most used criteria have been artistically, typological, functional, technological, statistical, and contextual. In the last years there is a growing interest in integrating ceramics into a wide analysis of finds assemblages. This must be the next step in ceramic analysis: having integrated the various aspects of ceramics investigations, paying special interest in the spatial and temporal context.

C. Grana and R. Cucchiara (Eds.): MM4CH 2011, CCIS 247, pp. 51–62, 2012.

In this contribution an on line system for storage, analysis, query and visualization of archaeological pottery is shown. Also this system is created as aggregating tool of pottery shapes (complete vessels or fragments from the rim or the base). This system is a useful tool for integrating all the information concerning to pottery sherds.

This paper is structured as it follows: first of all the spatial and temporal context is defined, then the methodology carried out for the systematization of the semantic and graphical information concerning to archaeology pottery is exposed, next the computer tools used for the realization of the ceramic reference collection are explained and finally the conclusions will be exposed.

2 A Computerized Method for Documentation of Ceramics: The Case of the CATA Project

2.1 The CATA Project: An Introduction

The CATA project (Archaeological Wheel Pottery of Andalusia) is an on line system for classifying and categorizing archaeological pottery.

The main goal of this project is to create a useful working tool in Internet, which would help to solve usual problems that archaeologists normally deal with. As has been mentioned, one of their more normal tasks is to classify thousand of pottery fragments retrieved in each archaeological work and select those ones, which give enough information for inferring shapes functions and chronologies.

The objectives of this virtual Corpus are:

- To achieve general valid protocols for the studying of the wheel-made pottery of Andalusia based on a selected reference array.
- To obtain a database with the pottery collections and the 2D drawings done until the moment and published or stored in archives.
- To develop useful communication channels on Internet to arrange a reference collections for the archaeologists and to make a database where professional archaeologists would be able of adding the results of their archaeological works.

The model is designed to be used as a professional tool in Archaeology; any archaeologist would have the opportunity of comparing or testing the materials of his/her excavation or surveys and obtain levels of similarity concerning the series include in this project.

2.2 Area of Study

The selected ceramic material comes from different archaeological sites located in the East area of Andalusia, specifically from the provinces of Jaén, Granada and Córdoba. Most of the ceramic vessels have been documented in the province of Jaén, since they pertaining to Iberian period (S. V B.C. I A.C.) In this area there is an expanded tradition with respect to the study of ceramic typologies of

Fig. 1. Studied Area

the Iberian period, emphasizing the work of Pereira [8] for the Iberian ceramics painted of the valley of Guadalquivir, see Fig. 1.

The combination of diverse archaeological sites, with different chronologies makes the accomplishment of a diachronic and synchronous study possible. (Table 1).

Table 1. N^o settlements, chronology and number of studied vessels

N^o of Settlements	Chronology	N^o of Vessels
2	VII BC - V BC	90
9	IV BC - III BC	829
4	II BC - II AC	255
1	III AC	85
TOTAL		1259

The sample for the analysis has been made in basis of 1259 complete forms whose chronology goes from the VII B.C to the S. II A.C., belonging to 16 archaeological sites from the previously mentioned area of Andalusia.

2.3 The Standardization of the Data

The first step in creating the CATA system is the definition of the protocols required for the analysis and study of pottery vessels found in Andalusia. These protocols are valid and applicable to different historical periods.

The second step is to define the key variables which synthesis the description and definition of vessels and sherds. The four most important variables are based on the work of Orton, Tyers and Vinci [7] date, distribution, functionality and state of preservation.

CATA adds an additional variable to the above:

Measurement variables. Measurements are based on a raster or vector image that is the drawing of the pottery vessel. The following subclassification is used:

- Basic measurements: vessel diameter, height, volume and weight.
- Complementary measurements: these define and numerically specify the most significant parts of the morphology of a vessel (rim, handle and base).

Qualitative variables are related to the manufacturing process of the vessel. Therefore inside this range of variables are included aspects regarding the shaped of the vessel, type of oven treatment, chemical composition of the clay and additives added to the clay. Also is considered the description of the morphology of the vessel, distinguishing rims, handles and bases; surface treatment and chemical analysis.

Preservation variables. The preservation variables are related to the physical state of the vessel (complete or fragmented), alterations suffered by the artifact, and the manufacturing treatments used to create the vessel (used propose to restoration and conservation of a pottery vessel).

Contextual variables. Finally, variables have been added to describe the context in which the artifact is found. A pottery vessel or fragment is associated with a temporal and a spatial context. The identification of the context allows correct dating, deduction of functionality, and the application of geographical significance.

Together with the systematization of the semantic information regarding to the archaeological pottery, graphical information has been standardized through a process of digitalization. This process can be divided into the following steps:

- Digitalization of drawings from archives.
- Vectorization of the contours.
- Separation of the profiles for its later computer processing.
- Export of the drawings of the profiles to a raster format without compression (PNG) for their subsequent comparison.

The sample of the reference collection is formed by drawings of complete vessels, understanding as such drawings of complete profiles or fragment drawings which had enough graphical information to reconstruct the complete section of the vessel, see Fig. 2.

The drawings of the complete vessels come mainly from archives of scientific literature. The documentation available has been compiled to homogenize the

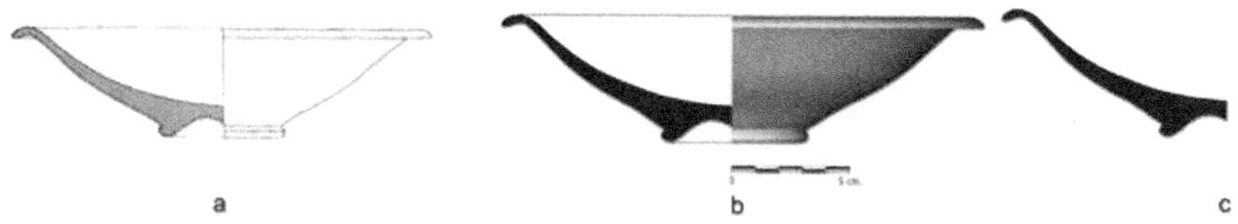

Fig. 2. a) Digitized drawing from a publication; b) Previous image vectorization; c) Vessel's profile

graphical information, which is not standardized and does not follow canons at the time of its study and publication.

Once compiled all the publications in which appear drawings of ceramic vessels it carries out a task of digitalization of these drawings to homogenize the visual reconnaissance of all the drawings, to convert images into vectors and to compress the space of each image for its later computer processing.

3 Computer Tools for on Line Reference Collection

In this section is exposed the main computer tools for the construction of the ceramic reference collection developed in this project.

3.1 Databases

Data archaeology is a skilled human task, in which the knowledge sought depends on the goals of the analyst, cannot be specified in advance, and emerges only through an interactive process of data segmentation and analysis.

Data from archaeological excavation is suitable for computerization although they bring challenges typical of working in non-scientific subjective areas. Meaning and significance within data are established on-site and afterwards by a heuristic process of discussion and contestation, a process at odds with the rigorous demands of database design.

A common and powerful method for organizing data for computerization is the relational data model. Relational databases have a very well-known and proven underlying mathematical theory, which makes possible automatic query optimization, schema generation from high-level models and many other features that are now vital for mission-critical Information Systems development and operations [2].

The database engine selected for CATA system is MySQL due to the facilities given for Web design and the easy implementation with programming language such PHP.

Once the above mentioned variables are defined and clarified, the next step is to create the table schemas using these variables and defining the relation amongst them, see Fig. 3.

In this case has been differentiated between two main levels: a high level, the archaeological site; and an artifact level represented by the pottery vessels. The systematization of the documentation is made using different types of fields for storing and searching numerical values, text, images and videos.

3.2 Image Comparison

There are different methodologies for the estimation of the similarity of vessels profiles. Maiza and Gaildrat [3] propose the use of an automated methodology to establish the relationship of relating a sherd to a known pottery vessel model in basis of 3D models forms and semantic information.

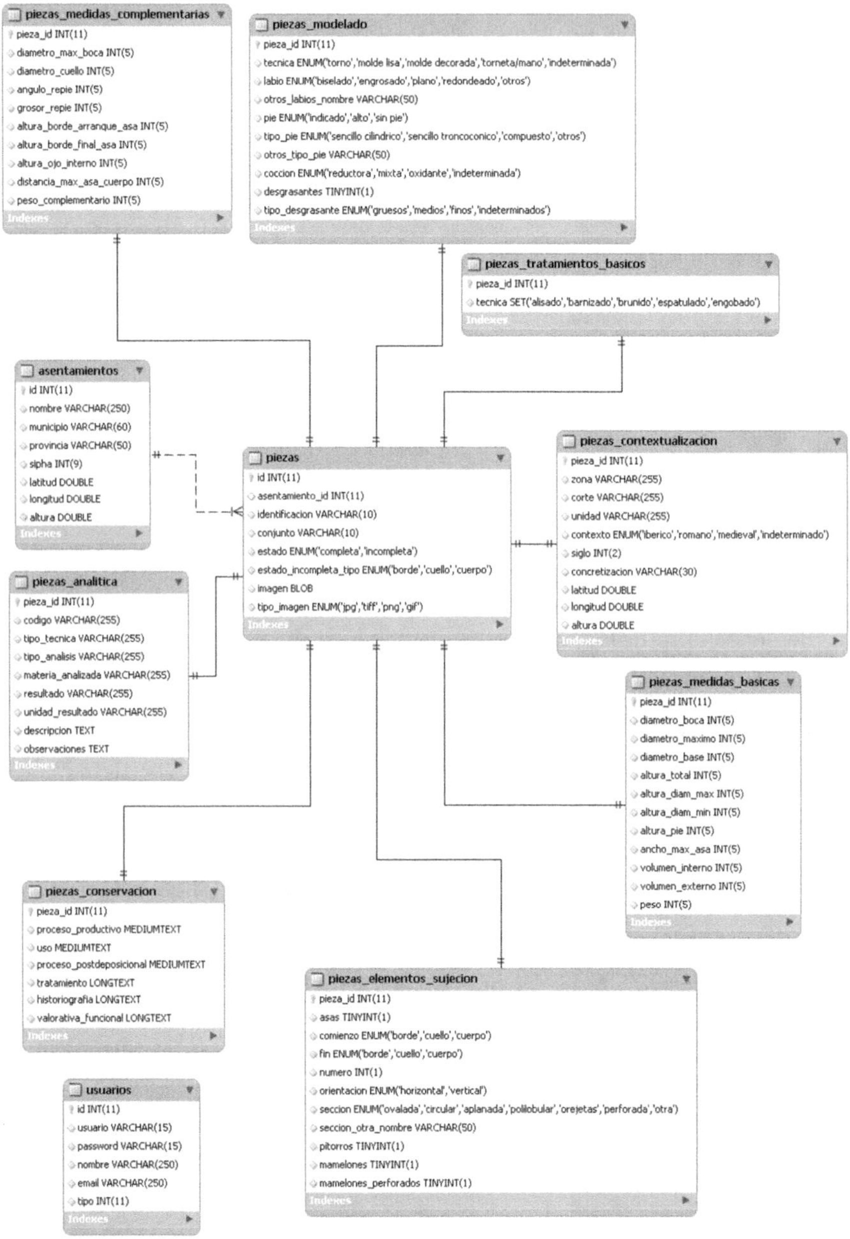

Fig. 3. Table schemas for the relational database used in CATA system

Bishop, Cha and Tappert [1] combine information of shapes forms, textures and colours for obtaining degrees of similarity between ceramics shapes.

In order to estimate the similarity between two profiles, a comparison technique based on non-rigid deformation analysis is designed and developed in CATA project [4].

First of all, a measure to evaluate the effort or deformation energy needed to apply to a given contour in order to adapt it to another is defined. The deformable model given by Nastar [5][6] is used, which is described briefly below.

This model was first used for analyzing the non-rigid motion of structures in temporal sequences of 2D and 3D biomedical images. The mechanical formulation of the problem consists in assuming that the contour is made up of a set of points (or nodes) with mass, joined together by springs. These elastic springs provide a polygonal approach of the contour and are supposedly identical, without mass, with stiffness k and length l_0. These springs modelize the surface elasticity of the object.

For the comparison of the complete profiles, being that is already known the number of points of the simple, a reference prototype is used. Each profile can be classified in relation to its deformation spectrum to the prototype. This way, similarity between two profiles can be computed as the Euclidean distance between their associated deformation spectra.

$$d(D_1, D_2) = \frac{1}{p}\sqrt{\sum_{i=1}^{p}(\tilde{u}_i(D_1) - \tilde{u}_i(D_2))^2} \tag{1}$$

The prototype C (Figure 4) is the circumference centred in (0.5, 0.5) and that passes through the point (0, 0) subsampled uniformly in N points. All the profiles should be scaled in relationship to the prototype. This makes our measure of deformation invariant to scale.

First the profile P is aligned over the profile to calculate the spectrum, the lowest point of the axis of rotation is aligned with the point (0, 0). Next, P is scaled uniformly so that its highest point corresponds with the edge of the piece that belongs to the circumference C.

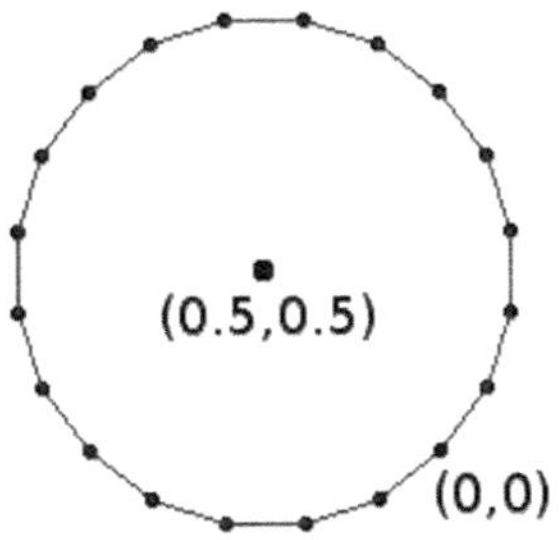

Fig. 4. Circumference C used as prototype figure

Different techniques are designed to establish the correspondence between the points (nodes) of the profile and the points of the prototype. The best results have been achieved when the profile is divided in exterior and interior halves that connect the origin with the edge of the piece. Both curves have been subsampled uniformly in N/2 points (Figure 5).

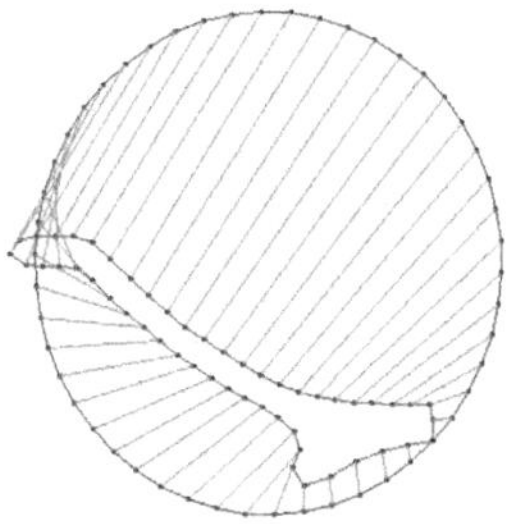

Fig. 5. Correspondence between profile and prototype nodes

Finally some results are shown (Figures 6 and 7).

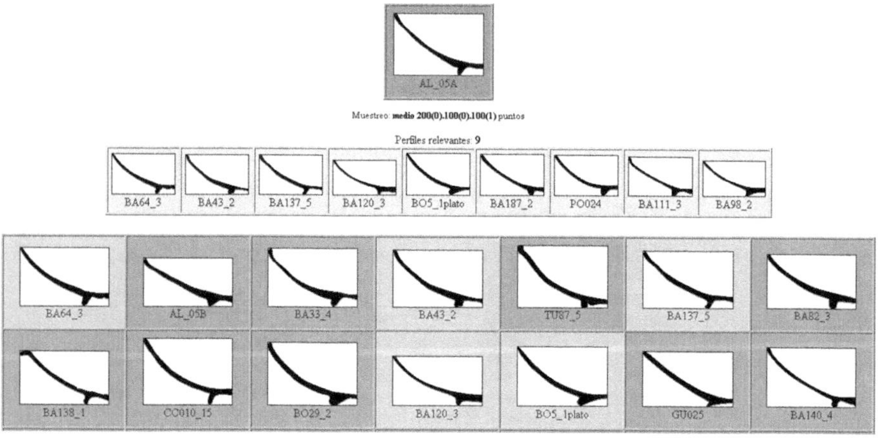

Fig. 6. Output obtained from the system. First row: query profile. Second row: related profiles (ground truth) provided by an expert. Third an fourth rows: first fourteen profiles returned by the system, with the ones belonging to the related profiles set marked in light gray.

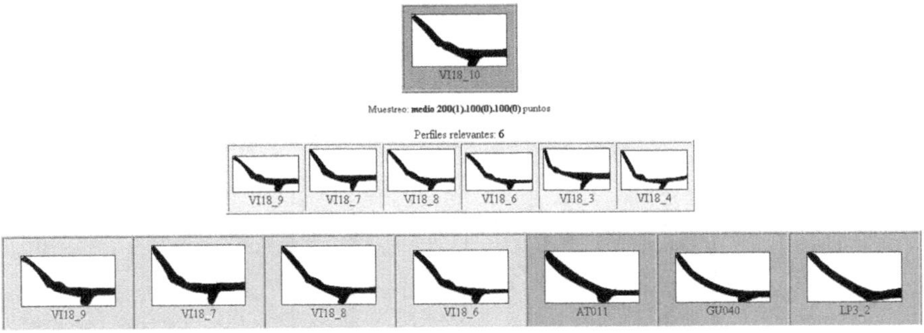

Fig. 7. Output obtained from the system. First row: query profile. Second row: related profiles (ground truth) provided by an expert. Third row: first seven profiles returned by the system, with the ones belonging to the related profiles set marked in light gray.

3.3 User Interface

The Internet interface is oriented on the one hand to implement the computerization tools to storage, retrieval and compare ceramic shapes and by another one to offer to the users an interactive access to the system. The results and the access on line to the application of this project are exposed in the following URL: http://cata.cica.es/.

First of all, different categories of users are defined:

- Invited: they can consult all the information available in the reference collection.
- Registered: they can add and edit information in the system with data of fragments or complete vessels from their own archaeological interventions.

The data uploaded in the system is controlled and validated by an administrator to guarantee the quality of the contents (Figure 8).

Once the user has accessed into the application, the information concerning to the archaeological sites is showed. In this section are exposed the administrative data and their geographical situation through Google maps. In another screen the information of the complete vessels and the fragments is available. The first level of information of the pieces is a list with the identification of each one, their historical period and the site in which they are documented. Also, more specific information within the descriptions of the variables above mentioned and the graphical materials (drawings and videos) is exposed (Figure 9)and (Figure 10).

Besides, it is possible to search information on line. There are two systems for retrieving information:

- Search by predetermined data (chronology, site, type of rim, base or handle and type of surface treatment).

- Search by image profile. The above mentioned module for image profile comparison is implemented in the system.

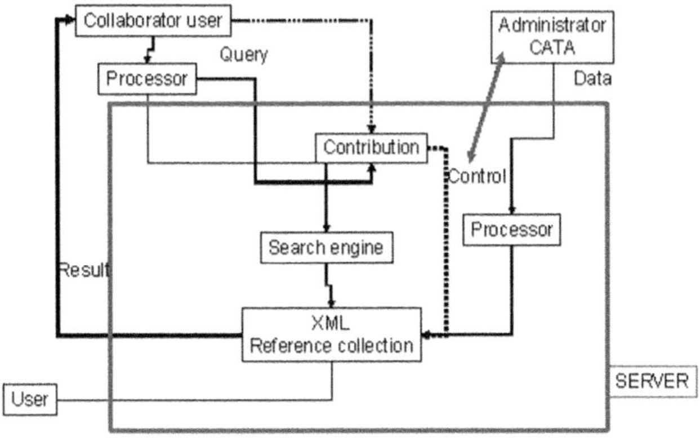

Fig. 8. Schema of CATA

Fig. 9. CATA web application screenshot

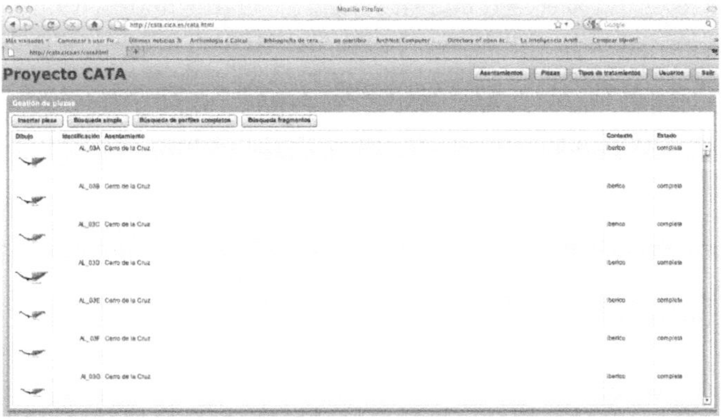

Fig. 10. CATA web application screenshot

Also, this system can be considered a 2.0 on line application, since this type of systems is defined as *all those utilities and services of Internet that contain a database, which can be modified by the users (adding, editing or deleting information or associating data to the existing information* [10].

4 Conclusions

To resume, the investigation of this project is focused on the development of a methodology for the classification, storage and management of archaeological pottery sets. In this sense, the collaboration between archaeologist and computer scientists permits the development of useful applications. There is, however, still a need for further development of information systems specifically targeted at using the full range of applied computation mathematics in archaeological pottery analysis.

This application can be considered an on line reference collection of archaeological ceramic. One of the advantages of the use of this systems is that make possible the unification and standardization of different criteria.

Nevertheless, there must be agreement on common standards for sharing information and the use of controlled vocabularies. This is the reason why standardized data interchange formats should be used and enforced for Internet knowledge transactions. In this direction, it is important to achieve full interoperability though the contents translation into multiple languages and to develop multi-lingual thesauri.

Other challenge is to ensure that e-reference collections must be developed in ways that are suitable for long-term digital preservation.

The work involved in re-purposing reference collections for multiple audiences is not trivial. Reference collections are generally developing by specialists for specialists and may required layers of supporting information to render them comprehensible to general users [10]. In this way it is necessary make available contents on line taking into account the different profiles of all the possible users that can access.

Acknowledgment. This work was has been supported by the Excellent Projects Program of CICE (regional government) and the European Union ERDF funds under research projects P07-TIC-02773 and Project HUM-890 *Corpus Virtual de Cerámica Arqueológica.*

References

1. Bishop, G., Cha, S.-H., Tappert, C.: A Greek Pottery Shape and School Identification and Classification System Using Image Retrieval Techniques. In: Proceedings of Student/Faculty Research Day CSIS. Pace University (2005)
2. Kadar, M.: Data connection and manipulation of archaeological database created in visual environment. In: Proceedings of theInternational Conference on Theory and Applications of Mathematics and Informatics - ICTAMI 2004, Thessaloniki, Greece (2004)

3. Maiza, C., Gaildrat, V.: Automatic Classification of Archaeological Potsherds. In: The 8th International Conference on Computer Graphics and Artificial Intelligence (2005)
4. Martínez-Carrillo, A.L., Lucena, M.J., Fuertes, J.M., Ruiz, A.: Morphometric Analysis Applied to the Archaeological Pottery of the Valley of Guadalquivir. Lecture Notes in Earth Sciences, vol. 124, pp. 307–323 (2010)
5. Nastar, C.: Modèles physiques déformables et modes vibratoires pour l'analyse du mouvement non-rigide dans les images multidimensionelles. PhD thesis, INRIA (1994)
6. Nastar, C., Ayache, N.: Frequency-based nonrigid motion analysis: application to four dimensional medical images. IEEE Trans. on Pattern Analysis and Machine Intelligence 18(11), 1067–1079 (1996)
7. Orton, C., Tyers, P., Vinci, A.: Pottery in archaeology. Cambrige University Press, Cambridge (1993)
8. Pereira, J.: La Cerámica ibérica de la Cuenca del Guadalquivir. I, Propuesta de clasificación. Trabajos de prehistoria, 45 (1989)
9. Shepard, A.: Ceramics for the archaeologist. Carnegie Institution of Washington, Washington D.C. (1956)
10. Yehuda, E., Kvan, T., Affleck, J.: New heritage: new media and cultural heritage. Routledge (2007)

Multimodal Interactive Transcription of Ancient Text Images

Verónica Romero, Joan Andreu Sánchez,
Alejandro H. Toselli, and Enrique Vidal

Instituto Tecnológico de Informática (ITI),
Universidad Politécnica de Valencia, Spain
{vromero,jandreu,ahector,evidal}@iti.upv.es

Abstract. The amount of digitized legacy documents has been rising dramatically over the last years due mainly to the increasing number of on-line digital libraries publishing this kind of documents. On one hand, the vast majority of these documents remain waiting to be transcribed into a textual electronic format (such as ASCII or PDF) that would provide historians and other researchers new ways of indexing, consulting and querying these documents. On the other hand, in some cases, adequate transcriptions of the handwritten text images are already available. This drives an increasing need to align images and transcriptions in order to make it more comfortable the consulting of these documents. In this work two systems are presented to deal with these issues. The first one aims at transcribing these documents using a interactive-predictive approach, which integrates user corrective-feedback actions in the proper recognition process. The second one presents an alignment method based on the Viterbi algorithm to find mappings between word images of a given handwritten document and their respective (ASCII) words on its given transcription.

Keywords: Handwritten text recognition, Multimodal interactive framework, Viterbi alignment.

1 Introduction

The task of transcribing old handwritten documents is becoming an important research topic, specially because of the increasing number of on-line digital libraries publishing large quantities of digitized legacy documents. The vast majority of these documents, hundreds of terabytes worth of digital image data, remain waiting to be transcribed into a textual electronic format (such as ASCII or PDF) that would provide researchers and general public new ways of indexing, consulting and querying these documents.

The transcription of handwritten text in these documents is usually carried out by experts in paleography, who are specialized in reading ancient scripts, characterized, among other things, by different calligraphy/print styles from diverse places and time periods. In general, this is a slow and very expensive activity.

C. Grana and R. Cucchiara (Eds.): MM4CH 2011, CCIS 247, pp. 63–73, 2012.

Up-to-date handwritten text recognition (HTR) systems are not accurate enough to substitute the experts in these transcription tasks. The variability of the handwriting, the complexity of the styles and the open vocabulary, explain most of the difficulties encountered by these recognition systems [12,17,7,3]. In order to produce adequately good transcriptions using these systems, once the full recognition process of one document has finished, heavy human expert revision is required to really produce a transcription of standard quality. The human transcriber is then responsible for verifying and correcting the mistakes made by the system. Given the high error rates involved, such a post-editing solution is quite inefficient and uncomfortable for the human corrector.

An effective alternative to post-editing is an interactive approach called "Multimodal Computer Assisted Transcription of Text Images" (MM-CATTI) proposed in [15]. Here, the automatic HTR system and the human transcriber cooperate to generate the final transcription, thereby combining the accuracy provided by the human operator with the efficiency of the HTR system. The implemented MM-CATTI system is presented in section 2.

While the vast majority of legacy documents are currently only available in the form of digital images, for a significant amount of these documents (manually produced) transcriptions are already available. In these cases, digital libraries typically offer both the original images and the corresponding transcriptions. Generally speaking, most documents have transcriptions aligned only at the page level (not at the level of individual text lines or words), which renders the visualization and consulting of these documents rather uncomfortable for the historians and general public[1]. This fact has suggested the development of *automatic alignment* techniques which generate a mapping between each line and word on a document image and its respective line and word on its electronic transcription [16,13]. These alignments can help quickly locating text images while reading a transcription, with useful applications to editing, indexing, etc. In the opposite direction, the alignment is useful for people trying to read the text image directly, when arriving to complex or damaged parts of the document. Section 3 presents an image-transcription alignment system which carries out this task.

2 Multimodal Computer Assisted Transcription of Handwritten Text Images

When transcribing a document image, usually a post-edition process is carried out when error-free transcriptions are expected. An interactive on-line scenario has been presented in previous works [15] as an alternative to post-editing. This scenario is called "Computer Assisted Transcription of Handwritten Text Images" (CATTI) and, rather than full automation, aims at assisting the human in the proper recognition-transcription process; that is, to facilitate and to speed up the transcription task of handwritten texts.

[1] See for example `http://darwin-online.org.uk/manuscripts.html`

In the CATTI framework, the user is involved in the transcription process since she is responsible of validating and/or correcting the Handwritten Text Recognition (HTR) output [15]. The protocol that rules this process can be formulated in the following steps, which are iterated until a correct transcription is obtained (see Figure 1):

(a) The HTR system proposes a full transcription ($\hat{s}$) of an input handwritten text line image. (b) The user validates the longest prefix of $\hat{s}$ which is error-free and enters some keystrokes (word v) to correct the first error in the suffix. (c) An extended correct prefix (p) is produced based on the previously validated prefix and the corrections made by the user. (d) Using this new prefix, the system suggests a suitable continuation ($\hat{s}$) and the process goes on from (b) above.

In order to improve human transcriber productivity and to make the previous defined protocol friendlier for the user, "pure" *mouse action feedback* was studied in detail in [11]. As soon as the user points to the next system error, the system proposes a new, hopefully more correct continuation, thereby trying to anticipate the intended user correction. This way, many explicit user corrections are avoided, saving significant amounts of expected human effort.

Furthering the goal of making the iteration process friendlier to the user led us to the development of *Multimodal CATTI* (MM-CATTI) [15,14]. Traditional peripherals like keyboard and mouse are used in CATTI to unambiguously provide the feedback associated with the validation and correction of the successive system predictions. Nevertheless, using more ergonomic multimodal interfaces

	x	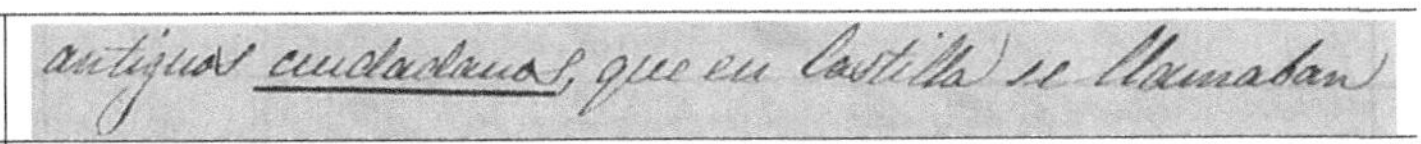						
INTER-0	p							
INTER-1	$\hat{s} \equiv \hat{w}$	**antiguos**	**cuidadores**	**que**	**en**	**el Castillo**	**sus**	**llamadas**
	p'	**antiguos**						
	v		ciudadanos					
	p	**antiguos**	**ciudadanos**					
INTER-2	$\hat{s}$			**que**	**en**	**el Castillo**	**sus**	**llamadas**
	p'	**antiguos**	**ciudadanos**	**que**	**en**			
	v					Castilla		
	p	**antiguos**	**ciudadanos**	**que**	**en**	**Castilla**		
FINAL	$\hat{s}$						**se**	**llamaban**
	v							#
	$p \equiv t$	**antiguos**	***ciudadanos***	**que**	**en**	***Castilla***	**se**	**llamaban**

Fig. 1. Example of CATTI interaction to transcribe an image of the Spanish sentence *"antiguos ciudadanos que en Castilla se llamaban"*. Initially the prefix p is empty, and the system proposes a complete transcription $\hat{s} \equiv \hat{w}$ of the input image x. In each interaction step the user reads this transcription, accepting a prefix p' of it. Then, he or she types in some word, v, to correct the erroneous text that follows the validated prefix, thereby generating a new prefix p (the accepted one p' plus the word v added by the user). At this point, the system suggests a suitable continuation $\hat{s}$ of this prefix p and this process is repeated until a complete and correct transcription of the input signal is reached. In the final transcription, T, the underlined boldface words are the words typed by the user. In this example the estimated post-editing effort is 5/7 (71%), while the corresponding interactive estimate is 2/7 (29%). This results in an estimated effort reduction of 59%.

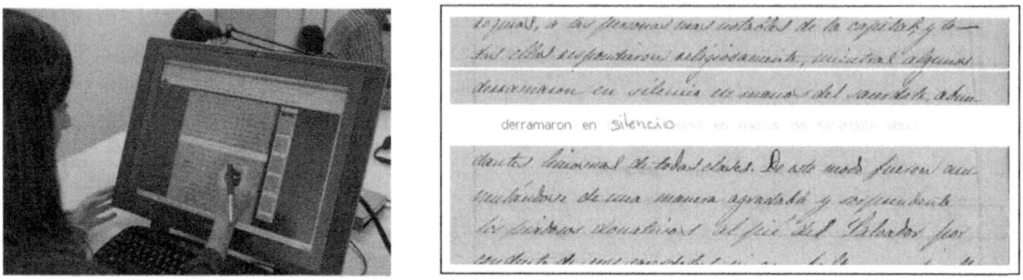

Fig. 2. Left: illustration of CATTI multimodal user-interaction using a touch-screen. Right: page fragment showing a line image being processed.

should result in an easier and more comfortable human-computer interaction, at the expense of the feedback being less deterministic to the system. This is the idea underlying MM-CATTI, which focus on touchscreen communication, perhaps the most natural modality to provide the required feedback in CATTI systems. It is worth noting, however, that the use of this more ergonomic feedback modality comes at the cost of new, additional interaction steps needed to correct possible feedback decoding errors. Therefore, solving the multimodal interaction problem amounts to achieving a modality synergy where both main and feedback data streams help each-other to optimize overall accuracy. Several experiments carried out in [15] show that the number of additional interaction steps is kept very small thanks to the MM-CATTI ability to use interaction-derived constraints to considerably improve the on-line HTR feedback decoding accuracy. More specifically, MM-CATTI feedback decoding accuracy increases by around 20% with respect to using just a conventional, off-the-shelf on-line HTR decoder for the correction steps.

Figure 2 (left) shows a user interacting with the MM-CATTI system by means of a touchscreen. Both the original image and the system's transcription hypotheses can be easily aligned and jointly displayed on the touchscreen (Figure 2, right). A publicly available[2] web-based demonstrator of this system has recently been presented in [9]. It provides a socket based, client-server multiuser environment, where several users across the globe can work concurrently on the same task. In addition, the web server and the MM-CATTI engine do not need to be physically at the same place. To work with the demonstrator, first a document and a page to transcribe are selected. Then, the user transcribes the handwritten text images line by line, using the keyboard and mouse to make corrections. If an *e-pen* is available, the MM-CATTI engine additionally uses its on-line HTR feedback decoder to recognize the user corrective pen-strokes. Then, taking into account the (multimodal) user corrections, the MM-CATTI engine responds with a suitable continuation to the prefix validated by the user. Figure 3 shows different MM-CATTI *e-pen* interaction gestures: the user can explicitly write the correct word, make a diagonal line to delete an erroneous word, make a vertical

[2] See `catti.iti.upv.es`

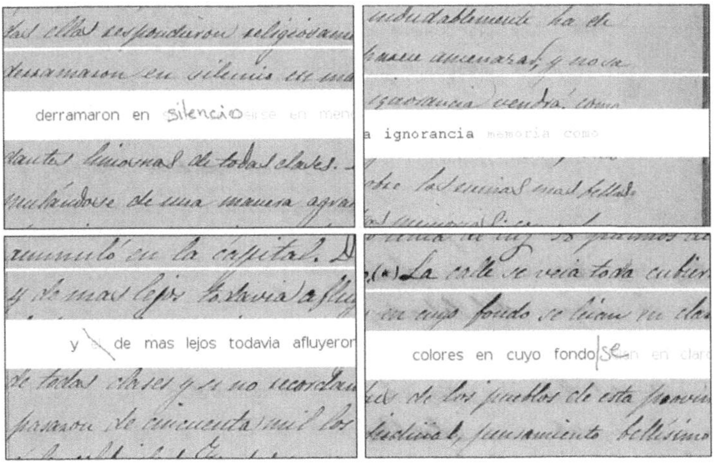

Fig. 3. Four interaction gestures to generate and/or validate an error-free prefix. From left to right, top to bottom: substitution, single click validation, deletion, and insertion.

line followed by text to be inserted, or make a single click to ask for another suitable continuation.

3 Aligning Text-Images and Transcriptions

As mentioned in the introduction, several handwritten documents include both, the handwritten material and its proper transcription (in ASCII or PDF format). This fact has motivated the development of methodologies to align these documents and their transcriptions, i.e. to generate a mapping between each word image on a document page with its respective ASCII word on its transcription [13].

Two different levels of alignment can be defined: line level and word level. Line alignments attempt to obtain beginning and end positions of lines in transcribed pages that do not have synchronized line breaks. This information allows users to easily visualize the page image documents and their corresponding transcriptions. Moreover, using these alignments as segmentation ground truth, large amounts of training and test data for segmentation-free cursive handwriting recognition systems become available. On the other hand, word alignments allow users to easily find the place of a word in the manuscript when reading the corresponding transcription. For example, one could display both the handwritten page and the transcription and whenever the mouse is held over a word in the transcription, the corresponding word in the handwritten image would be outlined using a box. In a similar way, whenever the mouse is held over a word in the handwritten image, the corresponding word in the transcription would be highlighted (see figure 4).

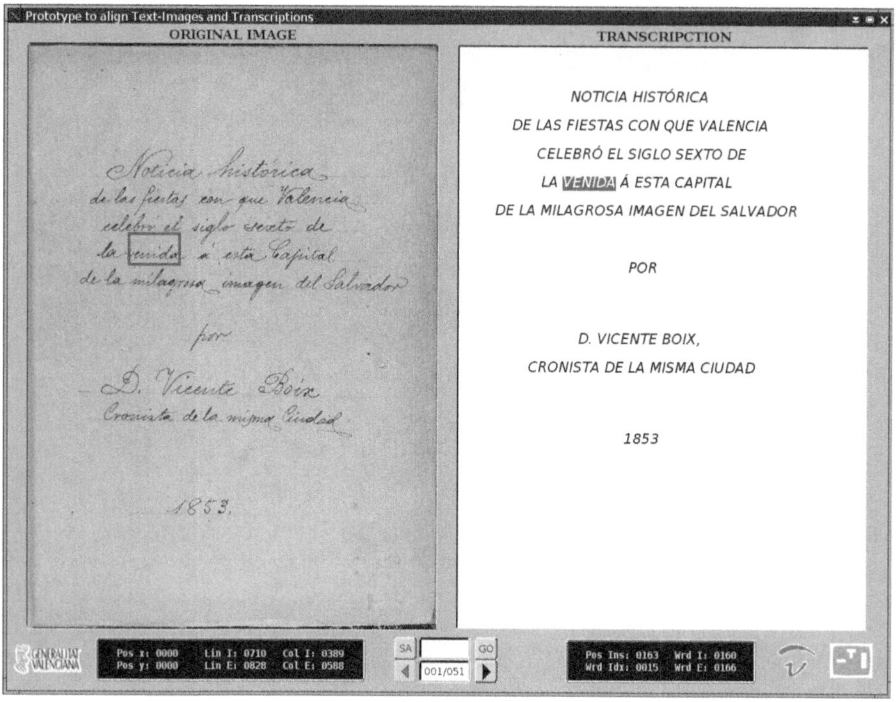

Fig. 4. Screen-shot of the alignment prototype interface displaying an outlined word (using a box) in the manuscript (left) and the corresponding highlighted word in the transcription (right)

Creating such alignments is challenging since the transcription is an ASCII text file while the manuscript page is an image. The alignment method implemented here (henceforward called Viterbi alignment), relies on the Viterbi decoding approach to Handwritten Text Recognition (HTR) based on Hidden Markov Models (HMMs) [1,12]. These techniques are based on methods originally introduced for speech recognition [2]. In such HTR systems, the alignment is actually a byproduct of the proper recognition process, i.e. an implicit segmentation of each text image line is obtained where each segment successively corresponds to one recognized word. In our case, word recognition is not actually needed, as we do already have the correct transcription. Therefore, to obtain the segmentations for the *given* word sequences, the so-called "forced-recognition" approach is employed, which consists in recognizing an imposed known sequence of words and get in this way their underlying segmentations.

4 HTR Technology Overview

The implementation of the systems described in this work involved three common different parts: document image preprocessing, line image feature extraction and Hidden Markov Model training/decoding.

It is quite common for ancient documents to suffer from degradation problems. Among these are the presence of smear, background of big variations and uneven illumination, spots due to the humidity or marks resulting from the ink that goes through the paper (generally called bleed-through). In addition, other kinds of difficulties appear in these pages as different font types and sizes in the words, underlined and/or crossed-out words, etc. The combination of these problems contributes to make the recognition process difficult, therefore a preprocessing module becomes essential.

Concerning the preprocessing module used in this work, the following steps take place: first, skew correction is carried out on each document page image; then background removal and noise reduction is performed by applying adequate filters [4] on the whole page image. Next, a text line extraction process based on local minima of the horizontal projection profile of the page image, divides the page into separate line images [8,6]. In addition, connected components are used to solve the situations where local minima alone do not allow to obtain a clear text line separation. Finally, slant correction and non-linear size normalization are applied [12] on each extracted line image.

As our alignment and recognition system is based on Hidden Markov Models (HMMs), each preprocessed text line image has to be represented as a sequence of feature vectors. To do this, the feature extraction module applies a grid to divide the text line image into squared cells. From each cell, three features are calculated: normalized gray level, horizontal gray level derivative and vertical gray level derivative. The way these three features are determined is described in [12]. Columns of cells or frames are processed from left to right and a feature vector is constructed for each frame by stacking the three features computed in its constituent cells. Hence, at the end of this process, a sequence of 60-dimensional feature vectors (20 normalized gray-level components, 20 horizontal and 20 vertical derivatives components) is obtained. An example of feature vectors sequence, representing an image of the Spanish word "Castilla" is shown in the upper part of figure 5.

Characters are modeled by continuous density left-to-right HMMs, with 6 states and 64 Gaussian mixture components per state. This topology (number of HMM states and Gaussian densities per state) was determined by tuning empirically the system on several corpora. Once a HMM "topology" has been adopted, the model parameters can be easily trained from images of continuously handwritten text lines (without any kind of word or character segmentation) accompanied by the transcription of these images into the corresponding sequence of characters. This training process is carried out using a well known instance of the EM algorithm called forward-backward or Baum-Welch re-estimation [2]. Figure 5 (bottom) shows an example of HMM character modeling.

Each lexical word is modelled by a stochastic finite-state automaton which represents all possible concatenations of individual characters that may compose the word. On the other hand, text line sentences are modelled using backoff bi-grams, with Kneser-Ney back-off smoothing [5], which are estimated using the given transcriptions of the trained set.

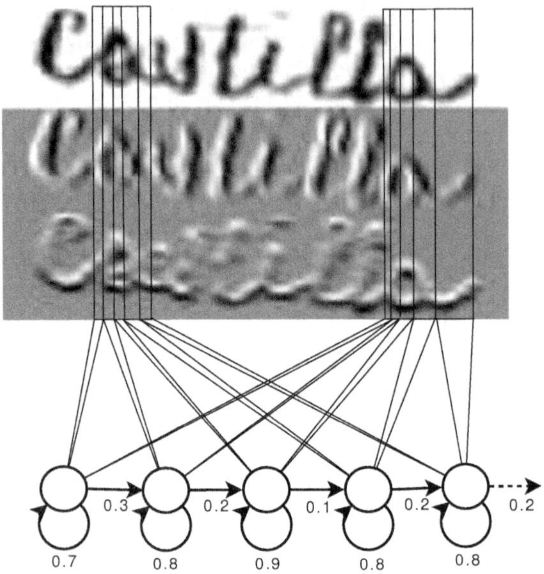

Fig. 5. Example of 5-states HMM modelling (sequences of feature vectors of) instances of the character "a" within the Spanish word "Castilla". The states are shared among all in- stances of characters of the same class. The zones modelled by each state show graphically subsequences of feature vectors (see details in the magnifying-glass view) compounded by stacking the normalized grey level and its both derivatives features.

All these finite-state (HMM character, word and sentence) models can be easily integrated into a single global model on which the search for decoding the input feature vectors sequence into the output words sequence is performed. This search is optimally done by using the Viterbi algorithm [2], which provides detailed word alignment information as a byproduct.

5 Evaluation Results

MM-CATTI: Experiments were carried out on several corpora [15,14,10]. According to the results of these experiments, when CATTI is compared with totally manual transcription, the estimated user effort reductions range from 68% to 80%. And, if compared with *post-editing* the results of a totally automatic HTR output, the expected effort savings range from 5% to 23%.

For a typical transcription task, this means that to produce 100 words of a correct transcription, a CATTI user should have to type only less than 20 words; the remaining 80 are automatically predicted by CATTI, thereby saving a considerable amount of the (typing and, in part thinking) effort needed to produce all the text manually. On the other hand, when compared with *post-editing*, from every 100 (non-interactive) word errors, the CATTI user should

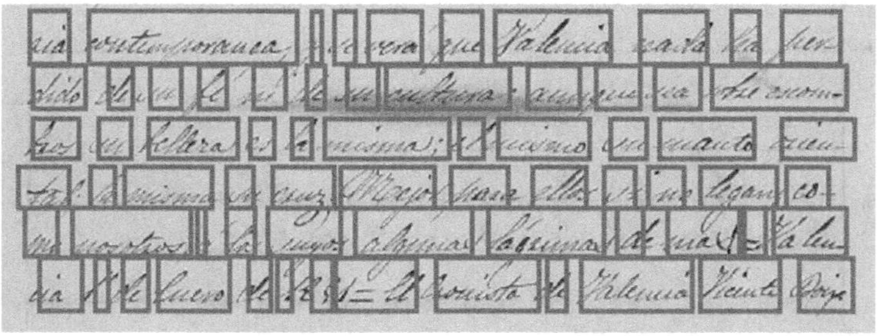

Fig. 6. Word alignment for 6 lines of a particularly noisy part of the corpus. The four last words on the second line as well as the last line illustrate some of over-segmentation and under-segmentation error types.

have to interactively correct only less than 77. The remaining 23 errors would be automatically corrected by CATTI, thanks to the feedback information derived from other interactive corrections [15].

Alignment System: One kind of measure adopted to evaluate the quality of alignments is the so-called *alignment error rate* (AER) [13], which measures mismatches between word-images and ASCII transcriptions (tokens), excluding word-space tokens. Preliminary results around 7% of AER were obtained on a set of 53 pages from the "Cristo-Salvador" [10] handwritten old-document.

The two typical alignment errors are known as over-segmentation and under-segmentation respectively. The over-segmentation error is when one word image is separated into two or more fragments. The under-segmentation error occurs when two or more images are grouped together and returned as one word. Figure 6 shows some of them.

6 Conclusions

In this paper, two systems have been described: one of them aiming at assisting in the transcription of handwriting old documents, while the other one focusing on the alignment between handwritten text images and their corresponding transcriptions.

The assisted transcription system (MM-CATTI) is based on an interactive-predictive framework which combines the efficiency of automatic HTR systems with the accuracy of the experts in the transcription of ancient documents. In this case, the words corrected by the expert become part of a increasingly longer prefixes of the final target transcription. These prefixes are used by the MM-CATTI system to suggest new suffixes that the expert can iteratively accept or modify until a satisfactory, correct target transcription is produced. On the other hand, for handwritten manuscripts whose transcriptions are already available, the presented alignment system maps every line and word image on the manuscript with its respective line and word on the electronic (ASCII or PDF) transcription. This method takes advantage of the implicit alignments made by the Viterbi decoding used in forced text image recognition with HMMs.

For these systems, adequate demonstrators have been implemented, which clearly show the capabilities and potential benefits of using the proposed technologies. We believe these technologies are already pretty mature and we are currently seeking to undertake projects involving large-scale field tests that will allow us to validate and/or further develop these technologies.

Acknowledgment. Work supported by the Spanish Government (MICINN and "Plan E") under the MITTRAL (TIN2009-14633-C03-01) research project and under the research programme Consolider Ingenio 2010: MIPRCV (CSD2007-00018) and the Generalitat Valenciana under gran Prometeo/2009/14.

References

1. Bazzi, I., Schwartz, R., Makhoul, J.: An Omnifont Open-Vocabulary OCR System for English and Arabic. IEEE Transactions on Pattern Analysis and Machine Intelligence 21(6), 495–504 (1999)
2. Jelinek, F.: Statistical Methods for Speech Recognition. MIT Press (1998)
3. Kavallieratou, E., Fakotakis, N., Kokkinakis, G.: An unconstrained handwriting recognition system. International Journal on Document Analysis and Recognition 4(4), 226–242 (2002)
4. Kavallieratou, E., Stamatatos, E.: Improving the quality of degraded document images. In: Proceedings of the Second International Conference on Document Image Analysis for Libraries (DIAL 2006), pp. 340–349. IEEE Computer Society, Washington, DC, USA (2006)
5. Kneser, R., Ney, H.: Improved backing-off for m-gram language modeling. In: International Conference on Acoustics, Speech, and Signal Processing (ICASSP 1995), vol. 1, pp. 181–184. IEEE Computer Society, Los Alamitos (1995)
6. Likforman-Sulem, L., Zahour, A., Taconet, B.: Text line segmentation of historical documents: a survey. International Journal on Document Analysis and Recognition 9(2), 123–138 (2007)
7. Lorigo, L., Govindaraju, V.: Offline Arabic handwriting recognition: a survey. IEEE Transactions on Pattern Analysis and Machine Intelligence 28(5), 712–724 (2006)
8. Marti, U.V., Bunke, H.: Using a Statistical Language Model to improve the preformance of an HMM-Based Cursive Handwriting Recognition System. Int. Journal of Pattern Recognition and Artificial Intelligence 15(1), 65–90 (2001)
9. Romero, V., Levia, L.A., Toselli, A.H., Vidal, E.: Interactive multimodal transcription of text imagse using a web-based demo system. In: Procedings of the International Conference on Intelligent User Interfaces, Sanibel Island, Florida, pp. 477–478 (February 2009)
10. Romero, V., Toselli, A.H., Rodríguez, L., Vidal, E.: Computer Assisted Transcription for Ancient Text Images. In: Kamel, M.S., Campilho, A. (eds.) ICIAR 2007. LNCS, vol. 4633, pp. 1182–1193. Springer, Heidelberg (2007)
11. Romero, V., Toselli, A.H., Vidal, E.: Using mouse feedback in computer assisted transcription of handwritten text images. In: Proceedings of the 10th International Conference on Document Analysis and Recognition (ICDAR). IEEE Computer Society, Barcelona (2009)

12. Toselli, A.H., Juan, A., Keysers, D., González, J., Salvador, I., Ney, H., Vidal, E., Casacuberta, F.: Integrated Handwriting Recognition and Interpretation using Finite-State Models. International Journal of Pattern Recognition and Artificial Intelligence 18(4), 519–539 (2004)
13. Toselli, A.H., Romero, V., Vidal, E.: Viterbi Based alignment between Text Images and their Transcripts. In: Language Technology for Cultural Heritage Data (LaTeCH 2007), Prague, Czech Republic, pp. 9–16 (June 2007)
14. Toselli, A.H., Romero, V., Vidal, E.: Computer Assisted Transcription of Text Images and Multimodal Interaction. In: Popescu-Belis, A., Stiefelhagen, R. (eds.) MLMI 2008. LNCS, vol. 5237, pp. 296–308. Springer, Heidelberg (2008)
15. Toselli, A.H., Romero, V., Pastor, M., Vidal, E.: Multimodal interactive transcription of text images. Pattern Recognition 43(5), 1814–1825 (2009)
16. Zimmermann, M., Bunke, H.: Automatic segmentation of the iam off-line database for handwritten english text. In: Proceedings of the 16th International Conference on Pattern Recognition, vol. 4, pp. 35–39 (2000)
17. Zimmermann, M., Chappelier, J.C., Bunke, H.: Offline grammar-based recognition of handwritten sentences. IEEE Trans. Pattern Anal. Mach. Intell. 28(5), 818–821 (2006)

A Collaborative Knowledge Management System for Analyzing Non-verbal Markings in the Ancient Mediterranean World

Stefano Valtolina[1], Giovanna Bagnasco Gianni[2], Alessandra Gobbi[3], and Nancy T. de Grummond[4]

[1] Dipartimento Informatica e Comunicazione, Università degli Studi di Milano, Via Comelico 39, 20135, Milano, Italy
valtolin@dico.unimi.it

[2] Dipartimento di Scienze dell'Antichità, Università degli Studi di Milano, Via Festa del Perdono 7, 20122, Milano, Italy
giovanna.bagnasco@unimi.it

[3] Dipartimento di Scienze dell'Antichità, Università degli Studi di Pavia, P.za del Lino 2, 27100, Pavia, Italy
gobbialessandra@gmail.com

[4] Department of Classics,The Florida State University, 205A Dodd Hall, Tallahassee, FL 32306-1510, USA
ndegrummond@fsu.edu

Abstract. This paper presents the results of an international archaeological project aiming to the study of non-verbal markings, named sigla, found on objects discovered in different excavation sites distributed in the Mediterranean area. The project is based on the involvement of an interdisciplinary team of experts from American and Italian universities and its aim is to develop a collaborative knowledge management system for formulating new hypotheses about the meanings, functions and roles of sigla stored in distributed archives. The paper analyzes knowledge integration problems and describes the design the environment supporting collaborative activities among archaeologists. For analysis purposes, the system integrates multimedia information retrieval strategies for recovering sigla according to certain conditions of similarity and taking into account other factors such as date, provenance and context. The conditions of similarity are based on possible recurrent patterns of sigla, connections and their layout merging from archaeologists' descriptions or drawings of sigla.

Keywords: Cultural Heritage, Knowledge Management, Ontology-Based Model, User-centered Design, Participatory Design.

1 Introduction

A large percentage of studies of the classical world have been devoted to or based upon archaeological remains, epigraphic texts and ancient literary sources. Recent trends in scholarship [1,2,3], however, show a surge in interest in non-verbal

C. Grana and R. Cucchiara (Eds.): MM4CH 2011, CCIS 247, pp. 74–89, 2012.

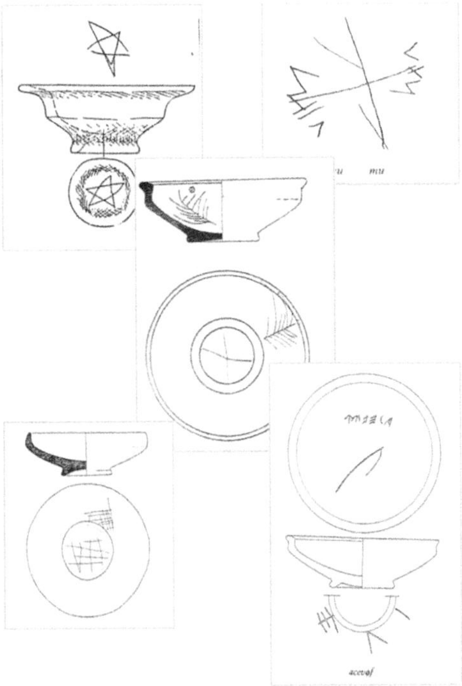

Fig. 1. A set of images depicting sketches of sigla used to store sigla representations

markings, that can be incised, painted or stamped; they can be numbers or letters, or abbreviations that can be considered part of a visual and non-verbal communication. Examples of sigla are presented in figure 1. In particular this paper reports a study about Etruscan markings as means of non-verbal communication (hereafter called sigla) discovered in Mediterranean archaeological excavations on objects of many different types and belonging to different contexts of the spheres of Etruscan life and afterlife. Sigla are usually poorly published, if at all, and receive little consideration in Etruscan studies in favor of letters that form words and can therefore be studied from a linguistic perspective. Nevertheless, non-verbal markings perform an important role for fostering studies about the Etruscan language or for supporting new hypotheses about aspects of the Etruscan culture.

In order to investigate the potential of communication in these markings, the Università degli Studi di Milano and the Florida State University collaborate in an international project called IESP - International Etruscan Sigla Project. The aim of this project is to put together independent studies on sigla carried out by an international team from the USA and Italy - archaeologists and computer scientists, professors and students - who by sharing their research have been able to experiment and to develop terminology and methodology for designing new systematic tools supporting their studies.

One of the goals of the IES project concerns the creation of an interactive system based on an integration of different knowledge sources, including databases of sigla and databases of archeological excavations able to recognize, group and compare similar sigla by means of matching scanned images and other factors such as date, provenance, context, descriptions, artifact type, artifact function, and location of the mark on the artifact. Another novelty of this system is to favor new forms of collaborative analyses in the archaeological field which require that different experts share their specialized knowledge, skills and work across different geographic and time zones. In these situations, one of the major problems to face and acknowledge is that these experts, belonging to different scientific communities, may have different views and opinions about sigla interpretations. Communicational and reasoning gaps arise among experts in the team due to their different cultural backgrounds. The IES project supports these types of cooperative activities through the definition of a collaborative knowledge management system in which each expert can express her/his opinions and interpretations externalizing the "why" and "how" of her/his idea by using an annotation tool. The IES project is also open to accept sigla from different areas outside Etruria in order to increase documentation, make comparisons possible among different cultural areas and better assess an contextualize Etruscan evidences.

The paper is organized as it follows. Section 2 summarizes current trends in studies upon archaeological non-verbal marking. Section 3 discusses our strategy for designing a collaborative environment. Section 4 presents the knowledge management model implemented to support archeologists in their analysis and collaboration activities and to integrate different databases. Finally, Section 5 reports conclusions and future works.

2 Context of Archaeological Sigla

There are in existence thousands of examples of Etruscan non-verbal writing, typically referred to as graffiti, a term that is found to be inadequate. The Latin word siglum (pl. sigla; the corresponding term in a Greek context is sema, semata) should be used instead to refer to such markings. The Etruscan examples, showing one or more symbols, numbers or letters, date from around 700 BCE to the first century BCE, and were incised, painted or stamped on objects of many different types. The sigla occur on a remarkable range of objects: pottery, weights, spindle whorls, sarcophagi, burial urns, roof tiles, architectural terracottas, boundary stones, stone walls, lead missiles, bone and ivory plaques, and a wide variety of artifacts in bronze (axes, fibulas, helmets, knives, razors, sickles). The contexts include cemeteries, sanctuaries, ports, artisans' quarters and habitations, i.e., the full spectrum of the spheres of Etruscan life and afterlife. The sites range widely in Italy, from the heartland of Etruria, to Etruscan expansion areas on the Bay of Naples and near Bologna and the Po Valley. Comparable phenomena can also be found in other sites in the Mediterranean area such as Greece, Crete and Turkey, now discussed and investigated during a recent conference at the Florida State University.

The goal of the studies on Etruscan sigla [1,2,3] is to assess the real consistency of archaeological indicators according to a deductive method taking into account a dialectic comparison between the ideas of function and role. If, on the one hand, the function of an object, used as support for sigla, can be suggested by its form, on the other, its role can be determined each time by the archaeological context retrieved both from the conditions of its discovery and from iconographic sources. As a consequence this attitude is also a priority in considering sigla because their meaning can change according to their archaeological context. This can be the case of the siglum in shape of V that can have the meaning of number 5 or letter U according to its context. This is also the case of the siglum formed by a cross inscribed in a circle that can have the meaning of the Greek letter theta or be the graphic representation of sacred space, based on principles of division and orientation. Therefore a first phase in the IES project was to study the division and orientation of sigla that suggest such a concern on pottery dating from the Orientalising period (end of the 8° century BCE - first quarter of the 6° century). According to these studies, it was clear the need of a digital system:

- to support questions about function and role in the field of sigla and a according to a multifaceted perspective taking into account archaeological data to a larger extent,
- to analyze cases of recurrent sigla as cultural indicators of non-verbal communication within their different archaeological contexts.

The core of the system is a procedure to assess sigla with reference to their geographical range and chronology, to the nature of the objects and contexts to which they belong and to the layout of the graphic design. The enormous amount of data, the variety of the cultural background of archaeological experts involved, the wide span of different hypotheses about the interpretation of each siglum type and their relationships urge the design of a tool to support collaboration activities and dialectic comparisons.

3 Collaborative System

Nowadays several interactive systems are designed in order to support a shift of the user's role from that of passive consumer towards active producer of information and knowledge, i.e. from consumers to prosumers [4,5]. A common element at the base of these studies is an interest in user involvement in co-creative activities. A typical example of this type of this co-creative work is discoverable in the archeological activity carried out in the context of the IES project. Based on their experiences, archeologists analyzing a siglum are able to identify and infer information about its nature and possible meaning in respect to the function and role of the support on which the siglum is placed. The archeologist's experience is able to support her/him to discover particular features of the siglum or a particular combination of sigla leading to formulate specific interpretations.

Since non-verbal markings have been poorly published, and since the meanings of these sigla are largely unknown, it is important to offer an environment for fostering archeologists in creating a knowledge base useful to support studies in the context of the Etruscan language. Moreover, since the IES project sees involved two different communities of archaeologists, one Italian and one American, the final environment has to be able to support a dialectic comparison between different competences and knowledge related to the work of experts that operate in a specialized collaborative system. To achieve these results it is necessary to emphasize as, during the analysis process, different experts can acquire knowledge from each other, accepting and interpreting their points of view through multi-disciplinary and collaborative methodologies [6,7]. Therefore, different actors belonging to different archeological spheres and thus having different points of view and competences, sometimes not overlapping, cooperate to create a common awareness in order to achieve a common understanding and interpretation [8].

The archeologists' participation in co-creating knowledge is based on the definition of a social-media platform able to play a focal role in adding value to the Etruscan studies. This social-media-based tool enables mutual dialogues among archeologists allowing them to exchange ideas, impressions, interpretations rather than merely allowing to submit content. Forums, blogs and wiki-systems are examples of social-media tools for supporting debates and cooperative user-generated contents but the solution adopted in the context of the IES project is based on the use of annotation strategies. Annotations allow archaeologists to trigger a discussion in the same environment used for inserting, searching and visualizing sigla information.

Annotating an area of the interface the archaeologist can express his/her opinion about the piece of information currently visualized. Further details about the implemented solution are presented in section 4.3. However, the idea is to offer to each expert an annotation tool for commenting hypotheses, ideas, notes, and impressions of other members of the team [9]. The annotation tool as communicational medium for exchanging ideas and impressions is used in different situations [10,11,12,13].Whereas, the concept of annotation has been defined by several authors [13,14,15] and a comprehensive study on annotations is presented in [10,11]in which detailed contours and complexity of annotations are defined. Summarizing these studies is possible to said that an annotation is a note, added by way of comment or explanation [14] to a document or to a part of a document. In[12] the authors describe an annotation tool as a service that has to be characterized by the following requirements:

- nested annotation: that is, the possibility to annotate another annotation,
- unique reference: that is, an annotation has to be referable by an handle,
- a set of signs: that is, the multimedia representation of the annotation (by means of texts, graphics, images, sounds or combination of them),
- access policies: that is, if an annotation is public, private or sharable,
- indexing strategy: that is, the index structure used for supporting annotation-based retrieval.

Therefore, the idea at the base of this paper is to exploit an annotation tool to allow different experts to create and explain knowledge associated to the siglum, that is, the justifications that have brought to the definition of a specific hypotheses or at the base of the performed analysis.

4 Knowledge Management System

As said in the previous section, the collaborative environment at the base of the IES project is a virtual environment in which archaeologists work in a collaborative way during the various stages of the sigla analysis process. Within the framework of this collaboration it is necessary to design a knowledge management (KM) system able to manage:

- information regarding sigla and objects used as supports for sigla, discovered in different archaeological excavations in the Mediterranean area and stored in distributed archives,
- information regarding the analysis carried out by experts, using multimedia information retrieval strategy, for formulating hypotheses and interpretations of sigla,
- information related to the annotations for supporting the collaborative activities among archaeologists who externalize their reasoning using the annotation tool.

4.1 Knowledge Integration

A key inspiration for our KM system is the idea that modern archaeology would benefit significantly from having access to information from a variety of heterogeneous data sources and being able to have multiple participants visually observe factual and visual data in an intuitive and natural setting. The advantage is that the investigation of sigla is not done in isolation but in relation to historical, social, economical, and geographical contexts of the objects on which the sigla are incised, painted or stamped. To address such integration problems, our KM system yields fast and intuitive access to archaeological information from distributed sources of sigla and excavations and provides the ability to recognize, group and compare similar sigla features by means of matching scanned images or descriptions carried out by archaeologists and other factors such as date, provenance, context, type, function, and location of the siglum on the support. This KM model proposed in the IES project stems from the consideration that, the integration of different archives has to face the problem of defining a common terminology allowing the exchange of data in the right way. To solve this problem the use of an ontology [16,17] was proposed as a strategy to describe a given Etruscan domain and retrieve the associated context information from distributed data sources. This ontology undertakes the role of "lingua franca" able to integrate knowledge spread in different sigla and excavations databases in order to offer a unique view about the heritage to be disseminated to archeologists. This common view, represented by the ontology, provides a formal definition for the relevant domain's concepts in order to create suitable relations among different concepts and to adapt and interpret concepts and methodologies according to mutual interactions. Creating a new ontology from scratch is a time consuming task and, therefore, it is better to exploit a general ontology from which a customized ontology can be derived. Significant efforts have been made to provide standard data representations within cultural heritage domains in order to enable museums and cultural organizations to share their information across different information systems. Among the existing reference models, one the most used in the cultural context is the CIDOC Conceptual Reference Model [18]. In our approach the CIDOC-CRM acts as the backbone of the final ontology, which maintains the structure of the CIDOC-CRM ontology slicing and adapting its concepts according to the Etruscan culture that we have to take in consideration. This semantic model customized for a specific archeological context is then used to integrate information of heterogeneous data sources. In order to integrate heterogeneous data sources the elements defined in each logical schema has been expressed according to the classes forming the ontology and to a proper set of mapping information. A detailed explanation about the integration strategy adopted in the IES project is reported in [17,19]. This paper presents an extension of the previous work carried out for integrating into the final ontology concepts related to the sigla study such as: siglum context information, siglum typology, siglum position, direction and orientation, siglum images and descriptions and information about the possible combinations of sigla. Figure 2 depicts a portion of the CIDOC-CRM and how new concepts related to the sigla study (bordered using the red circle) are integrated into the ontology. The information describing the mappings between the ontology and the sigla databases are memorized in the classes of the ontology itself. Such classes are endowed with a set of new properties which refer the information related to the mapping between the ontology and the sigla database schema. From a technical point of view, the ontology uses a machine-readable format such as RDF. Therefore, class names and properties are encoded using RDF labels. The information mapping inserted in the ontology permits the defining of transformation algorithms (implemented in JAVA) which translate a semantic query (expressed in SeRQL, a RDF Query Language) into a set of SQL statements according to the number of databases integrated in the KM system. The obtained SQL statements enable the access to the integrated databases by means of Sesame, an open source semantic Java framework. Going beyond standard digital retrieval operations, the system exploits the ontology expressing the concepts relevant for the domain and uses it to integrate the available data sources, providing a uniform point of access to all information. A semantic mediator allows the user to formulate queries in terms of the domain's concepts rather than entities defined in the databases' logical schemas; e.g., "retrieve all sigla and relate them with findings or monuments stored in excavations or museum archives". Moreover this semantic mediator, putting in comparison sigla and excavations databases, gives to archaeologists the possibility to re-build contexts or to formulate hypotheses. A possible

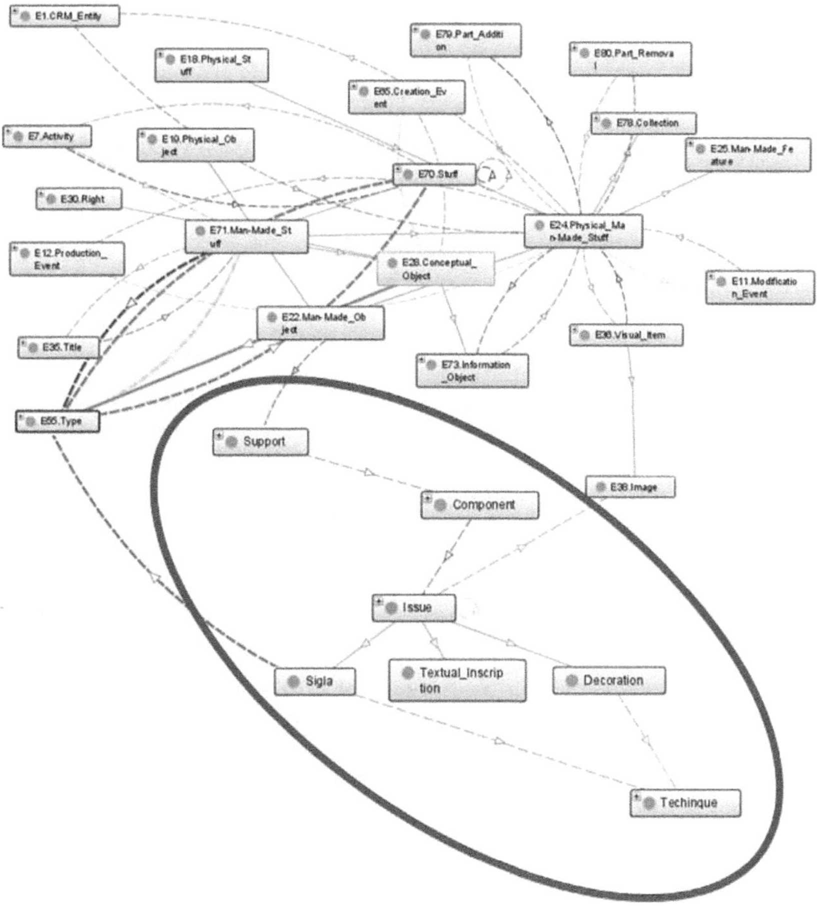

Fig. 2. A screenshot of the ontology adopted in the KM system. The sections bordered by the red circle concern sigla concepts. "Support" represents the object on which the non-verbal marks are placed. "Component" is the part of the object (neck, foot, side, ...). "Issue" represents the non-verbal marks that can be divided in "sigla", "decoration" and "textual_inscription". The two last concepts are important because, although they are not proper sigla, they have been often found in association with sigla and so they have to be considered together as parts of a whole communication system. Other concepts are related to techniques, images or types of the sigla. "Image" and "Type" are not new concepts because it is possible to use CIDOC-CRM classes for representing them.

re-building of a context could be: if a siglum is similar to others belonging to findings discovered in sacred places (i.e. tombs) then it is possible to infer that this siglum has a religious meaning even if the origin of the related finding is unknown. Instead a possible hypotheses formulation could be: if a set of similar sigla have been discovered in a specific place and all of them have the same chronology then it is possible to say that this siglum is a brand and then it is possible to trace its geographic distribution in order to understand something about its circulation. Therefore, the proposed ontology virtually unifies scattered archives containing sigla and excavation information. Using this system, archaeologists can retrieve data from different databases and can combine data in order to create a new hypotheses and interpretations.

4.2 Multimedia Information Retrieval

To exploit the KM system presented in the previous section, we designed and developed a system for offering multimedia research strategies of sigla according to certain conditions of similarity in appearance and taking into account other factors such as description, date, provenance and relationships with other sigla. The conditions of similarity are based on possible recurrent patterns of marking studied through comparisons of archaeologists' scientific descriptions or drawings of sigla. In particular our system integrates full-text retrieval strategies based on Oracle Text [20], a technology included in the Oracle11g DBMS. These full-text strategies enable one to carry out text analysis in descriptions of sigla, as well as text searches using a variety of approaches including keyword searching, linguistics features researches and thematic queries. Full-text searching provides the capability to identify descriptions of sigla that satisfy a query, and to sort them by relevance to the query. Notions of query and similarity are very flexible but the idea at the base of our system is to exploit Oracle Text features for normalizing query terms in order to retrieve all descriptions containing such terms according to specific factors of similarity. For example, the normalization phase includes folding upper-case letters to lower-case, and often involves removal of suffixes (such as s or es in English) or reduces each query term to its linguistic root (technique called stemming searching). Using stemming searching it is possible to reduce a set of words such as paint, painting, painted, painter to the same root term i.e. "paint". The use of the term "paint" allows to clear up the confusion between terms used for searching in respect with terms used for storing data enabling searches to find variant forms of the same term, without tediously entering all the possible variants. Another full-text searching technique is called fuzzy research and it is addressed to find words spelled in a similar way to the researched terms. This technique is helpful for finding more accurate results when the researched keywords contain mistakes e.g. Cuurve, cros, and so on. Besides the possibility of expanding a query to include all terms having the same linguistic root as the researched terms or terms which are spelled similarly, the originality of our system is addressed to support text researches based on a thematic dictionary (a thesaurus). A thesaurus is a classification of concepts useful for improving information retrieval strategies exploiting semantic relationships among terms belonging to a specific domain dictionary, in our case an Etruscan dictionary. This dictionary is a set of terms, generally used among archaeologists for discussing sigla. For example our Etruscan thesaurus contains terms used for describing the shape of siglum (e.g. Alphabetiform, Numeriform, Symbol) or other features such the typology (e.g. Craticula, Tridens Acutus, Forma

Quadrans, and so on) or the technique (e.g. incised, painted or stamped). Moreover the thesaurus is also used to put in relation each term with its synonyms or to define hierarchical or semantic relationships. In our case, these relationships are used to create a semantic network of terms arranged according to different conceptual associations. Examples of these associations are:

- SYN - synonyms: hook SYN hanger
- BT - broader term: sacred place BT tomb
- NT - narrower term: tomb NT sacred place
- RT - related term: sarcophagus RT tomb
- TR - translation in other languages (e.g. Italian): cup TR coppa

In this way the system is able to retrieve descriptions that contain relevant texts by expanding queries to include similar or related terms as defined in the thesaurus. For example, in figure 3 is depicted a screenshot in which the query submitted by the user "give me all sigla containing in the description field, the term 'buttonhole"' is extended with synonymous such as: "loop", "hole", "eyelet". The synonyms are terms used by other archaeologists for referring to

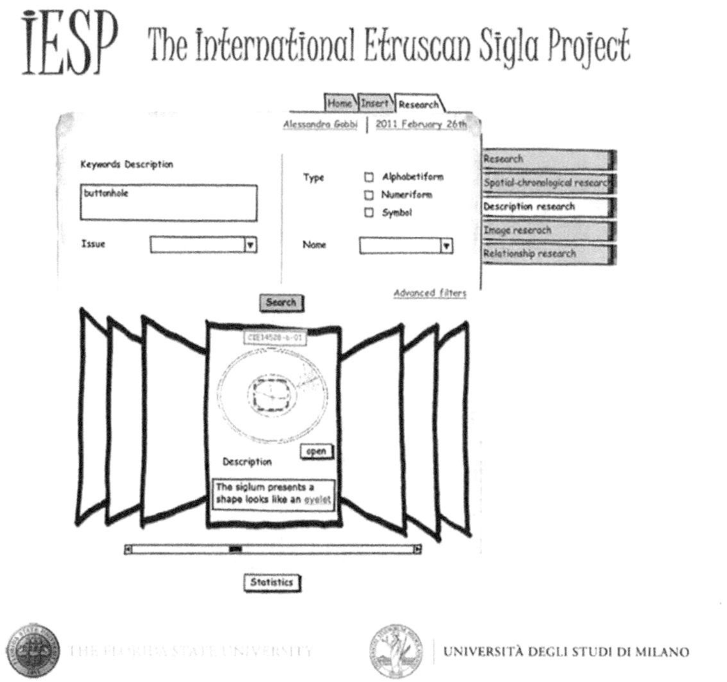

Fig. 3. In the screenshot the archaeologist uses the system for retrieving all sigla containing in the description field the term "buttonhole". The query is expanded using synonyms contained in the hesaurus. In this case the description of the recovered siglum contains the term: "eyelet".

similar shapes discoverable in sigla. Another feature of the information retrieval system developed in the IES project focuses on using automated image feature extraction solutions and object recognitions to classify image content. Such a content-based retrieval system processes the information contained in image data of each drawing of a siglum and creates an abstraction of that content in terms of visual attributes. These visual attributes concern textures, primitive shapes distributions (that is, the segmentations of the images in simple geometrical shapes) and their location, that is, the information about placements of shapes and textures in the image. These visual attributes are stored in the database using a specific memory structure called feature vectors, or signatures. Any query operations deal solely with this abstraction rather than with the image itself. Thus, each image inserted into the database is analyzed, and a compact representation of its content is stored in its feature vector. This image retrieval system is developed using MultiMedia services[18] that integrate the storage, retrieval, and management of media files in Oracle11g DBMS. Figure 4 presents an example of such image retrieval system in which some images are recovered due their similarity to the one inserted by the user (bordered using dashed line) in terms of textures, primitive shapes and their locations that, the Multimedia Oracle service has been able to process. The retrieving process is carried out

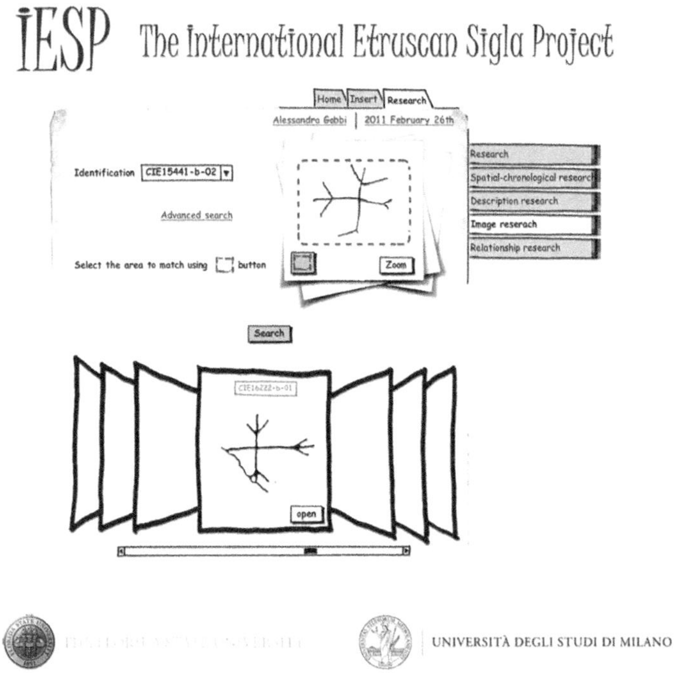

Fig. 4. In the screenshot the archaeologist uses the system for retrieving all images of sigla similar to the one loaded in the dashed area. The system compares the feature vector of this image with ones of the images contained in the IESP database.

comparing the feature vector of the inserted image with the feature vectors of the images contained in the IESP database. Therefore, Oracle processes the information of the researched image and creates an abstract content according to its visual attributes defining the signature. To set an importance to each visual attribute, Oracle allows to assign them a weight. In this way, the measures of similarity are calculated subtracting the features vectors of each image. Finally, the system is endowed with other information retrieval services for recovering geographical information based on Google maps in order to design an atlas for territorial reading of the sigla in the database. The combination of information about similarities and recurrent patterns with geographical contextualization allows for complex systemic readings that may lead to new insights and lines of investigation.

4.3 Annotation Tool

In the IESP system the annotation is thought of as author-attributable content placed within the virtual environment in association with (or reference to) a particular item of information of the sigla. Using annotation capabilities, the

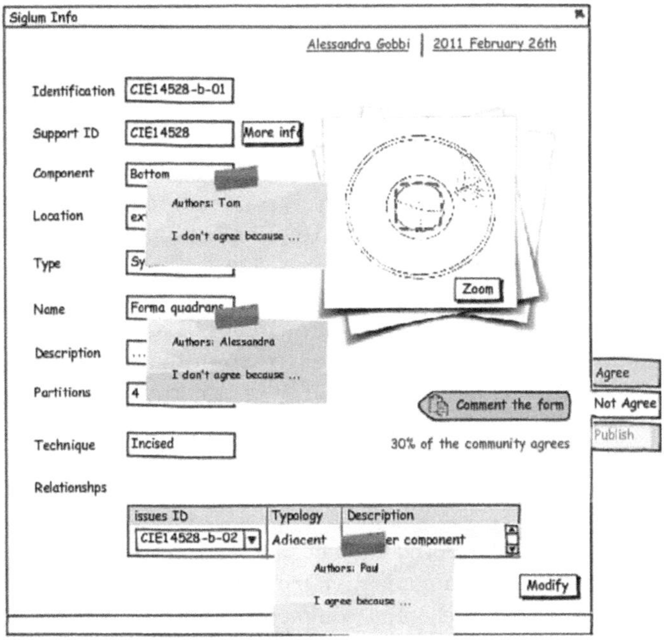

Fig. 5. In the screenshot is presented a collaborative scenario in which a set of archeologists have accessed the environment for commenting on the information of the visualized siglum. Each "post-it" is put on the screen in relation with the field that the archaeologist wants to comment on. For example, Alessandra disagrees about the fact that this siglum is a "forma quadrans" and so she has put a post-it on this field in order to express her disagreement.

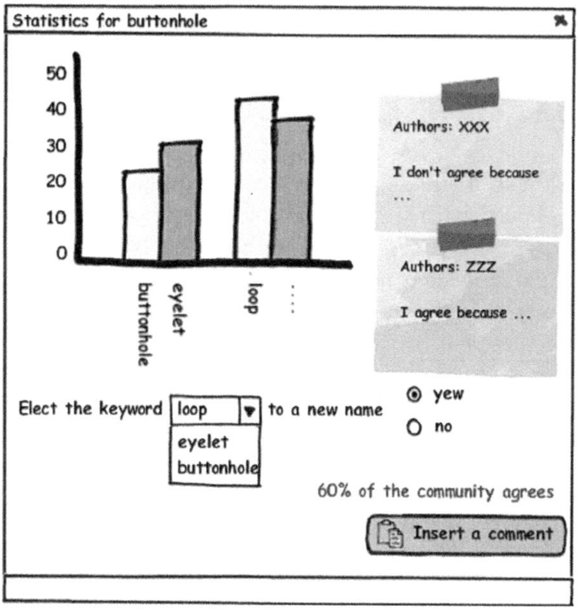

Fig. 6. In the screenshot is presented an annotation scenario in which a set of archeologists are discussing about the possibility to insert new terms in their Etruscan thesaurus

archaeologist is able to add commentary in association with specific data (or aspects) of the visualized siglum in order to comment on its content. These comments persist in the environment and are made available to other users as a form of annotation attributed to the author. In figure 5 a collaborative scenario is presented. Tom, Alessandra and Paul are archeologists who have commented on the visualized information in order to express agreement or disagreement and in this case for motivating and justifying it. The annotation can be organized as a thread of notes put one under the others in order to reply to previous comments posted by other users. This solution implements the concept of nested annotation [12] allowing the user to annotate another annotations in order to created a thread. In this way different archeologists can trigger a discussion process around the ideas exposed by the primary annotation's author. Thus, the annotation becomes a communication medium through which different users can exchange impressions, ideas and comments, that is the knowledge needful to achieve a shared solution about sigla interpretations. The annotation system also preserves the integrity of the archaeological data, without forcing it into a unique and absolute interpretation, but providing a fluid construction of hypotheses made by exchanges and comparisons between plural ideas, which remain clear and open in every step. From a technical point of view, when the archaeologist gets the information about a siglum he/she can switch the environment in an annotation mode in which the annotations are loaded and attached to the related pieces of information. Currently the annotations contain only textual descriptions but in future the idea is to extended the features of our system for enabling the insertion of images or other multimedia data in the annotations. Another example of annotation scenario is presented in figure 6. In this environment a statistic analysis is presented according to recurrences of terms used in sigla descriptions. Archeologists, discussing about this analysis, can insert in the Etruscan thesaurus a new term (e.g. in figure the term "loop") that in the future could be used for describing the typology of sigla.

5 Conclusions and Future Works

This paper describes the design and implementation strategies adopted to develop a collaborative knowledge management system for supporting archaeologists in the study of non-verbal markings discovered in numerous excavation sites in the Mediterranean area. These activities have been carried out in the context of an international project, the IES (International Etruscan Sigla) project, that involves experts in different disciplines and with different backgrounds (archaeologists and computer scientists, professors and students), from American and Italian universities. The aim of this project is to describe a methodology for designing new systematic tools in order to support the study of incised, painted or stamped symbols, numbers or letters found on different type of objects discovered in several cultural contexts, that can be considered essentially non-literary. The main problem is that such markings are normally poorly published, but they have an important role in the context of studies devoted to understanding the Etruscan language and culture. The idea presented in this paper is to support archaeologists' activities by means of a collaborative interactive environment taking advantage of sigla in cultural achievements. Therefore the collection, recognition and comparison of the features of sigla by means of matching scanned images or the archaeologists' descriptions or of other data such as date, provenance, context, type, function, and location of the siglum on the object is relevant. The paper describes these multimedia information retrieval strategies implemented using specific services provided by the Oracle DBMS and how these services enable the possibility to support the study of communication features of the Etruscan culture. Moreover these information retrieval services are able to recover data by a network of archives integrated through an ontology meant to describe a given Etruscan domain and retrieve multifaceted data sources belonging to other related domains. Finally, the system offers the possibility to involve archeologists in collaborative activities by means of an annotation tool. This tool allows to insert notes, comments and ideas to be disseminated and shared in order to enhance the discussion on sigla and achieve a common knowledge on current thesis or interpretations in progress.

Future works are designed to test the system in the context of the IES project for assessing its efficacy, efficiency and usability during collaborative activities among archeologists from different international universities. Further studies are expected to focus on innovative information retrieval solutions for supporting semantic researches combining heterogeneous data sources in order to put in relation information of sigla with information about the discovery contexts of the supports on which the sigla have been found. The idea is to design a semantic engine using which the archaeologist can submit semantic queries for information that is not contained in, or cannot be searched in only one database but that has to be recovered combining knowledge contained in the network of the integrated databases using the ontology after a period of testing held by a community of archaeologists.

References

1. de Grummond, N.T., Bare, C., Meilleur, A.: Etruscan sigla ("graffiti"): Prolegomena and some case studies. Archaeologia Transatlantica 18, 25–38 (2000)
2. Bagnasco Gianni, G., Gobbi, A., Scoccimarro, N.: Segni eloquenti in necropolis e abitato, In. L'écriture et l'espace de la mort Recontres internationales, Roma, Mars 5-7 (2009) (in press)
3. Gobbi, A.: Oggetti iscritti e contesti in Campania. In: Bagnasco Gianni, G., Biella, M.C., Cantù, M., Gobbi, A. (eds.) Quali Etruschi maestri di scrittura?, in Convivenze etniche e contatti di culture. Mamerco impara a scrivere, Atti del Seminario di Studi, Milano, Aristonothos, Novembre 23-24, 2009 (in press, 2011)
4. Bruns, A.: Blogs, Wikipedia, Second Life, and Beyond: From Production To Produsage. Peter Lang, New York (2008)
5. Fischer, G.: End-User Development and Meta-Design: Foundations for Cultures of Participation. In: Pipek, V., Rosson, M.B., de Ruyter, B., Wulf, V. (eds.) IS-EUD 2009. LNCS, vol. 5435, pp. 3–14. Springer, Heidelberg (2009)
6. Snow, C.P.: The Two Cultures. C. P. Cambridge University Press, New York (1993)
7. Valtolina, S., Mussio, P., Mazzoleni, P., Franzoni, S., Bagnasco, G., Geroli, M., Ridi, C.: Media for Knowledge Creation and Dissemination. Semantic Model and Narrations for a New Accessibility to Cultural Heritage. In: 6th Creativity & Cognition Conference, Washington DC, USA, June 13-15 (2007)
8. Fischer, G.: Symmetry of ignorance, social creativity, and meta-design. Knowledge-Based Systems 13(7-8), 527–537 (2000)
9. Valtolina, S., Mussio, P., Barricelli, B.R., Bordegoni, M., Ferrise, F., Ambrogio, M.: Distributed knowledge creation, recording and improvement in collaborative design. In: 2nd International Symposium on Intelligent Interactive Multimedia Systems and Services-KES IIMSS 2009, Mogliano Veneto, Italy, July 16-17 (2009)
10. Agosti, M., Ferro, N.: A Formal Model of Annotations of Digital Content. ACM Transactions on Information Systems (TOIS) 26(1), 3:1–3:57 (2008)
11. Agosti, M., Bonfiglio-Dosio, G., Ferro, N.: A historical and contemporary study on annotations to derive key features for systems design. International Journal on Digital Libraries 8(1), 1–19 (2007), doi:10.1007/s00799-007-0010-0
12. Agosti, M., Ferro, N., Albrechtsen, H., Frommholz, I., Panizzi, E., Thiel, U.: Design, Implementation and Evaluation of the Use of Annotations in Interactive and Collaborative DL Access. In: Thanos, C. (ed.) DELOS Research Activities 2005, pp. 47–48. ISTI-CNR at Gruppo ALI, Pisa, Italy (2005); In the present state of development of the work, the work could be presented as a poster
13. Marshall, C.C., Bernheim Brush, A.J.: Exploring the Relationship between Personal and Public Annotations. In: Proceedings of the 4th ACM/IEEE-CS Joint Conference on Digital Libraries (JCDL 2004) (2004)

14. Marcante, A., Mussio, P.: Electronic Interactive Documents and Knowledge Enhancing: a Semiotic Approach, the Document Academy, UC Berkeley, Berkeley, CA, USA, October 13-15 (2006)
15. Costabile, M.F., Fogli, D., Marcante, A., Mussio, P., Parasiliti Provenza, L., Piccinno, A.: Designing Customized and Tailorable Visual Interactive Systems. International Journal of Software Engineering and Knowledge Engineering (IJSEKE) 18(3), 305–325 (2008)
16. Wexler, M.N.: The Who, What and Why of Knowledge Mapping. Journal of Knowledge Management 5(3), 249–263 (2001)
17. Valtolina, S.: Design of Knowledge Driven Interfacesin Cultural Contexts. International Journal on Semantic Computing 5(3), 525–553 (2008)
18. Crofts, N., Doerr, M., Gill, T., Stead, S., Stiff, M.: Current Official Version of the CIDOC CRM version 4.2 of the reference document. Definition of the CIDOC Conceptual Reference Model (June 2005)
19. Valtolina, S.: Design of Knowledge Driven Interfaces in Cultural Contexts. International Journal on Semantic Computing - Special Issue on Human Centric Communications 2(4), 525–553 (2008) ISSN: 1793-351X
20. Shea, C., Faisal, M., Ford, R., Lin, W., Matsuda, Y.: Oracle Text Application Developer's Guide, 11g Release 1 (11.1), Oracle (2007)
21. Pelski, S., Abbott, R., Chen, F., Gettys, B., Guo, D., Lin, D., Mavris, S., Parida, P., Steiner, J., Sun, Y., Watt, S., Yalavarthy, M., Zhang, J.: Oracle Multimedia Reference, 11g Release 1 (11.1), Oracle (2007)

New World, New Worlds: Visual Analysis of Pre-columbian Pictorial Collections

Daniel Gatica-Perez[1,2], Edgar Roman-Rangel[1,2], Jean-Marc Odobez[1,2], and Carlos Pallan[3]

[1] Idiap Research Institute, Switzerland
[2] École Polytechnique Fédérale de Lausanne (EPFL), Switzerland
[3] National Anthropology and History Institute of Mexico (INAH), Mexico
{gatica,eroman,odobez}@idiap.ch
http://www.idiap.ch/project/codices/

Abstract. We present an overview of the CODICES project, an interdisciplinary approach for analysis of pre-Columbian collections of pictorial materials – more specifically, of Maya hieroglyphics. We discuss some of the main scientific and technical challenges that we have found in our work, and present a summary of our current technical achievements. This overview stresses the importance of thinking globally and acting both locally and globally with respect to developing approaches for cultural heritage preservation, research, and education.

1 Introduction

The work presented in this paper arises from the collaboration between Switzerland's Idiap Research Institute and Mexico's National Institute of Anthropology and History (INAH). The initial ideas and contacts were established as early as 2005, and the resulting CODICES project started in the summer of 2008 with the support of the Swiss National Science Foundation (SNSF). Our interdisciplinary work aims to design, implement, and test computational tools that allow for automatic and semi-automatic description, localization, retrieval, and classification of hieroglyphs of a large digital Maya corpus collected in Mexico.

The Maya is one of several pre-Hispanic cultures that flourished in ancient Mesoamerica. It originated and developed in the mid-Preclassic period (c.a., 1,500 - 400 BC), in the territories that currently spread between the Gulf of Mexico and the Isthmus of Tehuantepec, and southern portions of Mesoamerica including Guatemala, Belize, and Honduras (Fig. 1). This culture reached its climax during the late Classic period (c.a., 600 - 900 AD), when some of their activities achieved impressive levels of refinement, including agriculture, astronomy, architecture, arts, and writing. Our work is contributing tools to facilitate the management and analysis of large collections of photographs of artifacts, monuments, and buildings within the Maya Mexican territory, which have been collected by INAH over a number of years.

This overview discusses some of the main scientific and technical challenges that we have found during our work in the project, and presents a summary

C. Grana and R. Cucchiara (Eds.): MM4CH 2011, CCIS 247, pp. 90–102, 2012.

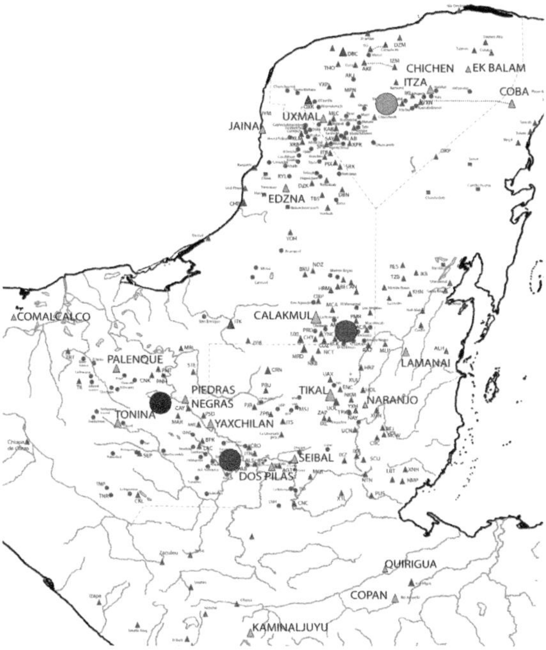

Fig. 1. Maya territories

of our work so far [7] [8]. Our goal here is to illustrate the kind of computer vision techniques that can be developed to analyze digital versions of ancient materials produced by a culture that, while praised and studied in depth by scholars worldwide – history, archaeology, the arts –, has received less attention from the perspective of multimedia analysis. Our work can be seen as an instance of the local/global research activities that could be envisioned for the future of this domain.

The paper is organized as follows. In Section 2, we briefly introduce the Maya writing system. Section 3 describes the tasks involved in the collection of a Maya hieroglyphic corpus. Section 4 presents a summary of our technical work. Section 5 provides some concluding remarks.

2 The Maya Writing System

According to [10], the Maya writing system derives from a large group of languages that developed in southern Mesoamerica. Some of the earliest Maya inscriptions have been dated to be from the late Preclassic period (c.a., 400 BC - 250 AD). During the late Classic period (c.a., 600 - 900 AD), this script system spread all over the entire Maya world, reaching its maximum in the terminal Classic period (c.a., 800 - 950 AD). Since then on it started to diminish, although it continued operational even after the so-called "Maya Collapse" [9] in few northern sites. Roughly, this writing tradition stayed operational during 17 centuries.

Linguists classify the Maya writing system as a member of the so-called logo-syllabic writing systems. The systems in this class encompass two distinct types of signs: syllabographs and logographs. The former are visual elements without specific meaning, only used to represent phonetic values (i.e., sounds or phonemes), and they usually correspond to a consonant-vowel (CV) or single aspirated vowel structure (Vh). The latter are visual symbols encoding high-level meaning: they approximate our notion of "word-signs", and the majority of them have a consonant-vowel-consonant (CVC) structure. Fig. 2 shows 5 visual examples of syllabographs and logographs. Roughly speaking, logographs account for 80% of all the Maya hieroglyphs currently known.

(a) b'a (b) 'a (c) KAB' (d) SUUTZ' (e) K'AHK'

Fig. 2. Examples of Maya hieroglyphs. Syllabographs b'a and 'a; and logographs KAB' (earth), SUUTZ' (bat) and K'AHK' (fire). Images taken from [4] and [11].

Syllabographs might be thought to be simpler than logographs since they only encode sounds instead of ideas. However, this is not true in terms of visual complexity: both syllabographs and logographs may be rich in visual details. Besides the intrinsic complexity of each Maya hieroglyph, the challenge can be increased by additional resources that enrich the inscriptions. Just to mention few examples: *conflation* occurs when two glyphs are visually fused, while retaining their same relative size; *infixation* occurs when one glyph is reduced in size and inserted within another; *superimposition* appears when one glyph partially covers another whose main characteristics remain visible as background; and *pars pro toto* occurs when one glyph is represented by only a fraction of its characteristic or diagnostic features. Fig. 3 shows examples of these phenomena.

Usually Maya hieroglyphs do not appear as single instances but they are arranged inside glyph-blocks where usually logographs are phonetically complemented by syllabographs, either on initial position (prefix or superfix) or in final position (postfix or suffix). In turn, glyph-blocks are found inside complex inscriptions whose organization resembles to a set of pairs of columns. Reading an inscription can be thought as following a scanning pattern in a grid indexed by a system of coordinates, where letters refer to columns and number refer to rows. For instance, the reading of the inscription showed in Fig. 4, with 4 columns and 2 rows would be: A1, B1, A2, B2, C1, D1, C2, D2.

Currently an approximate of 1000 distinct signs have been cataloged, from which only 80% have been deciphered and are readable. Maya archeologists

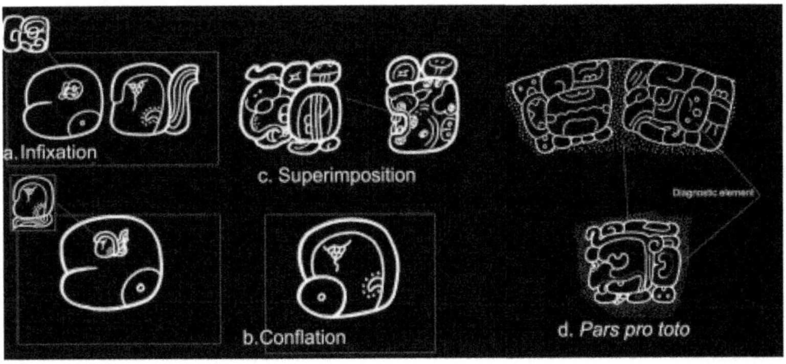

Fig. 3. Examples of complexity in the Maya writing system

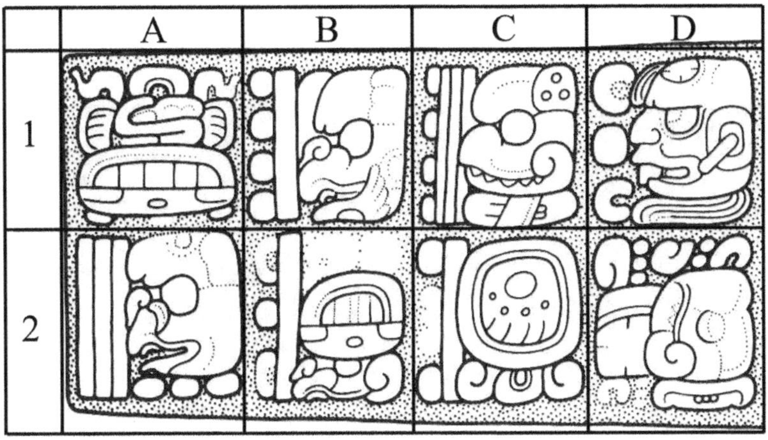

Fig. 4. Reading order of Maya inscriptions in a paired columnar format

continue exploring and discovering new hieroglyphs at sites and monuments, generating high-quality digital versions of them, which provides plenty of data to researchers in the field of the Maya culture. However, this rapid generation of digital data also posits the need for automatic tools than can help them classify all the new signs discovered.

3 Constructing a Digital Maya Hieroglyphic Corpus

Through the project "Hieroglyphic and Iconographic Maya Heritage" (*Acervo Jeroglífico e Iconográfico Maya*, AJIMAYA), INAH has collected a large collection of photographs of monuments and other buildings within the Maya Mexican territory. Deciphering the inscriptions in these images is an eight-step laborious process:

1. Digital photographs, taken at night under raking-light illumination to bring out the level of detail that facilitates the study of eroded monuments.
2. Line drawings, traced on top of photographs taken under different light conditions, to capture the inner features that are diagnostic.
3. Manual identification of glyphic signs with the aid of glyphic catalogs.
4. Manual transcription, i.e., rendering the phonetic value of each Maya sign into alphabetical conventions.
5. Transliteration, i.e., representing ancient Maya speech into alphabetic form.
6. Morphological segmentation, which breaks down recorded Maya words into their minimal grammatical constituents (morphemes and lexemes).
7. Grammatical analysis to indicate the function of each segmented element.
8. Translation, which involves rendering ancient Maya text on a modern target language, e.g., English.

In Fig. 5 we show an example of the first, second and third steps. Some of the data used in this work has been generated through this process.

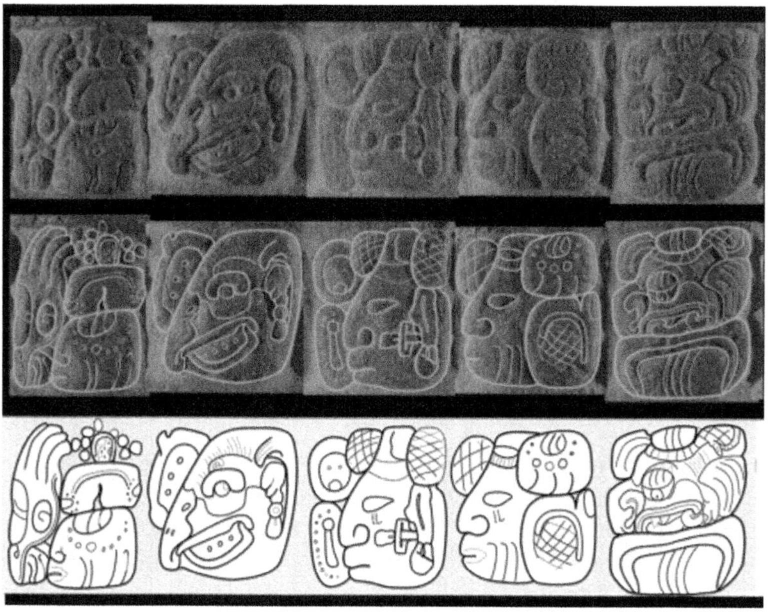

Fig. 5. First, second and third steps in the deciphering process of Maya inscriptions

4 Our Contribution

As part of the CODICES project, we have focused on shape representation approaches for retrieval of hieroglyphs. In this section we explain our two main contributions to the area of cultural heritage. First, we provide details about the syllabic dataset that has been collected. Then, we briefly explain a shape descriptor (HOOSC) that has been designed to deal with the Maya dataset. We follow the explanation by commenting our current results. Finally, we discuss about the need of automatic tools to support archaeological research.

4.1 Compilation of a Syllabic Dataset

The first contribution of our project is the compilation of a dataset of segmented instances of Maya syllabographs, which is meant to be used as testbed for computer vision techniques. Due to the difficulty of manually locating, segmenting, and annotating these instances, we focus only on syllabographs, reserving logographs for future work. With the goal of gathering enough data, this dataset contains instances of the 24 most popular syllabic classes within the AJIMAYA corpus. To the best of our knowledge, this is the biggest dataset of Maya syllabographs that has been analyzed with automatic techniques.

More precisely, the Maya syllabic dataset comprises 1270 segmented syllabographs distributed over 24 visual classes, where each class is referred to by its Thompson catalog number [11]. The dataset also contains 2128 extra segmented glyphs in a "negative class". The sources for the selected instances are: the AJIMAYA project, the Macri and Looper syllabic catalog [4], the Thompson catalog [11], and the website of the Foundation for the Advancement of Mesoamerican Studies (FAMSI) [6]. Table 1 shows one visual example for each positive class.

Table 1. Thompson numeration, visual examples, and syllabic values (sounds) for the 24 classes of the Maya syllabographs in our dataset

T1	T17	T23	T24	T25	T59

/u/	*/yi/*	*/na/*	*/li/*	*/ka/*	*/ti/*
T61	T82	T92	T102	T103	T106
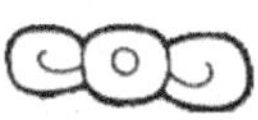	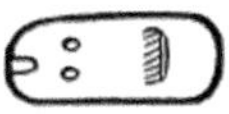				
/yu/	*/li/*	*/tu/*	*/ki/*	*/ta/*	*/nu/*
T110	T116	T117	T126	T136	T173
	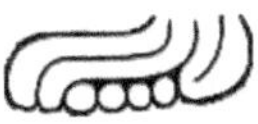				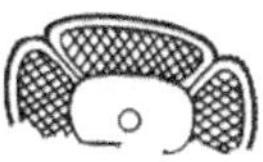
/ko/	*/ni/*	*/wi/*	*/ya/*	*/ji/*	*/mi/*
T178	T181	T229	T501	T534	T671
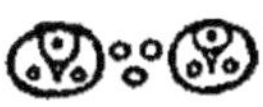					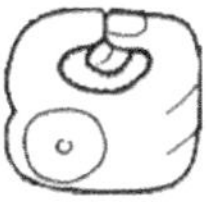
/la/	*/ja/*	*/'a/*	*/b'a/*	*/la/*	*/chi/*

For experiments, we have divided the dataset into two subsets, selecting at random 80% of the instances from each positive class and labeling them as "candidates" (G_C), and labeling the remaining 20% as "queries" (G_Q). The purpose of this segmentation is to evaluate the generalization, from candidates to queries, of any computer vision method that is tested on this dataset.

4.2 The HOOSC Descriptor

The Histogram of Orientation Shape-Context (HOOSC) descriptor has been proposed in [8] to describe and retrieve Maya syllabographs in small datasets. This descriptors is robust as it takes advantage of two traditional approaches for image description: a log-polar regional formulation from the Shape Context (SC) [1], and a distribution of orientations from the HOG descriptor [3].

In a nutshell, the HOOSC represents the same shape (glyph) several times from different points; these points are uniformly and randomly selected along the contours of the shape. This can be thought of as looking at the same shape from different perspectives, thus resulting in an aggregated robust description.

More specifically, using a log-polar grid divided in 12 angular and 5 spatial intervals as in [1] (Fig. 6), and whose external boundary spans twice the average pairwise distances of all the points to be described, a feature vector representing each of the selected points is computed as follows:

1. Impose the current point in the center of the log-polar grid, such that all the remaining points are placed around, and the grid includes only those points that are up to twice the average pairwise distances away from the center.
2. Compute the distribution of local orientations of all the points contained in each of the log-polar regions. To take into account uncertainty in orientation estimation and to avoid hard binning effects, this distribution is calculated through a kernel-based approach for orientation density estimation [8].
3. Normalize the resulting vector for each of the 5 spatial intervals, independently for one another, such that the resulting vector sums up to 5.

Since there are 60 log-polar regions and each of them is characterized by a 8-bins histogram of local orientations, the resulting vector has 480 dimensions.

Shape retrieval with the HOOSC. Different shapes might have different degrees of complexity, and therefore different number of points when sampled from their contours. Therefore, a direct comparison of two shapes is rather difficult, and solving a point-to-point correspondence matching could be computationally expensive in some cases. To avoid this, we have used a bag-of-visual-words representation (*bov*) which efficiently compare glyphs.

More precisely, we use the k-means algorithm to quantize the descriptors and to build a bag of visual words. Then we compare pairs of shapes based on the distance between their respective *bovs*. To perform retrieval experiments, we rank the *bov* of candidate-shapes according to their L1 similarity with respect to the *bov* of a given query-shape [5] [8]. We found empirically that 2500 visual words perform well for the HOOSC descriptor.

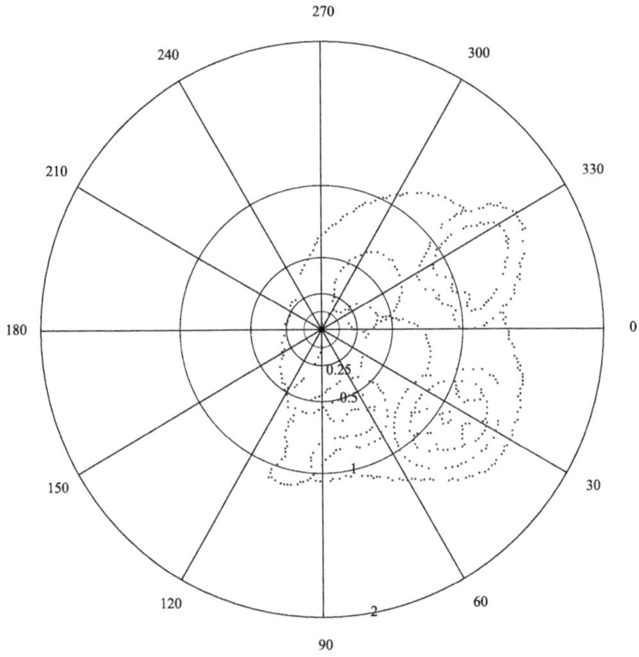

Fig. 6. Log-polar grid with 60 regions used for shape description

Improving the HOOSC descriptor The HOOSC descriptor was tested in a small dataset in [8]. However, when its performance is evaluated on the larger syllabic Maya dataset, a drop of almost 10% in the retrieval precision was detected. Recently, we have worked in an improved version of the HOOSC, which not only allows to maintain the retrieval performance but also to improve it in almost 20% compared with the original HOOSC descriptor.

The recent improvements are: a preprocessing filter to thin the contours of the glyphs which results in more stable inputs; an efficient approach to select only key points for the description while remaining accurate; an effective detection and selection of the most informative spatial scope of the descriptor, which allows for shorter feature vectors; and the inclusion of the explicit spatial position of each described point.

4.3 Results

Initially, we compared the performance of different shape descriptors in retrieval tasks [1] [5] [8]. This comparison is made in terms of mean average precision (mAP), computed after querying and retrieving candidate hieroglyphs in a small dataset in the order of hundreds of glyphs [8]. The initial results obtained with these descriptors indicate that our method is more suitable to describe complex shapes than the other two approaches. Namely, the SC and the Generalized

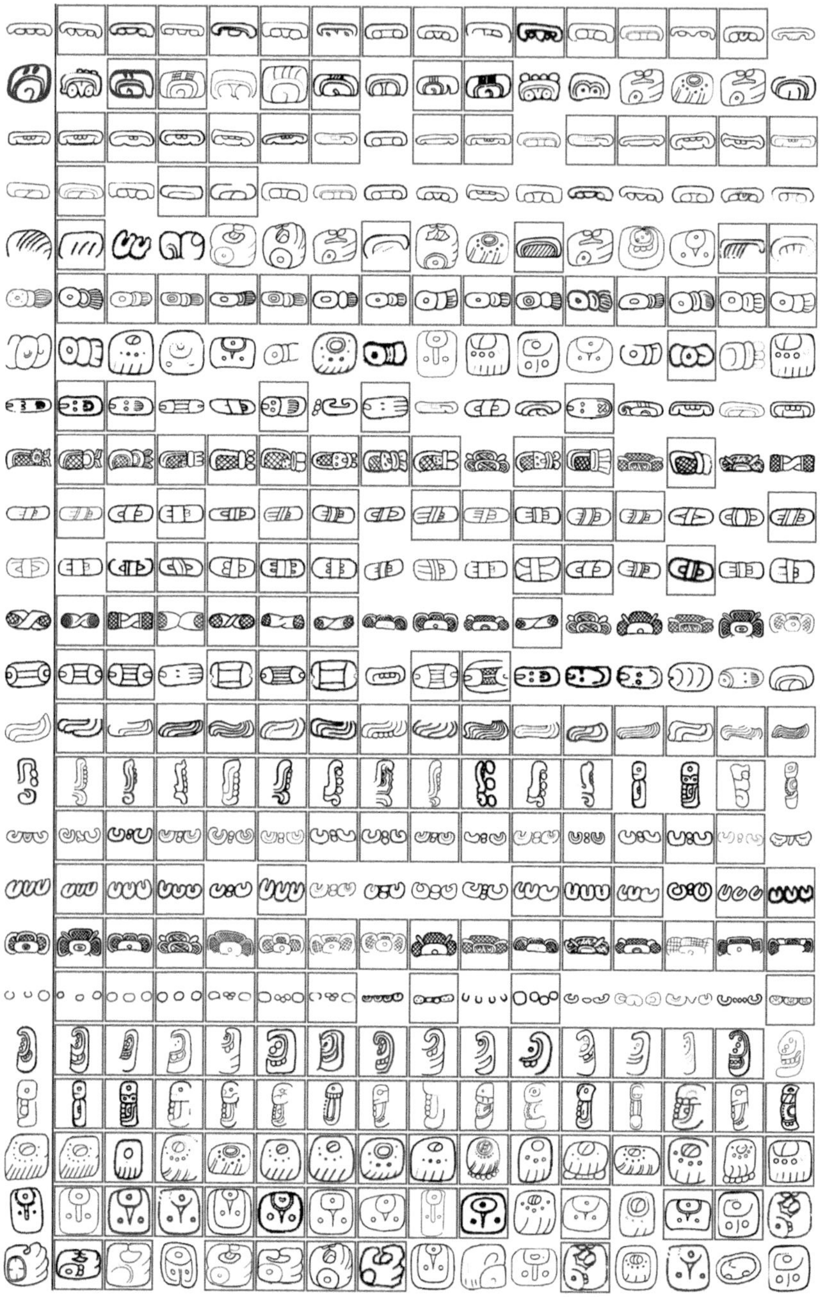

Fig. 7. Retrieval results. The First column shows one random query for each class, followed by its Top 15 retrieved candidate-glyphs shown in terms of decreasing similarity. Relevant glyphs are enclosed in a square.

Shape Context (GSC) result in a mAP value of 0.322 and 0.279, respectively, whereas the HOOSC descriptor reached a mAP of 0.39.

More recently, the experiments performed on the compiled syllabic Maya dataset, using an improved version of the HOOSC descriptor, resulted in a mAP of 0.54. Fig. 7 shows one query example randomly chosen from each syllabic class and the 15 candidates best ranked by the improved HOOSC. Note that in most of the cases our method retrieves relevant glyphs within the first positions.

4.4 Towards a Tool for Learning about Maya Hieroglyphics

Multimedia and Computer Vision techniques can help facilitate the daily work of researchers in the field of Maya archaeology. In our research, we are targeting two specific tools: an automatic analyzer of visual variability and a visual retrieval system.

Automatic analyzer of visual variability. This tool will allow Maya researchers to analyze the visual evolution of the inscriptions through time and across different regions of the Maya territory. In [8] we conducted a preliminary analysis of the intra-class visual variability for 8 syllabic classes. The instances in these classes are labeled as belonging to one of three epochs and one of four distinct regions of the Maya territory. Table 2 shows the average intra-class variability computed for three different periods of time.

Table 2. Average intra-class visual variability for syllabographs over three time periods of the ancient Maya world

Period	Time (A.D.)	average
Early Classic	250 - 600	0.277
Late Classic	600 - 900	0.238
Terminal Classic	900 - 1500	0.228

Table 3 shows the average intra-class variability for the four Maya regions.

Table 3. Average intra-class visual variability for syllabographs across four regions of the ancient Maya world. The colors in the bullets correspond to the colors in the map of Fig. 1.

In map	Region	average
•	Petén	0.251
•	Motagua	0.258
•	Usumacinta	0.349
•	Yucatán	0.214

Overall, this preliminary analysis suggests that visual representations converged as time passed, but perhaps diverged as glyphs got spread towards the borders of the Maya world.

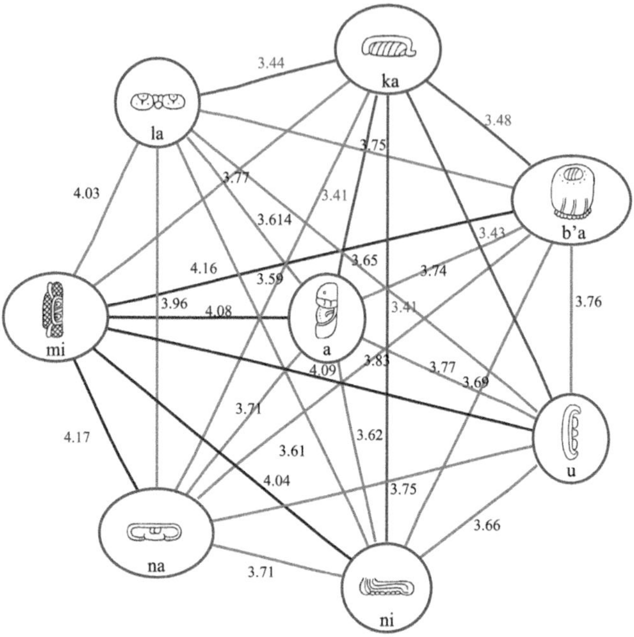

Fig. 8. Inter-class similarity. Each node shows an example of one syllabic class, edges are weighted with the similarity between the two classes it connects to.

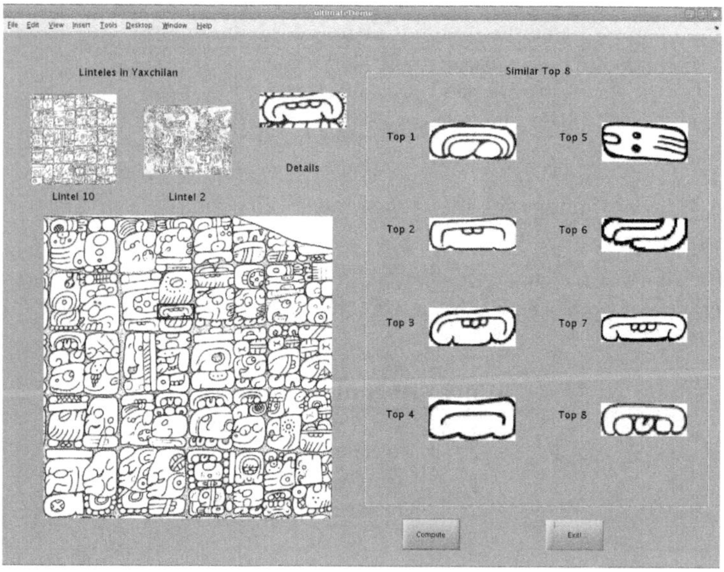

Fig. 9. The system retrieves, from a database, the segmented instances most similar to the selected glyph. Searching within an inscription given a segmented query is also possible.

A second possible analysis with this tool is that of inter-class similarity. We define a distance measure between classes A and B, as the average of all the distances from each instance of class A to each instance of class B. We use the inverse of this distance as similarity measure and as link strength to construct the graph shown in Fig. 8.

Visual retrieval machine. An accurate visual retrieval system is the main motivation for our current research. This tool will allow archaeologists to quickly search in large collections for instances of a given visual query. Fig. 9 shows one snapshot taken from the first version of this system.

When such a tool is further improved, it will ameliorate the time usually invested by archaeologists in manual search, and it also could help as a training tool for novice scholars learning about the Maya writing system. A video demo of this preliminary tool is available at the website of the project [2].

5 Conclusions

In this overview, we have presented the main developments of the CODICES project. Our work has spanned data collection, shape-based analysis, and the initial steps towards a visual retrieval tool that can be used by archaeologists. In particular, the HOOSC descriptor is an approach that has shown competitive performance w.r.t. state-of-the-art approaches, and represents a suitable starting point to address some of the complexities of Maya hieroglyphics. Further technical details, and future research opportunities were discussed at the workshop.

Acknowledgments. We thank the support of the Swiss National Science Foundation through the CODICES project (grant 200021-116702), and to INAH through the AJIMAYA project.

References

1. Belongie, S., Malik, J., Puzicha, J.: Shape Matching and Object Recognition Using Shape Contexts. IEEE Transactions on Pattern Analysis and Machine Intelligence 24(4), 509–522 (2002)
2. CODICES, `http://www.idiap.ch/project/codices`
3. Dalal, N., Triggs, B.: Histograms of Oriented Gradients for Human Detection. In: Proceedings of the IEEE Conference on Computer Vision and Pattern Recognition, pp. 886–893. IEEE Computer Society (2005)
4. Macri, M., Looper, M.: The New Catalog of Maya Hieroglyphs. The Classic Period Inscriptions, vol. 1. University of Oklahoma Press, Norman (2003)
5. Mori, G., Belongie, S., Malik, J.: Efficient Shape Matching Using Shape Contexts. IEEE Transactions on Pattern Analysis and Machine Intelligence 27(11), 1832–1837 (2005)
6. Pitts, M., Matson, L.: Writing in Maya Glyphs. Foundation for the Advancement of Mesoamerican Studies, Inc. (2008)

7. Roman-Rangel, E., Pallan, C., Odobez, J.-M., Gatica-Perez, D.: Retrieving Ancient Maya Glyphs with Shape Context. In: Proceedings of the IEEE Workshop on eHeritage and Digital Art Preservation, 12th International Conference on Computer Vision, Kyoto (2009)
8. Roman-Rangel, E., Pallan, C., Odobez, J.-M., Gatica-Perez, D.: Analyzing Ancient Maya Glyph Collections with Contextual Shape Descriptors. International Journal of Computer Vision, Special Issue in Cultural Heritage and Art Preservation 94(1), 101–117 (2011)
9. Sharer, R.: Daily Life in Maya Civilization. Daily life through history. Greenwood, Westport (1996)
10. Stuart, S.D., MacLeod, B., Martin, S., Polyukhovich, Y.: Glyphs on Pots: Decoding Classic Maya Ceramics. In: Sourcebook for the 29th Maya Hieroglyphic Forum. The University of Texas at Austin, Department of Art and Art History (2005)
11. Thompson, J.E.S.: A Catalog of Maya Hieroglyphs. University of Oklahoma Press, Norman (1962)

Towards a Procedure for Quality Control on Large Collections of Digitized Audio Data: The Case of the "Fondazione Arena di Verona"

Federica Bressan[1] and Sergio Canazza[2]

[1] University of Verona, Department of Computer Science
Strada Le Grazie 15, 34134 Verona, Italy
federica.bressan_01@univr.it
[2] University of Padova, Department of Information Engineering
Via G. Gradenigo 6/b, 35131 Padova, Italy

Abstract. Audio recordings are an important documentary source for academic studies in many fields, from linguistics to anthropology. During the last decades, great efforts were made to develop guidelines and best practices for the preservation of audio documents, but not as much attention have been paid to quality controls on the re-mediation process and the output data.

This article presents the experience of the research project REVIVAL, aimed at the preservation of the audio documents stored in the archive of the Fondazione Arena di Verona, Italy, where a quality protocol was defined, and original software tools for automation of control were developed.

Keywords: Preservation, methodology, automatization, quality control.

1 Introduction

The importance of audio recordings (speech and music) as documentary sources for disciplines such as linguistics, musicology, ethnomusicology, anthropology and the like is fully recognized today. Accordingly, much efforts have been spent on the preservation of audio documents over the past decades (see [13] and [12] for an overview), and a variety of methodologies and best practices is currently made available by the international community (see [10,9,14,1]). However, the awareness that audio/visual carriers have an alarmingly short life expectancy compared to other pieces of cultural material, which can be measured in decades or years, caused a "rush" to digitization and an overall underestimation of the importance of quality controls during the process of *re-mediation* (the process of transferring the acoustic information from a medium onto another medium). This approach may have dramatic consequences on the authority of a document as a source for academic studies, besides invalidating the re-mediation process that needs to be repeated, which is not always possible as explained in Section 2.

This article presents the experience of the research project REVIVAL (REstoration of the VIcentini archive in Verona and its accessibility as an Audio e-Library), aimed at the preservation of the audio documents stored in the archive

C. Grana and R. Cucchiara (Eds.): MM4CH 2011, CCIS 247, pp. 103–113, 2012.

of the Fondazione Arena di Verona, Italy, with a special attention to the development of protocols and tools for quality control during the re-mediation process of audio documents.

Section 2 introduces the problem of unreliable data as output of unsafe preservation programmes. Section 3 presents the REVIVAL project, where algorithms for quality control and software tools, respectively presented in Sections 4 and 5, were developed.

2 The Threat of Unreliable Data

Poor methodologies for preservation may nullify the audio document as a source for scholarly studies or, worse, lay a doubt over analysis and theories that were based on those documents. In this sense, reliable repositories of documents should be a major concern for academics and specialized communities. They should be aware of the risks, and demand that preservation programmes are planned in order "to save history, not rewrite it" [5].

The process of re-mediation is fatally error prone (at technical, planning and operative level) and it often tends to indulge to the present aesthetical taste. These are factors that clearly motivate the definition of a strict protocol for the re-mediation of audio documents.

Secondly, preservation is not limited to "safeguarding the world's documentary heritage, [but it is aims at] democratizing access to it, and raising awareness of its significance and of the need to preserve it" [4]. In this sense, the creation of "preservation copies" (or "archive copies"), as defined in Subsection 4.1, is not enough: the data needs to be (unrestrictedly) accessed, meaning that tools for retrieval are needed, from low-level (locating and associating data) to high-level (Content Based Retrieval (CBR)).

Performing controls on digital data is not straightforward, especially for large collections. Producing invalid data during the re-mediation process means that the process needs to be repeated, which is not only time consuming, but may not be possible if the original carrier got physically damaged during playback, and it cannot be played again. The signal extraction from the original carrier is one of the most, if not the most, delicate step of the process, but all steps must be carried out with equal attention. Each step is closely related to the others, and early mistakes propagate in the workflow with ambiguous effects.

The preparation of the carrier (physical restoration) and playback allow for errors that damage the carrier directly, but the definition of the format for playback (e.g., speed, equalization curve and noise reduction system for analog recordings) is crucial, as wrong calibrations during the extraction of the signal invalidate the entire procedure.

What has been underestimated during the last few decades is the complexity of the audio re-mediation process, which does not coincide with simple A/D transfer, as is unfortunately often thought. In other words, in fact there are many different things can go wrong during the re-mediation process, and each step should always be performed in optimal conditions.

An additional reason for wanting quality data is that algorithms and tools for automatic classification and tagging, analysis and processing, generally perform better with quality data sets. Subsequently, it is convenient to control the process of producing data in order to feed these tools, which are being developed very fast, with good data sets.

3 The REVIVAL Project

REVIVAL (REstoration of the VIcentini archive in Verona and its accessibility as an Audio e-Library) is a national joint project between the Fondazione Arena di Verona and the Department of Computer Science of the University of Verona, with the scientific support of Eye-Tech[1]. It started in January 2009 and by the end of the second year, in December 2010, the partners agreed to extend it throughout 2011, basing on the quality of the objectives achieved that opened the way for further work.

Its main objective is the development of a HW/SW platform with the purpose of preserving and restoring and audio documents stored in the archive of the Fondazione Arena. The estimated value of the archive is 2, 300, 000 Euros. It comprises tens of thousands of audio documents stored on different carriers (from wax cylinders to digital carriers), hundreds of pieces of equipment for playback and recording (from wire to magnetic tape recorders and phonographs) and bibliographic publications (including monographs and all issues of more than sixty music journals from the 1940's to 1999). Along with a history of the recording techniques, the archive traces the evolution of a composite genre such as opera, with one of the largest collections of live and studio recordings in Italy. The most precious section of the archive is represented by the live recordings of the operas staged every year during the summer season at the Arena. The first opera festival was organized back in 1913 by the tenor Giovanni Zenatello and the theatre impresario Ottone Rovato, to celebrate the centenary of the birth of Giuseppe Verdi. Since 1936 the festival was organized by the "Ente Lirico Arena di Verona" (autonomous organization for lyrical productions), until the Ente Lirico was transformed into a private law foundation in 1998, the Fondazione Arena di Verona. The oldest recording available of the opera festival dates back to July 30th, 1968, and it is a performance of "Trovatore" by Giuseppe Verdi, featuring Leyla Gencer as Leonora and Carlo Bergonzi as Manrico. Figure 1 shows some of the open-reel tapes stored by the archive: all of them are unique copies. The archive is constantly growing with the new recordings of the current seasons, stored on HDD devices.

The first task of REVIVAL consisted in the development of an operational protocol aimed at the preservation of the audio documents stored by the archive [2]. The main international guidelines were considered ([14,1]) and trade-offs were made to meet the characteristics of the Arena archive, in terms of number and type of documents, genre of the recordings, objectives of the digitization. The documents for the re-mediation were selected according to the following criteria,

[1] http://www.eye-tech.it/

(a) Audio documents (b) The laboratory

Fig. 1. Left (a): some of the open-reel tapes stored by the archive of the Fondazione Arena di Verona. All of them are unique copies. Right (b): a view of the laboratory that was set up withing the archive. Several tape recorders (in particular a Studer A-812 in the bottom right corner) and the A/D-D/A device can be seen. Between the loudspeakers for monitoring, on a lower shelf, the incubator for the thermal treatment of the tapes.

inspired by the (conflicting) classifications provided by the International Federation of Library Associations and Institutions (IFLA) [10] and the International Association of Sound and Audiovisual Archives (IASA) [9]:

1. original carriers in immediate risk / on endangered media;
2. documents in regular demand;
3. documents which depend on obsolete or commercially unsupported systems.

Figure 1 shows a view of the laboratory, which is equipped to fully support the preservation process, from the restoration of the physical carriers (e.g., thermal treatment in incubator) to the A/D-D/D transfer, from metadata extraction to multimedia processing. With the experience matured on the number of documents digitized, some experiments were planned 1) to have a better understanding on how magnetic tapes respond to thermal treatment (commonly used to compensate for the sticky shed syndrome [7]), in collaboration with the Department of Mathematical, Physical and Natural Science of the University of Verona and the Department of Chemical and Process Engineering of the University of Padova, and consequently plan better treatments; and 2) to find out if the audio signal obtained from a tape played in the intended direction (sound forward) equals the one obtained with the same tape running the opposite direction (sound backwards). The rationale for this experiment is that extracting the signal in one playback session for tapes showing two independent mono tracks using a stereo head (then splitting the stereo signal and reversing one channel by means of a wave editor) would save half of the time employed to read the tape (which may last up to 4 hours) and would prevent fragile carriers from being played back twice.

4 The Re-mediation Process

Two types of preservation can be distinguished for audio documents: passive, meant to defend the carrier from external agents without altering its structure, and active, which involves information transfer onto new media. A protocol for the re-mediation of audio documents consists in the formalization of the steps for active preservation.

The purpose of this protocol is to ensure that the loss of information during the re-mediation process is minimized. A number of different tasks are necessary to ensure that *all* information is read/generated, interpreted, represented and described adequately. The required input is: 1) the original document; 2) knowledge about the recording technique; 3) knowledge about the history of the recording. The output is the preservation copy, as defined in Subsection 4.1.

The process is structured in three steps (before playback, playback and after playback), each of which is articulated in procedures and sub-procedures. The output of each procedure and sub-procedure is either data, a report or a different state of the system.

The first level is general and applies to all types of carriers. The second must be occasionally adapted to the type of carrier that is being treated, and the third is completely carrier type dependent. Figure 2 shows the general scheme of the re-mediation process.

The re-mediation process requires a combination of conceptual, technical and also manual skills that result in a complex professional profile. Besides, during the process things can go wrong in very many ways. Therefore, each procedure was divided into simple tasks, described by a separate workflow, and each block is extensively commented. Exceptions are managed, and the precision of the

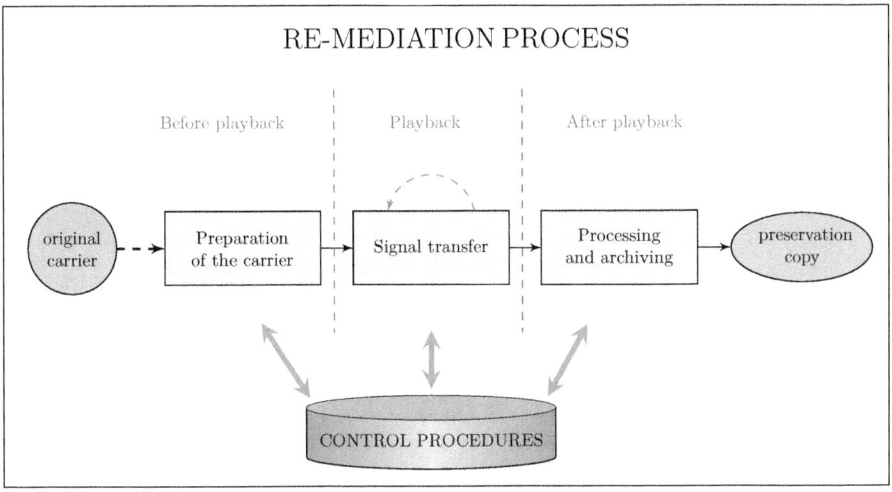

Fig. 2. General scheme of the re-mediation process, from the original carrier to the preservation copy

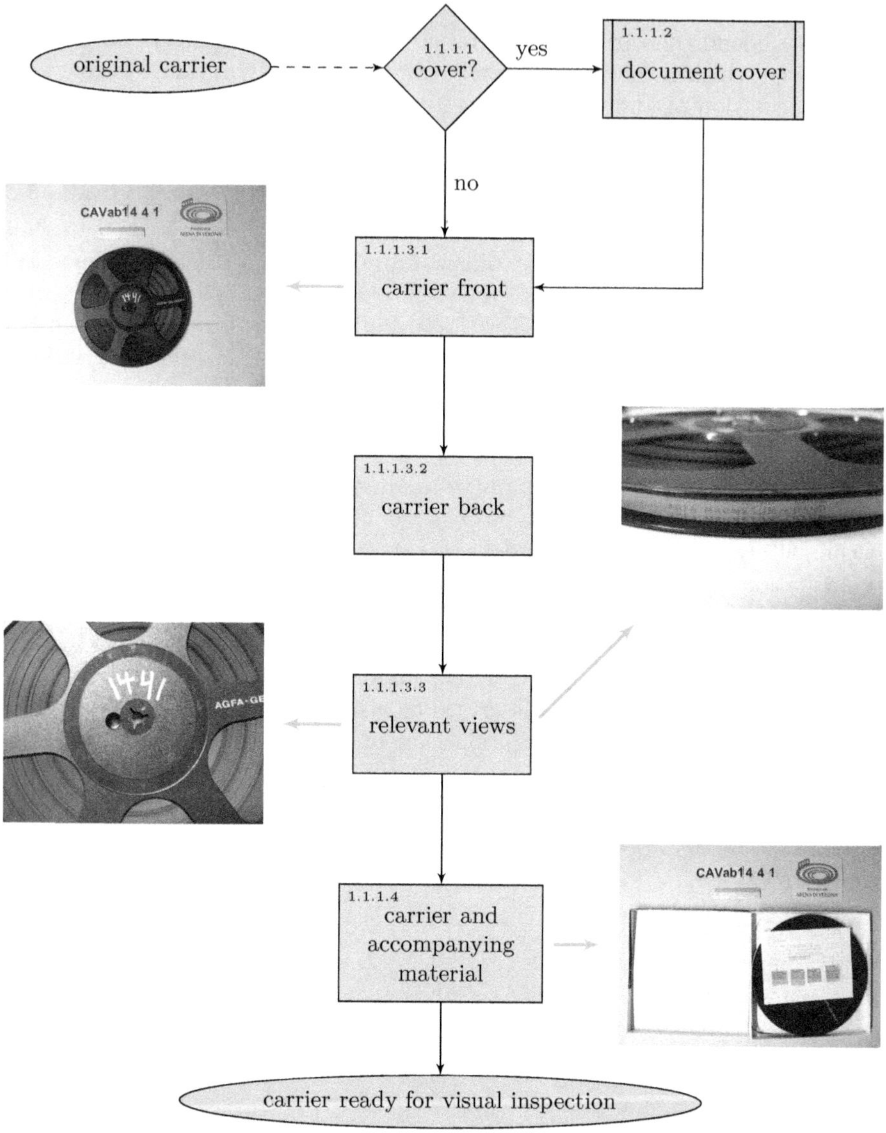

Fig. 3. Example of flowchart, describing procedure 1.1.1 (Preparation of the carrier → Physical documentation → Pictures of the document) mentioned in Section 3. Blocks marked with double lines (such as 1.1.1.2) are sub-functions with a separate description. Each block is extensively commented and exceptions are managed.

descriptions is as rich as possible in order to reduce the indecision that comes from the large variety of carriers and the numberless combinations of symptoms presented by the carriers.

Figure 3 provides an example of a very simple workflow: it represents the step 1.1.1 of the process (Preparation of the carrier → Physical documentation → Pictures of the document). In the notation adopted by the project reports, blocks marked with double lines are sub-functions described separately.

The structure of the workflow in Figure 3 is straightforward, but the example is representative because the aim of the document is to provide precise descriptions of each task. To achieve this goal, visual material and notes are associated to the blocks, with several references to separate sections where more material is presented and commented. This workflow describes the physical documentation of the carrier, and it comes with a section where guidelines for visual documentation of cultural heritage are presented [6], along with suggestions for the setup of a photographic workspace and a number of warning and tips that make a difference in the quality of the output data.

If all of the workflows reach the end successfully, the re-mediation process is complete. The expected output is a preservation copy of the original document, of which a general description is provided in the next Subsection.

4.1 Preservation Copy

The preservation copy (or Archive copy) is defined in [8] as the "artifact designated to be stored and maintained as the preservation master. ... Such a designation means that the item is used only under exceptional circumstances." In concrete terms, the preservation copy is a data set that groups all the information carried by the original document. This is not limited to the audio signal,

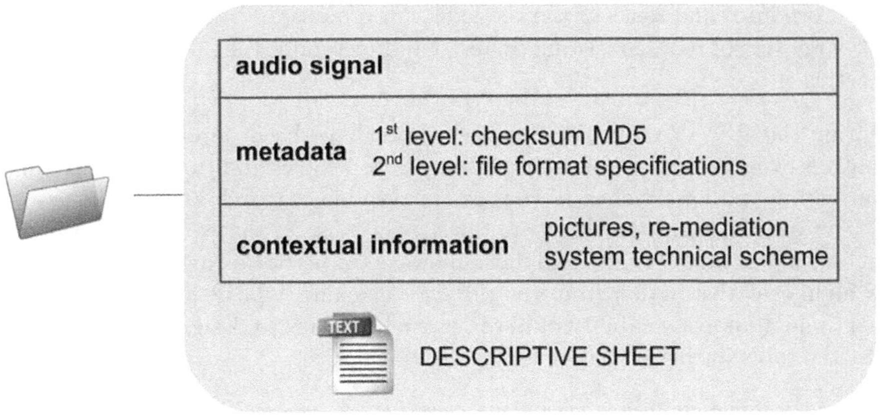

Fig. 4. Logical representation of the elements contained in a preservation copy

but it comprises metadata and contextual information[2], that is a complete documentation of the physical carrier and the accompanying material, plus a set of metadata that are are produced during the re-mediation process. Figure 4 shows the logical representation of a preservation copy. For further descriptions and background, see [3].

5 Automation

A quality re-mediation of audio documents requires specialized infrastructures, multi-disciplinary trained personnel for preservation and long-term maintenance, resulting in a system of resources that not all archives in the real world are able or willing to afford. This entails that many institutions may start digitization campaigns with technological makeshifts and inadequate methodologies, resulting in invalid documentary corpora. To avoid this risk, it is important to make cultural actors aware of the consequences of an uncontrolled use of technology, and thus to encourage them to maximize the quality of their preservation programme, according to the international standards and best practices.

Where applicable, automation is often a good solution to the problem of reducing costs. Moreover, automation brings several benefits that go beyond simple task delegation. It allows to minimize mistakes, perform (cross-)controls, and it allows people to concentrate on higher level tasks with better attention.

In this sense, automation can be of great help in preservation programmes both at local and national scale. However, it is to be noted that there are some crucial steps in the re-mediation process that are likely to remain refractory to full automation, such as the analysis and handling of the original carrier before playback. Nevertheless, some tools supporting semi-automation will be mentioned later in this paragraph.

In this context, automation mainly applies to:

1. procedures and tasks of the re-mediation process;
2. large sets of data consisting in audio and metadata (i.e., output of remediation process).

During the REVIVAL project, some utilities have been developed to perform controls over the entire collection of preservation copies and to automatize time-consuming and low-level tasks that are intrinsic in any archival routine.

The utilities were developed in Java [3], because i) the workstations of the archive mount different OS and Java allows cross-platform compatibility as well as high-level abstraction from the physical machine, and ii) fast code development and a large availability of libraries are necessary to design, implement and test the tools during the short life-cycles of a project.

[2] In this context, the term "metadata" refers to the content-dependent information that can be automatically extracted from the audio signal, and "contextual information" to the additional content-independent information.

[3] Java Version 1.6.0_24.

Although some of the tasks implemented by the utilities are not audio specific, meaning that some of them could be performed with a generic piece of free software, they got integrated in a tool especially designed for audio digital archives with the consequence that the level of automation got increased. At the same time, path variables and serialized objects have been kept as general as possible, making it easy for other archives to benefit from these tools in preservation programmes based on a similar approaches.

The personnel of the Fondazione Arena was asked for feedback during the development of each utility, defining the tasks that needed to be automated or controlled out of the real work in the laboratory. Another concern was that the utilities would be easy to use for people with little or no computer skills, which is often the case of archive personnel. Each piece of software was provided a GUI (an example is shown in Figure 5) and it can be launched by clicking on an icon as most desktop applications.

1. Utility to perform controls on the entire collection of preservation copies, searching for: empty directories, missing directories, anomalous directories, mismatch in file names and file formats, missing checksums.
2. Utility to rename audio and visual data pertaining to a preservation copy (based on a drag-and-drop interface).
3. Utility to perform a control on the checksums of the entire collection of preservation copies and calculate the missing ones (grouped in a single file

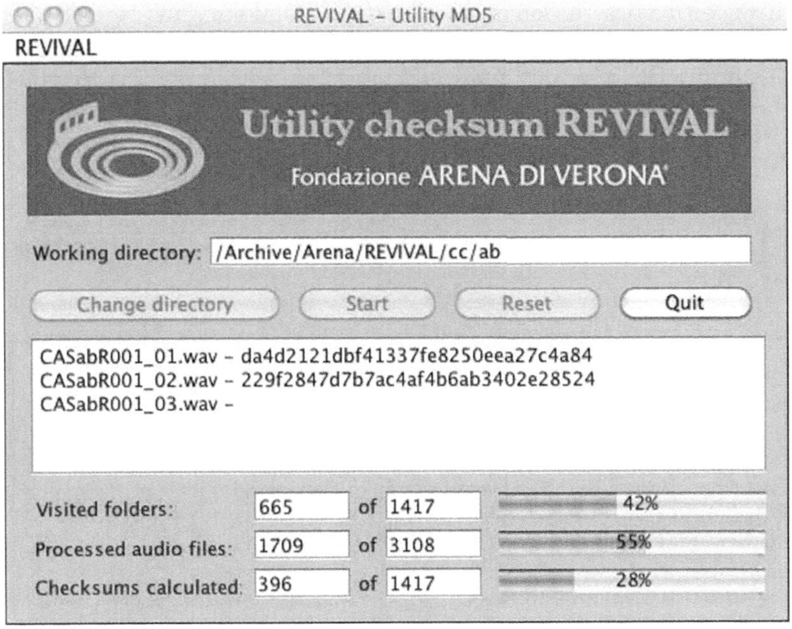

Fig. 5. One of the software tools developed for the Fondazione Arena di Verona

according to the structure of the preservation copy). Figure 5 shows this utility at work.
4. Utility for the long-term maintenance of the archive: it re-calculates the checksum of the audio files in each preservation copy and confronts it with the existing one.

Future work includes the integration of the functionalities described above into an independent work panel, in order to assist the personnel all along the re-mediation process. Besides the benefits of automation mentioned at the beginning of this Section, the work panel would ensure that procedures are carried out according to the protocol discussed in Section 4, and it would help dealing with problems and exceptions. The work panel would be able to extract and insert the data directly from a database, allowing i) additional cross-controls over the audio archive and the database; and ii) decreasing the possibility of introducing mistakes when a new record is created. A prototype implementing JHOVE[4] for metadata extraction is currently under test.

6 Conclusions

This article described the process of re-mediation for audio documents and pointed out the reasons why it is necessary to define procedures and perform controls on the process of A/D-D/D transfer and the subsequent management of digitized/digital data. In particular, the experience of the REVIVAL project was presented, with a description of the adopted methodology and the software tools that were developed to perform controls on the collection of preservation copies and to automatize time-consuming and low-level tasks have been described. The personnel of the archive of the Fondazione Arena di Verona got involved in each step of the process, and the software tools were progressively integrated in the archival routine. These tools will still be used after the end of the project, thus ensuring that the scientific protocol is maintained in the future.

References

1. Boston, G.: Safeguarding the Documentary Heritage. A guide to Standards, Recommended Practices and Reference Literature Related to the Preservation of Documents of all kinds. UNESCO (1988)
2. Bressan, F., Canazza, S., Salvati, D.: The vicentini sound archive of the arena di verona foundation: A preservation and restoration project. In: Workshop on Exploring Musical Information Spaces (WEMIS) in conjunction with ECDL 2009, Corfu, Greece, pp. 1–6 (October 2009)
3. Canazza, S., Orcalli, A.: Preserving musical cultural heritage at mirage. Journal of New Music Research 30(4), 365–374 (2001)
4. Edmonson, R.: Memory of the World: General Guidelines to Safeguard Documentary Heritage. UNESCO (February 2002)

[4] JHOVE is a Java based application developed by JSTOR and the Harvard University Library for the identification, validation and characterization of digital objects [11].

5. Edmonson, R.: Audiovisual Archiving: Philosophy and Principles. UNESCO, Paris, France (April 2004)
6. Galasso, R., Giffi, E.: La documentazione fotografica delle schede di catalogo - metodologie e tecniche di ripresa. Tech. rep., Istituto Centrale per il Catalogo e la Documentazione (ICCD) - Ministero per i Beni e le Attività Culturali (1998)
7. Hess, R.: Tape degradation factors and challenges in predicting tape life. ARSC Journal 39(2), 240–274 (2008)
8. IASA: The IASA Cataloguing Rules. IASA Editorial Group (1999)
9. IASA-TC 03: The safeguarding of the audio heritage: Ethics, principles and preservation strategy. Tech. rep. (2005)
10. IFLA - Audiovisual and Multimedia Section: Guidelines for digitization projects: for collections and holdings in the public domain, particularly those held by libraries and archives. Tech. rep., International Federation of Library Associations and Institutions (IFLA) (March 2002)
11. JSTOR, the Harvard University Library: Jhove – jstor/harvard object validation environment, `http://hul.harvard.edu/jhove/`
12. Orcalli, A.: On the methodologies of audio restoration. Journal of New Music Research 30(4), 307–322 (2001)
13. Orio, N., Snidaro, L., Canazza, S., Foresti, G.L.: Methodologies and tools for audio digital archives. International Journal on Digital Libraries 10, 201–220 (2009)
14. Storm, W.D.: The establishment of international re-recording standards. Phonographic Bulletin 27, 5–12 (1980)

A Web-Oriented Multi-layer Model to Interact with Theatrical Performances

Adriano Baratè, Goffredo Haus, Luca A. Ludovico, and Davide A. Mauro

Laboratorio di Informatica Musicale (LIM)
Dipartimento di Informatica e Comunicazione (DICo)
Università degli Studi di Milano
Via Comelico 39/41, I-20135 Milan, Italy
{barate,haus,ludovico,mauro}@dico.unimi.it

Abstract. This paper presents an innovative approach to online fruition of theater performances. Web applications like traditional viewers are already available for the wide audience of Internet users. Our proposal aims at adding both interactivity and multi-layer fruition, and a way to manipulate and create new media. The premise to reach these goals is digitizing a number of heterogeneous materials in order to describe a single performance comprehensively, e.g. different video and audio-takes from different perspectives, and a number of related materials such as scripts, fashion plates, playbills, etc. The format we adopt to encode such information is based on the XML international standard known as IEEE 1599. Finally, an advanced Web player supporting search and play functions for synchronized materials must be designed. This work describes the whole process, from the acquisition of materials directly on the stage to their publishing on a Web portal.

Keywords: IEEE 1599, Web application, multi-layer encoding, cultural heritage, collaborative approaches.

1 Introduction

The relationship between art and technology represents one of the research fields where advanced applications are emerging. Among the actors interested in this wide range of possibilities, it is worth to cite institutions such as theaters and opera houses. These cases are particularly relevant, since on the one side they go on staging new theatrical performances, but on the other side they usually keep archives with the related multimedia materials. As demonstrated by the case of the Teatro alla Scala [4], such materials and documents can include: scores and symbolic representations of music; audio and video recordings; fliers, playbills and posters; photos, sketches and fashion plates; costumes and related accessories; stage tools, maps and equipment; other textual documents, such as bibliography, discography, libretto, short descriptions and reviews of music works. This list does not claim completeness, however it illustrates the heterogeneity of data and metadata a potential database could store.

C. Grana and R. Cucchiara (Eds.): MM4CH 2011, CCIS 247, pp. 114–125, 2012.

The main goal of these institutions is still the realization of live shows, which are characterized by the occurrence in a given place at a given time. The audience physically attending the performance in a certain sense takes part into the show, even when their interaction is not explicitly indicated by the plot. Many theaters are experiencing activities such as the digitization and preservation of the documents related to theatrical performances. Some of them simply archive the original analog materials (e.g. playbills), some others produce ad hoc digital objects (e.g. stage photos), finally others perform digitization campaigns oriented to archiving. But usually such documents are stored for preservation purposes, whereas they could be used for the revivification of shows.

Our goal is transforming web users into interacting actors for theatrical performances, which implies geographical and temporal distribution as well as participation in creating new and enriched materials from the available ones. In fact, with no doubt archived documents have a historical function, but they can also play a participative role, since they allow the audience to be involved in interaction even if they were not physically present during the performance.

Current repositories for multimedia materials usually fall into two categories:

1. Extensive databases, geographically distributed but poor in relationships among contents or scarcely enjoyable from a multimedia perspective;
2. Databases very rich as regards heterogeneity of materials and semantic relationships among them, but having a data amount both limited and intrinsically difficult to increase.

This paper aims at presenting an innovative approach to overcome the mentioned limitations and to provide online fruition for theater performances. In the following, we will review the state of the art, by considering the approach of traditional theaters towards the use of new technologies. Then we will describe an XML-based format, namely the IEEE 1599 international standard, which is fit to represent heterogeneous multimedia information inside a unique document. Such a format will be employed to code digitized materials coming from live performances. Finally we will present a case study based on the *Prospettiva09* initiative.

2 State of the Art

Nowadays theaters and other cultural institutions are experiencing an increasing interest towards Social Media and Web 2.0. For example, [6] presents an accurate overview of issues and research related to creating semantic portals for publishing cultural heritage collections and other content on the Web. For theaters, this is a way to build a privileged relationship with both their traditional and fresh new audience through initiatives such as online advertising, mailing lists, etc. Besides, the huge amount of information (both analog and digital) usually archived into their repositories could attract investments from partners potentially concerned in its valorization. Due to these reasons, the interest in digitization campaigns as well as Web-oriented tools with multimodal interaction is arising.

The reaction of theaters to the rapidly changing world of digital communication is the subject of a survey by the *CoOPERARE* (Content Organization, Propagation, Evaluation and Reuse through Active Repositories) initiative [2]. This project reviews the use of social media for performing arts as instruments to involve the audience and to induce participation by taking advantage of audiovisual materials.

The survey, which analyzes the presence of 70 Italian theaters on the Web, illustrates the following results:

- 38 theaters manage a dedicated page on Facebook (they are all migrating to official profiles), where they publish news and information about the season and allow users to share comments. Other Social Networks are used by 12 theaters, while 7 institutions maintain a blog;
- 58 institutions have an online archive, either as a structured database or as iconographic material simply exposed in their official Web site;
- In their site, 36 theaters have a customized search engine that normally indexes the whole site and not only the online archive;
- Most common materials are texts (67 theaters) and photos (62 theaters), whereas only 6 theaters offer iconographic materials such as playbills and fashion plates;
- 30 theaters have a video archive, 15 present a proper video-gallery, 11 rely on YouTube channels and 4 broadcast contents through a WebTV;
- Only in one case (i.e. *Teatro dell'Opera di Roma*) users are allowed to process materials in order to make E-card and send them via email.

It is worth citing that Social Media can have a deep impact. For example the *Teatro San Carlo* of Naples (one of the earliest opera houses in the world) has 32000 fans on Facebook and normally sells half the available seats to the online community. *Ravenna Festival 2010* had an estimated participation of 25% of "novices" coming from Facebook.

In conclusion, Social Media are usually considered by theaters as a showcase to enlarge their own audience, attracting young people and offering better (but somehow traditional) services to regular customers. Only a limited number of them is exploring the new possibilities offered by techical improvements in order to create new fruition models and to involve Web users in their activities. Our proposal goes beyond the traditional approaches, as it strives to overcome the *hic et nunc* aspect typical of theatrical performances by involving Web users in the process of fruition, interaction, and creation of new materials.

3 An Overview of the IEEE 1599 Format

IEEE 1599 was originally designed as a standard format to encode a piece of music [3]. We have chosen it to describe theatrical performances, thus stretching its original goals, because of its intrinsic characteristics that will be reviewed in the following.

Based on XML (eXtensible Markup Language), this format follows the guidelines of IEEE P1599, "Recommended Practice Dealing With Applications and Representations of Symbolic Music Information Using the XML Language". This IEEE standard has been sponsored by the Computer Society Standards Activity Board and it was launched by the Technical Committee on Computer Generated Music (IEEE CS TC on CGM).

The innovative contribution of the format is providing a comprehensive description of music and music-related materials within a unique framework. In fact, the symbolic score - intended here as a sequence of music symbols - is only one of the many descriptions that can be provided for a piece. For instance, all the graphical and audio instances (scores and performances) available for a given music composition are further descriptions; but also text elements (e.g. catalogue metadata, lyrics, etc.), still images (e.g. photos, playbills, etc.), and moving images (e.g. video clips, movies with a soundtrack, etc.) can be related to the piece itself. Such a rich description allows the design and implementation of advanced browsers. Please refer to [5] for an in-depth discussion of the subject.

Before starting the discussion, a point should be clarified. In our work, a format to encode music information is adjusted to theatrical performances. This is made possible by the flexibility of the XML encoding we adopt, but the concepts of score and music event must be generalized. In the following we will introduce the key features of the standard comparing their traditional meaning in the music field to our new goals, thus exploring the applicability of IEEE 1599 to theatrical performances.

The mentioned comprehensiveness in music description is realized in IEEE 1599 through a multi-layer environment. The XML format provides a set of rules to create strongly structured documents. IEEE 1599 implements this characteristic by arranging music and music-related contents within six layers [7]:

- *General* - music-related metadata, i.e. catalogue information about the piece;
- *Logic* - the logical description of score in terms of symbols;
- *Structural* - identification of music objects and their mutual relationships;
- *Notational* - graphical representations of the score;
- *Performance* - computer-based descriptions and executions of music according to performance languages;
- *Audio* - digital or digitized recordings of the piece.

In IEEE 1599 code, this 6-layers layout corresponds to the one shown in Figure 1, where the root element `ieee1599` presents 6 sub-elements.

The previous list is strongly related to music contents, but in our work layers can be used in a wider context. Before discussing this matter in depth, we have to introduce a key concept of the format, namely the *spine*. This is a mean to organize contents into various layers allowing to keep heterogeneous descriptions together and to jump from one description to another. When a user encodes a piece in IEEE 1599 format, he/she must specify a list of music events to be organized in a linear structure called spine, located into the *Logic* layer. Inside this structure, music events are uniquely identified by the `id` attribute,

```
<?xml version="1.0" encoding="UTF-8"?>
<!DOCTYPE ieee1599 SYSTEM "http://standards.ieee.org/downloads
                                   /1599/1599-2008/ieee1599.dtd">
<ieee1599 version="1.0">
   <general>...</general>
   <logic>...</logic>
   <structural>...</structural>
   <notational>...</notational>
   <performance>...</performance>
   <audio>...</audio>
</ieee1599>
```

Fig. 1. The XML stub corresponding to the IEEE 1599 multi-layer structure

and located in space and time dimensions through `hpos` and `timing` attributes respectively. Please refer to Figure 2 for a simplified example of spine.

Each event is "spaced" from the previous one in a relative way. In other words, a 0 value means simultaneity in time and vertical overlapping in space, whereas a double value means a double duration of the previous music event with respect to a virtual unit. The measurement units are intentionally unspecified, as the logical values expressed in spine for time and space can correspond to many different absolute values in the digital objects available for the piece.

Let us consider the example shown in Figure 2, interpreting it as a music composition. Event `e3` forms a chord together with `e2`, belonging either to the same or to another part/voice, as the attributes' values of the former are 0s. Similarly, we can affirm that event `e3` happens after `e0` (and `e1`), as `e4` occurs after 2 time units whereas `e1` (and `e2`) occurs after only 1 time unit. For further details please refer to the official document about IEEE 1599 standard [1].

In conclusion, the role of the structure known as spine is central for an IEEE 1599 encoding: it provides a complete and sorted list of events which will be described in their heterogeneous meanings and forms inside other layers. Please note that only a correct identification inside spine structure allows an event to be described elsewhere in the document, and this is realized through references from other layers to its unique `id`. Inside the spine structure only the entities of some interest for the encoding have to be identified and sorted.

One of the most relevant aspects of the format consists in the loose but versatile definition of *event*. In the music field, an event is a clearly recognizable music entity (a note, a chord, a pattern, etc.) which presents aspects of interest for the author of the encoding. Nevertheless, this interpretation can be relaxed to be applied to other fields, as in the case we will present and in some previous works (e.g. see [8]). For example, each cue of an actor during a performance can be seen as the occurrence of an event. From this perspective, our work aims at discovering and exploiting the potentialities of IEEE 1599 format when applied to theatrical shows.

```
<ieee1599 version="1.0">
  ...
  <logic>
    <spine>
      <event id="e0" timing="0" hpos="0"/>
      <event id="e1" timing="1" hpos="1"/>
      <event id="e2" timing="1" hpos="1"/>
      <event id="e3" timing="0" hpos="0"/>
      <event id="e4" timing="2" hpos="2"/>
      <event id="e5" timing="2" hpos="2"/>
      ...
    </spine>
    ...
  </logic>
...
</ieee1599>
```

Fig. 2. An example of simplified spine

4 Case Study: The Prospettiva09 Application

An application has been developed for the festival called *Prospettiva09* in order to demonstrate the potentialities of our approach. This work is the result of the collaboration among the *Teatro Stabile di Torino* and two universities, namely the *Politecnico di Torino* and the *Università degli Studi di Milano*. The final goal was releasing a Web-oriented application that allows users to enjoy performance-related materials, interact with them, and create new ones starting from such materials. The three activities we have cited correspond to the macro-areas the application is subdivided into. Further details will be provided in the following subsections.

4.1 Background

Before describing the software, it is worth to clarify the framework in which it was developed. The application is focused on a subset of productions from *Prospettiva09* festival. This initiative, organized by the *Teatro Stabile di Torino*, took place in 4 locations in Turin: *Teatro Carignano*, *Cavallerizza reale*, *Teatro Gobetti*, and *Fonderie Limone*. *Prospettiva09* melted together different experiences and artistic forms, such as theater, dance, performing arts and music. It staged 50 contemporary productions - for a total amount of 72 performances - and hosted 350 artists and 40 companies from all over the world: Argentina, Belgium, Germany, Great Britain, Italy, United States, etc.

The experimentation was conducted on a small number of productions, heterogeneous as regards their artistic form but all characterized by the use of multimedia. In particular:

1. *Paranoia* (Teatro Carignano, 18/10/09) - A prose work using video projections in the background;
2. *I Pescecani, ovvero quello che resta di Bertolt Brecht* (Teatro Carignano, 28/10/09) - A prose work based on improvisation and live music, performed by prison inmates;
3. *Concerto Senza Titolo* (Teatro Carignano, 05/11/09) - A multimedia show with live music and video materials;
4. *Short Ride in a Fast Machine* (Cavallerizza Reale, 07/11/09) - A contemporary ballet celebrating the aesthetics of Futurism movement;
5. *Too Late! (Antigone) Contest #2* (Cavallerizza Reale 21/10/09) - A contemporary prose work.

For all the cited shows, some digital materials have been directly acquired during the performance. As a consequence, they all present stage photos and a number of audio recordings and video takes, from different points of view. Besides, all the preparatory materials have been retrieved, when present: scripts, synopses, video interviews, multimedia projections, music scores, etc.

4.2 IEEE 1599 Encoding

All the heterogeneous descriptions for the same performance have to be grouped and synchronized in order to provide a unique vision of the single show. This is the reason why IEEE 1599 standard was employed. In fact, as explained in Section 3, a unique XML document in such a format can incapsulate and synchronize heterogeneous information.

At this point, an example is called for. In Figure 3 a simplified IEEE 1599 code block is shown. The *General* layer contains a number of metadata about the show. As regard the *Logic* layer, the events listed and univocally identified within the spine correspond to script lines. In particular, the *Lyrics* sub-element is used to encode them. Of course, the document's author could choose any other granularity, either more accurate (e.g. syllables) or inaccurate (e.g. scenes). Needless to say, this choice has a deep impact on other layers, since it provides anchors to synchronize all materials, and ultimately also the fruition model to be implemented will be influenced. When graphical contents are available (e.g. scans of the script or the music score), ad hoc mappings are present within the *Notational* layer. Finally, the audio and video takes for each performance are synchronized with spine events through the *Audio* layer, which in our example performs the mapping of the script lines onto multimedia files. Finally, when graphical contents are available (e.g. scans of the script or the music score), ad hoc mappings are present within the *Notational* layer. Other types of description are available in an IEEE 1559 document, e.g. in the *Structural* layer, and they could be adopted to encode further aspects of theatrical performances, such as the structure of the plot.

When we analyze the terminology used inside IEEE 1599, its original goal - namely music-oriented description - clearly emerges. Here terms such as "notational" and "lyrics", the use of an "audio" layer mainly for video takes, etc.

```
<ieee1599 version="1.0">
  <general>
    <description>
      <main_title>La canzone di Marinella</main_title>
      <work_title>Concerto senza titolo</work_title>
      <author type="music and lyrics">Fabrizio De Andre'</author>
    </description>
  </general>
  <logic>
    <spine>
      <event id="e0" timing="0" hpos="0"/>
      <event id="e1" timing="3" hpos="3"/>
      ...
    </spine>
    <los>
      <lyrics>
        <syllable start_event_ref="e0">Questa di Marinella
          e' la storia vera</syllable>
        <syllable start_event_ref="e1">che scivolo' nel fiume
          a primavera</syllable>
        ...
      </lyrics>
    </los>
  </logic>
  <notational>
    <graphic_instance_group description="score">
      <graphic_instance file_name="score/page01.tif"
                  encoding_format="image_tiff" file_format="image_tiff"
                       measurement_unit="pixels" position_in_group="1">
        <graphic_event event_ref="e0"
                                      upper_left_x="1022" upper_left_y="1506"
                                 lower_right_x="1076" lower_right_y="1610" />
        <graphic_event event_ref="e1"
                                      upper_left_x="1670" upper_left_y="1526"
                                 lower_right_x="1724" lower_right_y="1630" />
        ...
      </graphic_instance>
    </graphic_instance_group>
  </notational>
  <audio>
    <track file_name="videos/marinella.mpg" encoding_format="video_mpeg"
                                                 file_format="video_mpeg">
      <track_indexing timing_type="seconds">
        <track_event event_ref="e0" start_time="2" />
        <track_event event_ref="e1" start_time="9" />
        ...
      </track_indexing>
    </track>
  </audio>
</ieee1599>
```

Fig. 3. The IEEE 1599 document which encodes a scene of *Concerto senza Titolo* strain the normal interpretation. Nevertheless, this case study demonstrates that IEEE 1599's multi-layer approach is suitable to the description of theatrical performances, too.

4.3 The Enjoy Section

The Enjoy section of the application implements a traditional way to enjoy available materials. In other words, heterogeneous documents are organized into specific categories by their type (e.g. texts, audios, videos, etc.), but they are not synchronized: user interaction is limited to their fruition. This can be a good example of what traditional archives usually offer to Web surfers. Even if not innovative at all, this section was implemented in order to showcase the variety and the amount of available materials. Besides, in this way occasional visitors - accustomed to traditional tools to interact with digital archives - are not forced to change their approach. This section of the application is devoted to the preservation of digitized documents and to their fruition, geographically distributed and deferred in time.

Figure 4 shows a screenshot of the interface.

Fig. 4. The Enjoy section

4.4 The Interact Section

By entering this section, it is possible to enjoy metadata, text and multimedia materials in a synchronized way, by exploring the relationships and the synchronizations among them. The interface, shown in Figure 5, presents a number of controls and windows to navigate materials in an innovative way. Different fruitions models are available through the interface. First, it is possible to select a show and simultaneously follow its plot on the script and on a video or audio track (one of the many available versions). Even if this is a basic level of fruition, it proposes a more advanced model with respect to other similar Web applications, since the performance in its many aspects can be watched in a synchronized fashion. But a second way to use the interface is even more interesting: it consists in switching from an aural/visual representation to another. In other words, it is possible to compare in real time different versions and perspectives of the multimedia contents related to the same performance. When the user decides to switch from one material to another, the execution continues just from the current point. Finally, the application allows a third way to enjoy the theatrical performance, namely the possibility to alter the original time sequence of events. This function is implemented by making all the parts of the interface sensitive to mouse clicks. For instance, it is possible to jump from a point to another in the plot or the music score, or dragging the scrollbar of the media player, and recreate the synchronization among materials in real time.

Such features of the interface are made possible by the IEEE 1599 standard, which encodes not only raw data about the theatrical performance but also all the information required to synchronize them.

First, this section gives to the Web audience some of the features typical of a live fruition, such as the possibility to change the point of view and to concentrate on a particular type of content, chosen by the user and not imposed by a director. Moreover, this model provides a sort of augmented reality if compared to a live view of the performance, since the elements mixed up on the stage can be enjoyed together - and from different perspectives - or even "ungrouped" and watched one by one. This possibility is particularly relevant for the shows with multimedia projections, which sometimes present an information overload very difficult to decode in real time.

4.5 The Create Section

The digital objects previously digitized and organized in a unique IEEE 1599 document can also originate new materials. This possibility is explored within the Create section, where already available materials can be re-used inside a video editing environment (see Figure 6). The idea is letting Web users create their own clip about the show, by picking contents from the built-in archive. For example, it is possible to create cross fadings among different moments of the performance, to mix the original audio with other tracks, to superimpose free texts or parts of the script, and so on. Finally, the user-produced materials can be shared with other surfers.

It is worth noting that the obtained results can be noticeably heterogeneous. As a trivial example, short clips with advertising purpose can be realized; but a more creative use of this tool can originate brand new forms of art, for example by mixing zoomed particulars from still images, extrapolating single words, breaking audio contents into small pieces and editing them in an original manner, and

Fig. 5. The Interact section

so on. In other words, through this section each user can communicate his/her own perspective on a show, thus recalling the name itself of the festival, namely *Prospettiva09*.

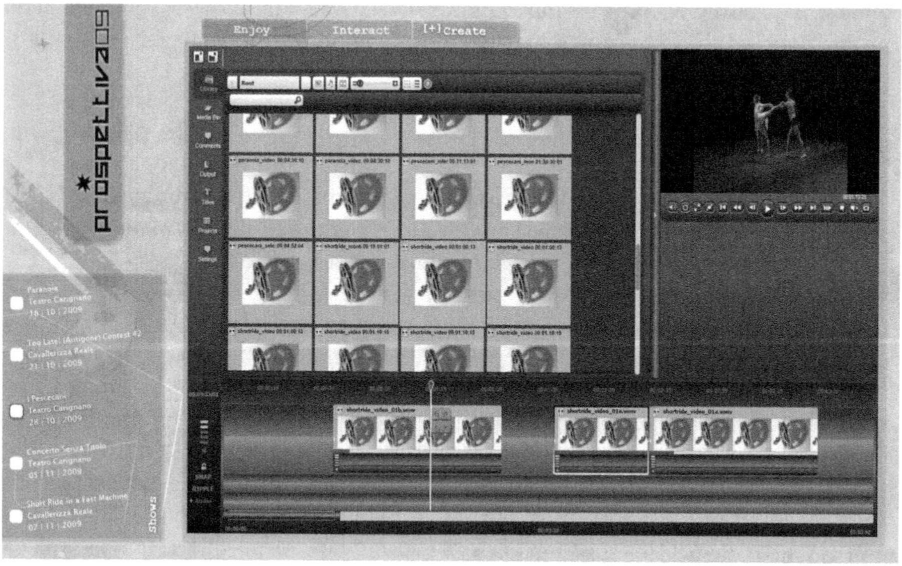

Fig. 6. The Create section

5 Conclusions

In this paper we have presented a proposal for the valorization of traditional theatrical performances through XML, network technologies and social media. First, materials have to be either digitized or directly acquired in digital format in order to create a *corpus* of heterogeneous descriptions for the same performance. Starting from such materials, all related to a single show, an XML format - namely IEEE 1599 - has been employed to describe them within a unique document in a synchronized way. The concept of *event*, originally related to the music field in IEEE 1599, here has been reinterpreted to take into account the occurence of given actions on the stage. Finally, a Web interface with advanced multi-modal functions has been designed and implemented. In this way, also Web users can participate to the performance and somehow interact with it.

Acknowledgement. The authors gratefully wish to acknowledge Vanessa Michielon, Elisabetta Ranieri and Mario Ricciardi from the *Politecnico di Torino* for their cooperation in *Prospettiva09*. This work has been made possible by the financial support of Regione Piemonte.

References

1. IEEE Std 1599-2008 - IEEE Recommended Practice for Defining a Commonly Acceptable Musical Application Using XML. The Institute of Electrical and Electronics Engineers, Inc. (2008)
2. Cooperare: Content organization, propagation, evaluation and reuse through active repositories. Torino (2010), `http://nexos.cisi.unito.it/joomla/cooperare/`
3. Baggi, D.L.: An IEEE standard for symbolic music. Computer 38(11), 100–102 (2005)
4. Haus, G., Paccagnini, A., Pelegrin, M.: Characterization of music archives contents. a case study: the archive at Teatro alla Scala. In: Proc. of the 3rd International Congress on Science and Technology for the Safeguard of Cultural Heritage in the Mediterranean Basin, Alcalà de Henares, Spain (2001)
5. Haus, G., Longari, M.: A multi-layered, timebased music description approach based on XML. Computer Music Journal 29(1), 70–85 (2005)
6. Hyvönen, E.: Semantic portals for cultural heritage. In: Handbook on Ontologies, pp. 757–778 (2009)
7. Ludovico, L.A.: Key concepts of the IEEE 1599 standard. In: Proceedings of the IEEE CS Conference The Use of Symbols To Represent Music And Multimedia Objects. IEEE CS, Lugano (2008)
8. Ludovico, L.A., Mauro, D.A.: Sound and the City: Multi-layer representation and navigation of audio scenarios. In: Proceedings of the 6th Sound and Music Computing Conference, SMC, Oporto (2009)

Augmented Perception of the Past: The Case of the Telamon from the Greek Theater of Syracuse

Filippo Stanco[1], Davide Tanasi[2], Matteo Buffa[1], and Beatrice Basile[3]

[1] University of Catania, Dipartimento di Matematica e Informatica,
Viale A. Doria, 6 - 95125 Catania, Italy
{fstanco,buffa}@dmi.unict.it
[2] Arcadia University, The College of Global Studies, MCAS
via Roma, 124 - 96100 Siracusa, Italy
dtanasi@mediterranencenter.it
[3] Servizio Museo archeologico regionale Paolo Orsi di Siracusa,
Viale Teocrito, 66 - 96100 Siracusa, Italy
museo.arche.orsi@regione.sicilia.it

Abstract. The paper presents a system of real–time interaction with ancient artifacts digitally restored in a virtual environment in which the perception of reality is augmented, through the provision of the visual data missing in the current conditions of the artifacts themselves. The application of this system will be through common mobile devices, like the Apple Iphone. The case study for this project is a Late Classical Greek statue of a Telamon from the Theater of Syracuse. Since the statue is subject to constant degradation, a virtual replica was created through the application of laser scanning techniques. Once the 3D model of the Telamon was produced, a process of digital restoration based on archetypes and photographic documentation of the statue was carried out. Then, the commercial framework for mobile devices, ARToolworks, was used for developing Augmented Reality applications. Using a pattern that is recognized by the device, a three-dimensional model is associated to that pattern and the virtual model is shown as it is in the real world.

Keywords: Augmented reality, Laser scanning, Real time interaction, Virtual heritage.

1 Introduction

In the last fifty years, the growing use of computer applications has become a main feature of archaeological research [1]. Since the '90s, when computer science was oriented to the creation of work tools and solutions for the storage and management of quantitative data, to the development of virtual models and to the dissemination of knowledge, this discipline has also developed a more theoretical approach to the problems of archaeology. In fact, it can now influence interpretation procedures and revolutionize the language and contents of the study of the past [2].

C. Grana and R. Cucchiara (Eds.): MM4CH 2011, CCIS 247, pp. 126–135, 2012.

From its first definition by Reilly in 1991 [3], virtual archaeology (VA) was intended as the use of digital reconstruction in archaeology. Recently, new communicative approaches to archaeological contents through the use of interactive strategies have been added. The development of VA is not simply caused by the proliferation of 3D modeling techniques in many fields of knowledge, but by the necessity to find new systems to store an ever-increasing amount of data and to create the best medium for communicating those data through a visual language. From this point of view, the application of 3D reconstructions, obtained with the different techniques available, has become the core area of study of VA with regards to the potential of cognitive interaction offered by a 3D model. In this way, virtuality becomes an even more effective communication method if applied to particular fields, such us archaeological areas that are well preserved but not accessible [4], sites that are not preserved but that are known through traditional documentation [5], destroyed sites but depicted in iconographical repertoires [6], contextualization in progressive dimensional scale (object, context, site, landscape), and functional simulations repeating the processes of experimental archaeology in a virtual environment.

The cognitive experiences of 3D computer graphics can essentially be divided into passive and active interactions. The first case refers mainly to applications related to research and study, where the primary need is of a documentation type, such as the archaeological excavation or the monitoring of degradation. In the second case, interaction with the virtually–recreated reality is further exploited in the enhancement of the archaeological heritage through the creation of a virtual museum, reachable on digital media or on the web, intended both as a virtual version of a real museum and as a closer study of an archaeological site. 3D modeling can also be extremely useful for the identification, monitoring, conservation, restoration, and promotion of archaeological artefacts. All archaeological heritage is (always) under constant threat and danger. Architectural structures and cultural and natural sites are exposed to pollution, tourists, and wars, as well as environmental disasters such as earthquakes, floods, or climatic changes. Hidden aspects of our cultural heritage are also affected by changes in agricultural regimes due to economic progress, mining, gravel extraction, construction of infrastructures, and the expansion of industrial areas. In this context, 3D computer graphics can support archaeology and the politics of cultural heritage by offering to scholars a "sixth sense" for understanding the traces of the past [8]. 3D documentation of extant archaeological remains or building elements is an important part of collecting the necessary data for a virtual archaeology project. New developments facilitate this phase of documentation, including the obtaining of correct measurements and ground plans from photography, through the use of readily-available equipment. This is important when restoring archaeological remains, when older phases are reconstructed in a virtual way. The original state, the restored state, and eventual in–between states can be recorded easily through this photo–modeling technique [9]. Furthermore, the recent application of 3D computer graphics has proved crucial in planning strategies of restoration and in conservation issues concerning monuments that are part of the world cultural heritage, about which there is still an open debate, as in the case of the restoration of the Parthenon on the Acropolis of Athens [10].

In this paper, we illustrate the application of some VA techniques to a late classical Greek statue depicting a satyr Telamon, from the stage-scenery of the Theater of Syracuse, now kept at the Archaeological Museum "Paolo Orsi" of Syracuse. The statue, recovered at the end of the 19th century, is made out of local calcarenite plastered with a mix of marble dust and sand. Due to the materials used, the statue is subject to cyclical degradation and even the restoration attempts seem unsuccessful, as can be observed in Fig. 1. We show how a virtual copy of the statue can be used to monitor the degradation and to present the statue in a new way.

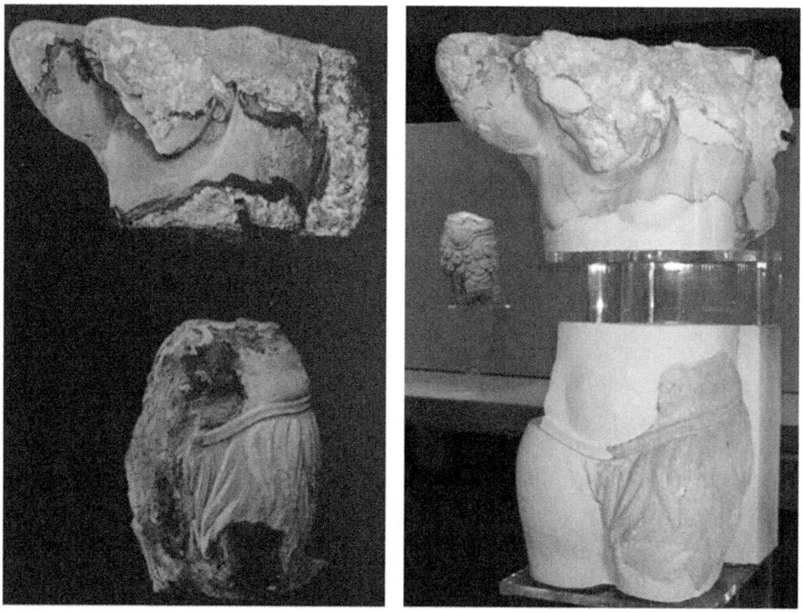

(a) (b)

Fig. 1. (a) Telamon in a picture of 1927; (b) Telamon today

2 The Archeomatica Project

This experience has been developed as part of the Archeomatica Project [11], a digital archaeology research project that was begun in late 2007 by researchers in image processing and computer graphics of the Image Processing Lab [12] of the University of Catania and scholars in archaeology joining the Lab. The project aims to develop new implements for archaeological research in prehistory and protohistory within the field of 2D digital imaging and 3D graphics [32]. Its main aim is to produce automatic systems of recognition and classification of graphic data, such as figurative pottery decoration, through the use of computer vision and pattern recognition techniques, and to develop virtual models of prehistoric sites and items with a high degree of accuracy through application of laser scanner and 3D modeling techniques. This cognitive process is based on peer-to-peer exchange of knowledge between experts of computer science and prehistory working side by side. The cooperative experience of the Archeomatica Project, which represents (through its scientific production) the most recent trends in digital archaeology and the modern politics of conservation of archaeological heritage, has also aimed to define a common multidisciplinary language for this new discipline to improve the quality of the message that reaches the outside world. In these first years, of research activity the Archeomatica Project has produced significant results in archaeological 3D modeling and 3D digital restoration, helping to improve the cognitive capacities of the archaeologists.

3 Digital Restoration

The technique of 3D digital restoration of archaeological objects is perhaps the most common trend in interdisciplinary projects related to the interpretation and dissemination of archaeological knowledge. This is because of the potential that 3D has in subtracting the archaeological goods from the destructive effects of atmospheric agents, of pollution, of time, and, in some cases, of natural disasters and wars. The high–definition 3D laser scanner is an instrument that collects 3D data from a given surface or object in a systematic, automated manner, at a relatively high rate, in near real time using a laser ray to establish the surface coordinates. Over the last decade, this technology has been applied to archaeological research to construct geometric models with different characteristics [13,14]. Most archaeological work has been carried out to digitize objects of an intermediate size, such as settlement structures, statues, and vessels. The most recent projects have been focused on modeling structures during the excavation of archaeological sites, either of one limited zone [7] or the complete ensemble [15]. These studies have been carried out from the ground surface or using helicopters and airplanes [16].

The possibility of obtaining a virtual, exact replica of reality in a limited amount of time makes the laser scanning method ideal for studies of 3D digital restoration, where the virtual recomposition of fragmented elements, both physically and narratively, is fundamental [17]. The Archeomatica Project team of researchers in this field has proposed integrating the Blender–based 3D modeling and image–based 3D modeling with the laser scanning technique, in order to solve the problems of possible data voids connected with complex scanning. The laser scanner used is the compact and handy Next Engine [18], and it is very versatile especially when the objects to be scanned are placed in restricted spaces or cannot be removed. It is an optical triangulation scanner that offers a high degree of precision, allowing the creation of good three-dimensional models

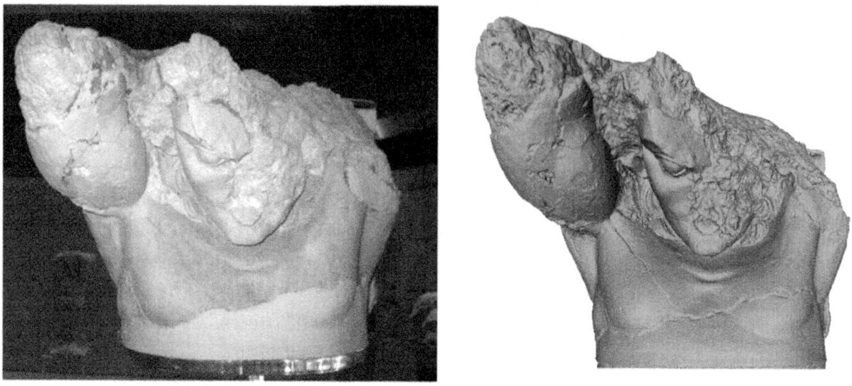

(a) (b)

Fig. 2. (a) Statue of Telamon, from Syracuse Museum; (b) 3D model of the statue obtained with laser scanning technique

of real subjects. Since the Telamon was very large, a tripod was used with the scanner in manual mode. Its proprietary software NextEngine ScanStudio offers an excellent interface for the alignment process. However, another software, Meshlab [30], was preferred as it is more suitable for this kind of work since it offers a wide range of specific filters to manipulate and improve data acquired in the previous phase.

As is customary, the alignment process produced a project file containing a significant amount of data (vertex and faces) that permits any type of transformation or filter application useful for completing the digital statue. First the digital statue was cleaned, by deleting scattered points and filling holes (Fig. 2(b)). Subsequently, a filter was applied to reconstruct those parts that were not scanned in the acquisition phase because they were considered insignificant, such as, for example, the back of the statue that is covered by plexiglass. Since the Telamon was symmetrical, later we tried to produce a symmetrical version of the 3D model, using just the laser scanner data (Fig. 3).

4 Augmented Reality

Virtual reality allows the 3D visualization of concepts, objects, or spaces and their contextualization through the creation of a visual framework in which data is displayed. VR also enables interaction with data organized in 3D, facilitating the interaction between operator, data, and information in order to enhance the sensorial perception [19]. It creates a virtual space that is a replica of the real space, where the information about every feature that constituted the different moments of life of the real space are "translated" into 3D data. The two crucial points of every project of VR are the selection of the information (pictures, drawings, geometrical measures) and the choice of which facet of the original

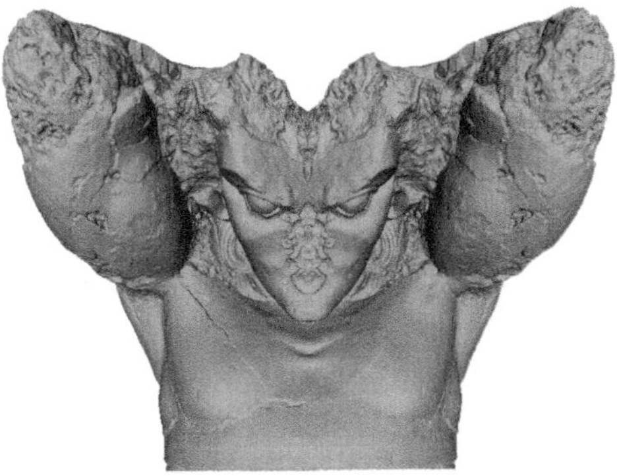

Fig. 3. Restoration analysis in virtual ambient of the Telamon acquired with laser scanning technique

object's nature must be captured and reconstructed. "Visual computer models should make clear their sources and the criteria on which they are based" [20]. In order to understand archaeological systems, much more than a visually "realistic" geometric model is needed. "Dynamism and interaction" are essential. A dynamic model is a model that changes in position, size, material properties, lighting, and viewing specification. If those changes are not static but respond to user input, we enter into the proper world of virtual reality, whose key feature is real-time (RT) interaction. Here real-time means that the computer is able to detect input and modify the virtual world "instantaneously" at user commands. By selectively transforming an object, that is, by interpolating shape transformations, archaeologists may be able to form an object hypothesis more quickly [21]. One field where the scholars in archaeology and computer science are recently getting involved is augmented reality (AR) where the simultaneous visualization of virtual data and the real world is performed [22,23,25,26]. One of the objectives of AR is to bring the computer out of the desktop environment and into the world of the user who works with a three-dimensional application. In contrast to VR, where the user is immersed in the world of the computer, AR incorporates the computer into the reality of the user. The user can then interact with the real world in a natural way, with the computer providing information and assistance. It is then a combination of the real scene viewed by the user and a virtual scene generated by the computer that augments the scene with additional information. The virtual world acts as an interface, which may not be used if it provides the same experience as face-to-face communication. AR enables users to go "beyond being there" and enhance the experience in order to achieve both the full interpretation of the traces of the past and the development of the best tool for the dissemination of their message [24].

In our example of a Greek Telamon in Syracuse, the system provides new ways of information access at the Museum in a user-friendly way through the use of 3D-visualization on mobile devices [27,28]. We have chosen as our device a common mobile Apple Iphone, with the commercial framework ARToolworks. Once the three-dimensional statue is obtained, it is necessary to adapt it to the hardware limitations imposed by the device. The graphical engine inside the mobile device is able to handle three-dimensional environments without loss of data and without any delay within a certain threshold. This limit has a maximum of seven million polygons per second. However, the statue is composed of thirty-nine million polygons and must necessarily be reduced to fit within the limitations of the device, without compromising the aspect of the statue. For this operation, a filter contained in Meshlab software [30] called "Quadric Edge Collapse Decimation" has been used. This filter has been applied many times by halving the number of faces each time instead of making only one application of this filter and obtaining a drastic decimation with bad results in terms of quality.

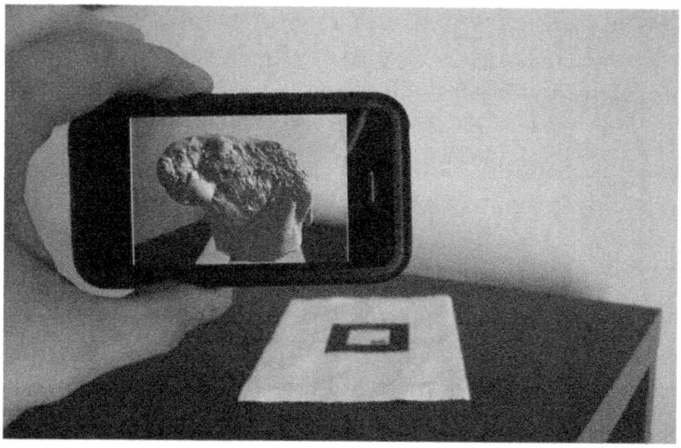

Fig. 4. The AR applied to the Telamon. The mobile phone gives the statue model when the pattern is found by the camera.

ARToolworks uses ARToolkit [31], an open source library for Augmented Reality that allows many easy-to-use functions of Computer Vision to be used for AR. It gives the possibility to create Augmented Reality applications on any mobile device using a high level programming environment that allows the developer to set and manipulate the Video Tracking process and three-dimensional overlapping in a few simple steps without having to delve into the world of deep programming and the theory of Computer Vision. ARToolworks is integrated in Xcode, an Apple Integrated Development Environment; it uses only API approved by Apple and any application is "App-Store" compatible. Using a pattern that is recognized by the device, a three-dimensional model is associated with the pattern and the virtual model is shown like it is in the real world (Figs. 4 and 5).

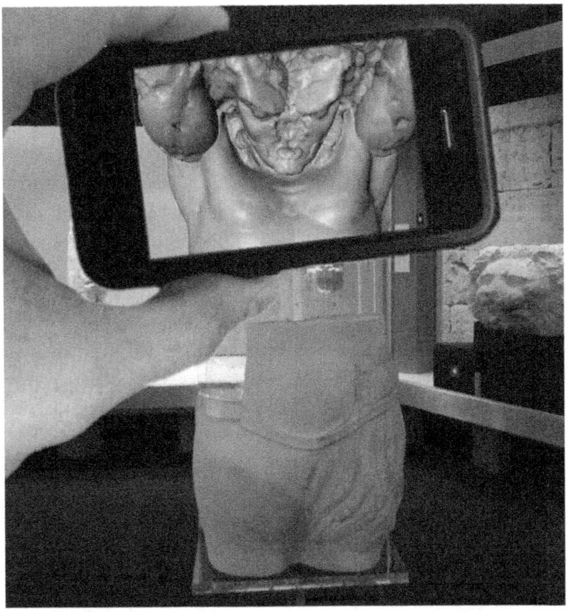

Fig. 5. The augmented reality in the Museum

5 Conclusions

The encouraging results of the application of AR to archaeological evidence has demonstrated that it is possible to use another "sense" to decrypt the traces of the past: the three-dimensional recreation of ancient life and visual images are extremely effective in explaining the past because they allow us to experience it.

The potential of this approach in the future could be enhanced by investing much more in the five fundamental elements of an AR environment, namely virtuality (objects that don't exist in the real world can be viewed and examined), augmentation (real objects can be augmented by virtual annotations), cooperation (multiple users can see each other and cooperate in a natural way), independence (each user controls his own independent viewpoint), and individuality (displayed data can be different for each viewer) [29].

Future works will include to create of visual pattern less "invasive", hopefully based on natural geometry of the artefacts, to integrate of two 3D models in an overall virtual replica of the altar as it was at the time of its use, the simplify the entire model in order to be run on mobile devices and finally to develop other versions of the software to be used also in android environment.

Acknowledgments. Many thanks to Susanna Kimbell for the review of the English text.

References

1. Zubrow, E.B.W.: Digital Archaeology. A Historical Context. In: Evans, T.L., Daly, P. (eds.) Digital Archaeology. Bridging Method and Theory. Routledge, London (2006)

2. Vannini, G.: Informatica per l'Archeologia o Archeologia per l'Informatica? Archeologia e Calcolatori 11, 311–315 (2000)
3. Reilly, P.: Towards a Virtual Archaeology. In: Lockyear, K., Rahtz, S. (eds.) Computer Applications and Quantitative Methods in Archaeology 1990, Oxford. BAR International Series, vol. 565 (1990)
4. Cultraro, M., Gabellone, F., Scarrozzi, G.: The Virtual Musealization of Archaeological Sites: Between Documentation and Comunication. In: Remondino, F., El-Hakim, S., Gonzo, L. (eds.) Proceedings of the 3rd ISPRS International Workshop 3D-ARCH 2009, 3D Virtual Reconstruction and Visualization of Complex Architectures, Trento, Italy, February 25-28. International Archives of Photogrammetry, Remote Sensing and Spatial Information Sciences, vol. XXXVIII-5/W1 (2009)
5. Cultraro, M., Gabellone, F., Scardozzi, G.: Integrated Methodologies and Technologies for the Reconstructive Study of Dur-Sharrukin (Iraq). In: Remondino, F., El-Hakim, S., Gonzo, L. (eds.) Proceedings of the 3rd ISPRS International Workshop 3D-ARCH 2009, 3D Virtual Reconstruction and Visualization of Complex Architectures, Trento, Italy, February 25-28. International Archives of Photogrammetry, Remote Sensing and Spatial Information Sciences, vol. XXXVIII-5/W1 (2009)
6. Stojakovic, V., Tepavcevica, B.: Optimal Methods for 3D Modeling of Devastated Architectural Objects. In: Remondino, F., El-Hakim, S., Gonzo, L. (eds.) Proceedings of the 3rd ISPRS International Workshop 3D-ARCH 2009, 3D Virtual Reconstruction and Visualization of Complex Architectures, Trento, Italy, February 25-28. International Archives of Photogrammetry, Remote Sensing and Spatial Information Sciences, vol. XXXVIII-5/W1 (2009)
7. Doneus, M., Neubauer, W.: Laser Scanners for 3D Documentation of Stratigraphic Excavations. In: Baltsavias, M., Gruen, A., Van Gool, L., Pateraki, M. (eds.) Recording, Modeling and Visualization of Cultural Heritage. Taylor and Francis, London (2006)
8. Moser, S.: Archaeological Representation. The virtual Conventions for Constructing Knowledge about the Past. In: Hodder, I. (ed.) Archaeological Theory Today. Polity Press, Malden (2005)
9. Pletinckx, D.: Virtual Archaeology as an Integrated Preservation Method. In: Arqueologica 2.0, Proceedings of 1st International Meeting on Graphic Archaeology and Informatics, Cultural Heritage and Innovation, Seville, June 17-20, pp. 51–55 (2009)
10. Toganidis, N.: Parthenon Restoration Project. In: Georgopoulos, A., Agriantonis, N. (eds.) Anticipating the Future of the Cultural Past, Proceedings of the XXI International CIPA Symposium, Athens, pp. 1–6 (2007)
11. `http://www.archeomatica.unict.it`
12. `http://iplab.dmi.unict.it`
13. Peloso, D.: Tecniche Laser Scanner per il Rilievo dei Beni Culturali. Archeologia e Calcolatori 16, 199–224 (2005)
14. Boeheler, W.: Comparison of 3D Laser Scanning and other 3D Measurement Techniques. In: Baltsavias, M., Gruen, A., Van Gool, L., Pateraki, M. (eds.) Recording, Modeling and Visualization of Cultural Heritage, pp. 89–100. Taylor and Francis, London
15. Gaisecker, T.: Pinchango Alto. 3D Archaeology Documentation Using the Hybrid 3D Laser Scan System of RIEGL. In: Baltsavias, M., Gruen, A., Van Gool, L., Pateraki, M. (eds.) Recording, Modeling and Visualization of Cultural Heritage. Taylor and Francis, London (2006)
16. Doneus, M., Brieseb, C., Feraa, M., Fornwagnera, U., Griebla, M., Jannera, M., Zingerlea, M.C.: Documentation and Analysis of Archaeological Sites Using Aerial Reconnaissance and Airborne Laser Scanning. In: Georgopoulos, A., Agriantonis, N. (eds.) Proceedings of the XXI International CIPA Symposium on Anticipating the Future of the Cultural Past, pp. 1–6 (2007)

17. Cain, K., Sobieralski, C., Martinez, P.: Reconstructing a Colossus of Ramesses II from Laser Scan Data. In: SIGGRAPH 2003: ACM SIGGRAPH 2003 Sketches & Applications, p. 1. ACM, New York (2003)
18. http://www.nextengine.com
19. Hermon, S., Kalisperis, L.: Between the Real and the Virtual: 3D Visualization in the Cultural Heritage Domain - Expectations and Prospects. In: Arqueologica 2.0, Proceedings of 1st International Meeting on Graphic Archaeology and Informatics, Cultural Heritage and Innovation, pp. 99–103 (June 2009)
20. Niccolucci, F.: Virtual Archaology: an Introduction. In: Niccolucci, F. (ed.) Proceedings of the VAST Euroconference on Virtual Archaeology, Arezzo, November 24-25. BAR I.S. 1075, pp. 3–6. Archaeopress, Oxford (2000)
21. Barceló, J.: Virtual Reality for Archaeological Explanation Beyond "Picturesque" Reconstruction. Archeologia e Calcolatori 12, 221–244 (2001)
22. Milgram, P., Yin, S.: An Augmented Reality Based Teleoperation Interface for Unstructured Environments. In: ANS 7th Meeting on Robotics and Remote Systems, pp. 101–123 (August 1997)
23. Magnenat-Thalmann, N., Papagiannakis, G.: Virtual Worlds and Augmented Reality in Cultural Heritage Applications. In: Baltsavias, M., Gruen, A., Van Gool, L., Pateraki, M. (eds.) Recording, Modeling and Visualization of Cultural Heritage. Taylor and Francis, London
24. Billinghurst, M., Kato, H.: Collaborative Mixed Reality. In: Proceedings of the First International Symposium on Mixed Reality (ISMR 1999), Mixed Reality - Merging Real and Virtual Worlds, pp. 261–284. Springer, Berlin (1999)
25. Zollner, M., Keil, J., Wust, H., Pletinckx, D.: An Augmented Reality Presentation System for Remote Cultural Heritage Sites. In: Debattista, K., Perlingieri, C., Pitzalis, D., Spina, A. (eds.) Proceedings of the 10th International Symposium on Virtual Reality, Archaeology and Cultural Heritage VAST, pp. 112–116 (2009)
26. Ramic-Brkic, B., Karkin, Z., Sadzak, A., Selimovic, D., Rizvic, S.: Augmented Real-Time Enviroment of the Church of the Holy Trinity in Mostar. In: Debattista, K., Perlingieri, C., Pitzalis, D., Spina, A. (eds.) Proceedings of the 10th International Symposium on Virtual Reality, Archaeology and Cultural Heritage VAST, pp. 141–148 (2009)
27. Vlahakis, V., Ioannidis, N., Karigiannis, J., Tsotros, M., Gounaris, M., Stricker, D., Gleue, T., Daehne, P., Almeida, L.: Archeoguide: Challenges and Solutions of a Personalized Augmented Reality Guide for Archaeological Sites. IEEE Computer Graphics and Applications 22(5), 52–60 (2002)
28. Stricker, D., Pagani, A., Zoellner, M.: In-situ Visualization for Cultural Heritage Sites Using Novel, Augmented Reality Technologies. In: Arqueologica 2.0, Proceedings of 1st International Meeting on Graphic Archaeology and Informatics, Cultural Heritage and Innovation, pp. 141–145 (June 2009)
29. Schmalsteig, D., Fujrmann, A., Szalavari, Z., Gervautz, M., Studierstube, E.: An Environment for Collaboration in Augmented Reality. In: CVE 1996 Workshop Proceedings, Nottingham (September 1996)
30. http://meshlab.sourceforge.net/
31. http://www.hitl.washington.edu/artoolkit/
32. Stanco, F., Tanasi, D.: Experiencing the Past. Computer Graphics in Archaeology. In: Stanco, F., Battiato, S., Gallo, G. (eds.) Digital Imaging For Cultural Heritage Preservation. Analysis, Restoration and Reconstruction of Ancient Artworks, pp. 1–36. CRC Press (2011) ISBN: 978-1-4398217-3-2

Publishing Europe's Television Heritage on the Web: The EUscreen Project

Johan Oomen[1] and Vassilis Tzouvaras[2]

[1] Nederlands Instituut voor Beeld en Geluid, Sumatralaan 45, Hilversum, The Netherlands
joomen@beeldengeluid.nl
[2] National Technical University of Athens, Iroon Polytexneiou 9, 15780 Zografou, Greece
tzouvaras@image.ntua.gr

Abstract. The EUscreen project represents the European television archives and acts as a domain aggregator for Europeana, Europe's digital library. The man motivation for it is to provide unified access to a representative collection of television programs, secondary sources and articles, and in this way to allow students, scholars and the general public to study the history of television in its wider context. The main goals of EUscreen are to (i) develop a state-of-the-art workflow for content ingestion, (ii) define content selection and IPR management methodology, and (iii) provide a front-end that accommodates requirements from several user groups.

Keywords: TV on the Web, EBUcore, Europeana, Metadata Interoperability, Linked Open Data.

1 Introduction

Providing access to large integrated digital collections of cultural heritage objects is a challenging task. Multiple initiatives exist in different domains. For example, Europeana manages a state-of-the art technical infrastructure to manage the ingestion and management of data from a wide variety of content providers. It aims to give access to all of Europe's digitised cultural heritage by 2025. Europeana focuses on two main tasks (i) to act as a central index, aggregating and harmonising metadata following a common data model [1], and (ii) to provide persistent links to content hosted by trusted sources. The portal currently provides access to 15 million objects, primarily books and photographs; audiovisual collections are underrepresented. However, recent analysis of query logs from the Europeana portal indicated users have a special interest for this type of content. Television content is regarded a vital component of Europe's heritage, collective memory and identity – all our yesterdays – but it remains difficult to access. Even more than with the museum and library collections, the dealing with copyrights, encoding standards, costs for digitization and storage makes the process of its aggregated and contextualized publishing on the Web extra challenging.

In this paper, we will focus in outlining the ingestion workflow; the projects' main technical achievement. In Section 2, we outline the motivation of our work. In Section 2, we elaborate on the technical infrastructure.

C. Grana and R. Cucchiara (Eds.): MM4CH 2011, CCIS 247, pp. 136–142, 2012.

2 Motivation

The main motivation for our work is to overcome the current barriers and provide a unified access to a representative collection of television programs, secondary sources and articles, and in this way to allow students, scholars and the general public The multidisciplinary nature of the EUscreen project is mirrored in the composition of the socio-technical nature of the consortium; comprising of 20 collection owners, technical enablers, legal experts, educational technologists and media historians of 20 countries. EUscreen represents all major European television archives and acts as one of the key domain aggregators providing content to Europeana.

Several public reports on our work can be downloaded from the project blog. This paper reports on the results of the work performed over the past one and a half years, leading up to the launch of the first version of the portal. Notably, we analyze the design decisions from a Web Science perspective; zooming in on the interplay between user requirements, technical possibilities and societal issues, including intellectual property rights. We will show how EUscreen contributes to a so-called 'Cultural Commonwealth' [2] that emerges by bringing content from memory institutions and the knowledge of its heterogeneous constituency together.

Conceptually, EUscreen is built on the notion that knowledge is created through conversation [3]. Hence, ample attention is given to investigating how to stimulate and capture knowledge of its users. Combining organizational, expert and amateur contributions is a very timely topic in the heritage domain, requiring investigation of the technical, organizational and legal specificities.

The goals of the project are to (i) develop a state-of-the-art workflow for content ingestion, (ii) define content selection and IPR management methodology (35.000 items will be made available), and (iii) design and implement a front-end that accommodates requirements from several user groups. To reach these goals, close cooperation between the different stakeholders in the consortium is essential. For example, the selection policy needs to take in to account the available content, wishes from media historians and the copyright situation. The workflow will need to study the existing metadata structures, should support aggregation by Europeana and provide support for multilingual access.

2.1 Define Content Selection Methodoloy

In collaboration with leading television historians EUscreen has defined a content selection policy [4], divided into three strands:

1. Historical Topics: 14 important topics in history of Europe in the 20th Century (70% of content);
2. Comparative Virtual Exhibitions: two specially devised topics that explore more specialised aspects of European history in a more comparative manner (10% of content – include documents, stills, articles);
3. Content Provider Virtual Exhibitions: Each content provider selects content supported with other digital materials and textual information on subjects or topics of their own choosing (20 % of content).

EUscreen has written a set of guideless regarding management of intellectual property rights. The copyright situation of each and every item is investigated prior to uploading.

2.2 The Front-End

Representatives of the four primary user groups, e.g. secondary education, academic research, the general public and the cultural heritage domain were consulted in order to define user requirements and design fron-end functionality. The main challenge for the portal's front-end is to include advanced features for specific use cases without overwhelming the users with a complex interfaces. The Helsinki University of Arts and Design adapted a component-based conceptual model that accommodates this requirement (Figure 1.)

Fig. 1. EUscreen Homepage

Implementation of the front-end services is not done in the traditional way using serverside programming language like php, java or asp. EUscreen implemented a 'server-less' front-end APIs where a javascript/flash proxy system handles the communication with the back-end services. The result will be a front-end system that can be 'installed' on any plain html web server without any need for server-side technologies. This means it can be hosted and moved to any location or multiple locations. It also means partners can use these APIs to integrate parts of the functionality in their own intranet and internet systems using simple 'embed' ideas. This method is gaining more ground, for example companies like Google who provides these types of APIs for services like Google Maps.

3 Metadata Ingestion and Video Playout

The technical standards enabling interoperability form an important dimension of the technical achievements. In order to achieve semantic interoperability, a common automatic interpretation of the meaning of the exchanged information is needed, i.e. the ability to automatically process the information in a machine-understandable manner. The first step of achieving a certain level of common understanding is a representation language that exchanges the formal semantics of the information. Then, systems that understand these semantics can process the information and provide web services like searching, retrieval.

Many different metadata schemas or in a broader sense, sets of elements of information about resources, are being used in this domain, across a variety of technical environments and scientific disciplines. EUscreen has developed an ingestion mechanism providing a user friendly environment that allows for the extraction and presentation of all relevant and statistical information concerning input metadata together with an intuitive mapping service that uses the EUscreen Metadata schema, and provides all the functionality and documentation required for the providers to define their crosswalks. The workflow (Figure 2) consists of four phases, each responsible for specific services to ensure the quality of the ingestion process:

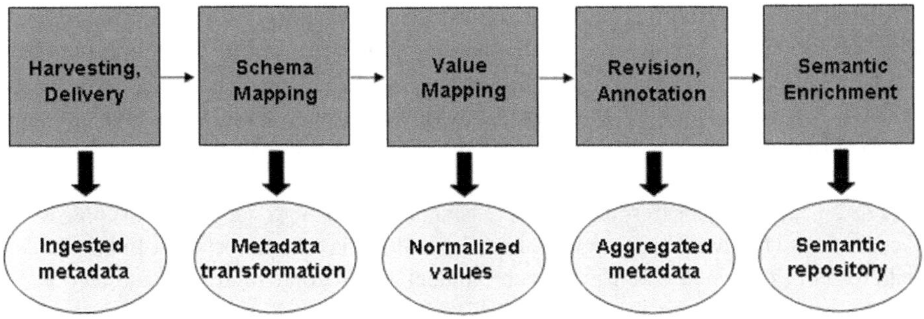

Fig. 2. Metadata Ingestion Workflow

The Workflow consists of five steps. The first is *harvesting/delivery*, which refers to collection of metadata from content providers through common data delivery protocols, such as OAI-PMH, HTTP and FTP. is implemented as a web service, where authentication is required to perform a series of tasks that correspond to work flow steps. The havesting service is an application written in the Java and hosted on a web server by the Tomcat servlet engine. Data is imported into a PostgreSQL database in xml format. Once uploaded, the xml structure is parsed and represented in a relational database table.

Second is the *Schema Mapping* that aligns harvested metadata to the common reference model. A graphical user interface assists content providers in mapping their metadata structures and instances to the EUsceen metadata model, using an underlying machine-understandable mapping language. It supports sharing and reuse of metadata crosswalks and establishment of template transformations.

The next step is *Value Mapping*, focusing on the alignment and transformation of a content provider's list of terms to the authority file or external source introduced by the reference model. It provides normalisation of dates, geographical locations or coordinates, country and language information or name writing conventions.

Revision/Annotation, being the fourth step, enables the addition of annotations, editing of a single or group of items in order to assign metadata not available in the original context and, further transformations and quality control checks (e.g. for URLs) according to the aggregation guidelines and scope.

Finally, the *Semantic Enrichment* step focuses on the transformation of data to a semantic data model, the extraction and identification of resources and the subsequent deployment of an RDF semantic repository.

3.1 EBUcore and Multilinguality

In order to achieve semantic interoperability with external web applications, EUscreen metadata are exported in EBUcore [5], which is an established standard in the area of audiovisual metadata. EBUCore has been purposefully designed as a minimum list of attributes to describe audio and video resources for a wide range of broadcasting applications including for archives, exchange and publication. It is also a Metadata schema with well-defined syntax and semantics for easier implementation. It is based on the Dublin Core to maximise interoperability with the community of Dublin Core users. EBUCore expands the list of elements originally defined in EBU Tech 3293-2001 for radio archives, also based on Dublin Core. The metadata is stored in RDF format to improve the search functionality and enable the alignment with external resources.

Finally, EUscreen has created a SKOS multilingual thesaurus (15 languages) based on the subject terms of IPTC standard and the geographical places of GeoNames. The thesaurus supports multilingual retrieval services and links to open data resources that could be used for enrichment and to contextualise the collection.

3.2 Video Playout

EUscreen requires content providers to provide MPEG 4 part 10 (normally known as H.264). EUscreen advises to encode in a bit rate between 500 and 1000 kb/sec, as this resembles SD quality video. Since the client playback method will be a Flash player with h.264 streaming, EUscreen demands that providers have streaming servers that are capable stream videos to a Flash client. In practice this means using one of the available Flash streaming servers.

This will leave room for the content providers themselves to add html5 or Silverlight server programs to create a 100% coverage of the possible technologies.

EUscreen supports four scenarios:

1. Content provider transcodes and files are hosted by service provider Noterik
2. Content provider transcodes and the content provider hosts
3. Noterik transcodes and Noterik hosts
4. Noterik transcodes, and the content provider hosts

3.3 The Mapping Tool

Metadata mapping is a crucial step of the ingestion procedure. It formalizes the notion of `crosswalk' by hiding technical details and permitting semantic equivalences to emerge as the centerpiece. It involves a graphical, web-based environment where interoperability is achieved by letting users create mappings between input and target elements. User metadata imports are not required to include the adopted XML schema. Moreover, the set of elements that have to be mapped are only those that are populated. As a consequence, the actual work for the user is easier, while avoiding expected inconsistencies between schema declaration and actual usage.

The structure that corresponds to a user's specific import is visualized in the mapping interface as an interactive tree that appears on the left hand side of the editor (Figure 3). The tree represents the snapshot of the XML schema that the user is using as input for the mapping process. The user is able to navigate and access element statistics for the specific import.

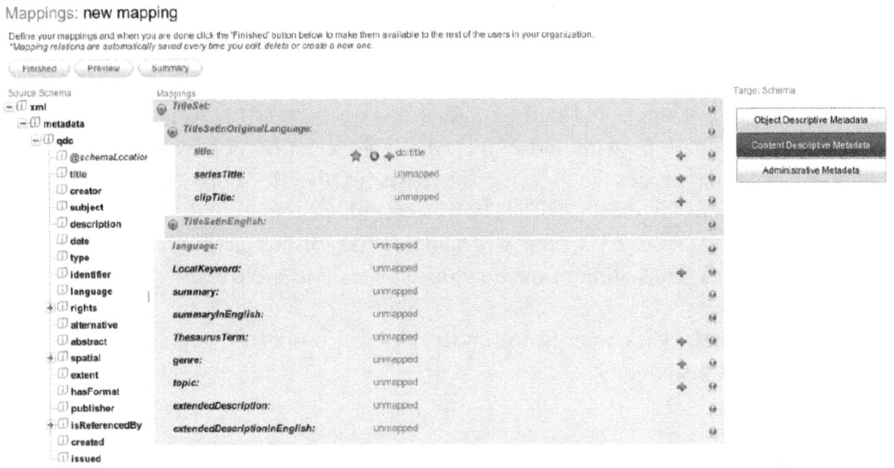

Fig. 3. Mapping Interface

The interface provides the user with groups of high-level elements that constitute separate semantic entities of the target schema. These are presented on the right hand side as buttons, which are then used to access the set of corresponding sub-elements. This set is visualized on the middle part of the screen as a tree structure of embedded boxes, representing the internal structure of the complex element. The user is able to interact with this structure by clicking to collapse and expand every embedded box that represents an element along with all relevant information (attributes, annotations) defined in the XML schema document. To perform an actual mapping between the input and the target schema, a user has to simply drag a source element and drop it on the respective target in the middle.

The user interface of the mapping editor is schema-aware regarding the target data model and enables or restricts certain operations accordingly, based on constraints for elements in the target XSD. For example, when an element can be repeated then an appropriate button appears to indicate and implement its duplication. User's mapping actions are expressed through XSLT stylesheets, i.e. a well-formed XML document conforming to the namespaces in XML recommendation. XSLT stylesheets are stored and can be applied to any user data, can be exported and published as a well-defined, machine understandable crosswalks and shared with other users to act as template for their mapping needs. Features of the language that are accessible to the user through actions on the interface include:

- string manipulation functions for input elements;
- 1-n mappings;
- m-1 mappings with the option between concatenation and element repetition;
- structural element mappings;
- constant or controlled value assignment;
- conditional mappings (with a complex condition editor);
- value mappings editor (for input and target element value lists).

4 Future Work

The first version of the portal will be launched in March 2011, followed by a period of extensive evaluations with end-users. Also, the selection policy will be reviewed. Outcomes of this process will form the basis of the development of the second release, scheduled for early 2012. The major enhancements will be related to the front-end. For instance, EUscreen will support the on-line creation of on so-called virtual exhibitions, consisting of media objects of various archives.

Acknowledgments. EUscreen is co-funded by the European Commission within the eContentplus Programme.

References

1. Isaac, A. (ed.) Europeana Data Model Primer. Europeana v1.0 Technical report (2010)
2. Scott, B.: Gordon Park's conversation theory: a domain independent constructivist model of human knowing. Foundations of Science 6(4), 343–360 (2001), National Center for Biotechnology Information, http://www.ncbi.nlm.nih.gov
3. Our Cultural Commonwealth: The report of the American Council of Learned Societies Commission on Cyberinfrastructure for the Humanities and Social Scences. American Council of Learned Societies (2006)
4. Kaye, L.: D3.1 Content Selection and Metadata Handbook (EUscreen 2011) (2011)
5. Evain, J.P. (ed.) EBU Core Metadata Set. EBU (2009)

Towards Artistic Collections Navigation Tools Based on Relevance Feedback

Daniele Borghesani, Costantino Grana, and Rita Cucchiara

Università degli Studi di Modena e Reggio Emilia
Via Vignolese 905/b - 41100 Modena
{daniele.borghesani,costantino.grana,rita.cucchiara}@unimore.it

Abstract. Artistic image collections are usually managed via textual metadata into standard content management systems. More sophisticated searches can be performed using image retrieval technologies based on visual content. Nevertheless, the problem of the information presentation remains. In this paper we try to move beyond the classic grid-styled presentation model, suggesting a novel use of relevance feedback as a navigation tool. Relevance feedback is therefore used to warp the view and allow the user to spatially navigate the image collection, and at the same time focus on his retrieval aim. This is obtained exploiting a distance based space warping on the 2D projection of the distance matrix. Multitouch gestures are employed to provide feedbacks by natural interaction with the system.

1 Introduction

The valorization of cultural heritage is probably one of the most interesting and useful applications of modern technologies of human-computer interaction and multimedia search. All the plurality of artistic masterpieces can live a complementary life through digitalization, which allows a significant reduction in management costs, an enormous expansion of public —therefore of money income— and, at the same time, a tremendous freedom of data elaboration, therefore a pleasure for the public and usefulness for experts.

One of the key aspects is the way in which information is presented, in other words how the results of a visual search, or an automatic classification based on content, is shown to users. This can constitute a significant gap between such systems and the final users, especially untrained ones. Instead an engaging user interaction design could impact positively on the success of these platforms, thus increasing the interest of people on the fruition of such artistic collection, with consequent positive spillovers on the culture, the society and the economy. Therefore, in this paper we are proposing an easy solution to solve this interface gap. Starting from a solid set of content analysis and indexing techniques (which can be eventually designed to fit the large scale requirements), we propose the relevance feedback not only as an effective tool to improve the raw performance of the retrieval system, but mainly as a mean to help the user navigating into

C. Grana and R. Cucchiara (Eds.): MM4CH 2011, CCIS 247, pp. 143–153, 2012.

the collection. In this way, we want to facilitate the user in the process of manipulation of the information: by visually surfing through images, the user can build connections and feel emotionally involved in the navigation experience, using the relevance feedback to warp the space around his needs, quickly learning the results content and possibly moving to a destination he did not even think about when he started.

Among the different forms of art, we focused our work on Renaissance illuminated manuscripts. Italy, in particular, has a significant collection of them, such as the *Bible of Borso d'Este* in Modena (which is currently the dataset considered in this work), the *Bible of Federico da Montefeltro* in Rome and the *Libro d'ore of Lorenzo de' Medici* in Florence. These masterpieces contain thousands of valuable illustrations with different mythological and real animals, biblical episodes, court life illustrations, and some of them even testify the first attempts in exploring perspectives for landscapes. For this reason, they represent a challenging dataset which allows testing the effectiveness of our proposal, not only in scientific terms (how a particular set of algorithms perform on these images) but also in "social" terms (how much interest this kind of multimedia application can gather). From now on, throughout the work, we will refer to illuminated manuscripts as the primary art collection form we are focused on.

The idea comes from the feedback we had about the project "Rerum Novarum" [1], a multimedia application we developed to enhance the fruition of artistic image collections, illuminated manuscripts in particular. Besides the combined use of visual search and relevance feedback to provide visually assisted tagging, people asked us a smart way to navigate the meaningful visual content, i.e. the pictures extracted by the illuminated pages. For this reason, we are proposing this novel interactive interface which aims at redefine the use of relevance feedback and image similarity for this kind of applications.

2 Background

The problem of image retrieval is two-fold. In the first place, we need fast and effective techniques to convey visual similarity to the user. In the second place, we need an effective technique to allow the user to manage the results.

Regarding the first problem, a great amount of literature has been proposed. Among it, we think that the natural choice is a global feature representation, providing a compact summary by aggregating some information extracted at every pixel location of the image. The bag-of-words approach, a global representation build of clustered local features like SIFT [2] or SURF [3] as a visual dictionary, is generally considered the state of the art. For a complete comparison of performance of local features in CBIR, please refer to [4]. Most of these local descriptors use luminance information only. Nevertheless, both color and shape are widely considered important visual characteristics in a cognitive context, so an interesting way to account this information is by using the *covariance region descriptor*, proposed by Tuzel *et al.* in [5], which aggregates the correlations of a custom amount of elementary sources of information (like color, shape, spatial information, gradients). Moreover, great interest was devoted to GIST feature, a statistical summary of the spatial layout properties (Spatial Envelope representation) of the scene [6].

To solve the second problem, a presentation strategy is required. The classical spatial arrangement of images is their placement on a grid, typically in row-major ordering based on relevance. Despite its simplicity, this visualization is unable to convey information on the structure of the collection, for example the availability of a cluster of similar images. As described in [7], alongside with more standard approaches based on static hierarchies or clustering, the main approaches are build around a network based or a dimensionality reduction based representations. Multi-Dimensional Scaling (MDS) solves a non linear optimization problem by determining the mapping that best approximates the high-dimensional pairwise distances between data points. One of the initial proposals was the Sammon mapping by [8]. An interesting proposal of this kind is the Hyperbolic-MDS by [9], which exploits the hyperbolic space $\mathbb{H}^2$ to map the most significant images in the center of the projection (thus visualizing them with a greater detail) while displacing the others along the curve $\mathbb{H}^2$ falling towards infinity with a smaller scale; moreover this projection has the advantage of allowing to focus the view in different points by applying the Möbius transformation. A number of other non-linear projections have been proposed to solve the prohibitive computational costs, for example the isometric mapping (ISOMAP) [10], the stochastic neighbor embedding (SNE) [11] and the local linear embedding (LLE) [12]. An older yet effective approach, especially in large scale contexts, is finally the FastMap [13] which exploits a set of pivot objects to project points in the reduced space. This technique, exploited also in this paper, has the advantage to allow easily a fast insertion of new objects within the map.

3 Rerum Novarum: Visually Assisted Tagging for Artistic Documents

Typically, the majority of the visual information retrieval systems follow the schema of Fig.1. Essentially, the system has a top-down design, and a professional effort (in terms of knowledge, documents and ontologies definition). It is necessary to provide the user with the full set of functionalities, potentially exploiting some image analysis and machine learning tools to facilitate the job. This authoritative experience of experts is used to create the annotated digital library (DL), often formalized as an ontology, that becomes the center of the application design. In this *content-centered* paradigm, the user has not got a real role of intervention inside the structure: he turns out to be a simple viewer of the retrieval results, having no real interaction with the system.

In this paper, we want to provide a more similar structure to the one in Fig.2. It is based on a *user-centered* paradigm, capable of putting together abilities, experiences and knowledge of different kinds of users, such as experts, art viewers, scholars and research communities. Instead of only assuming a static authoritative knowledge, needing a long and laborious work of visual data annotation,

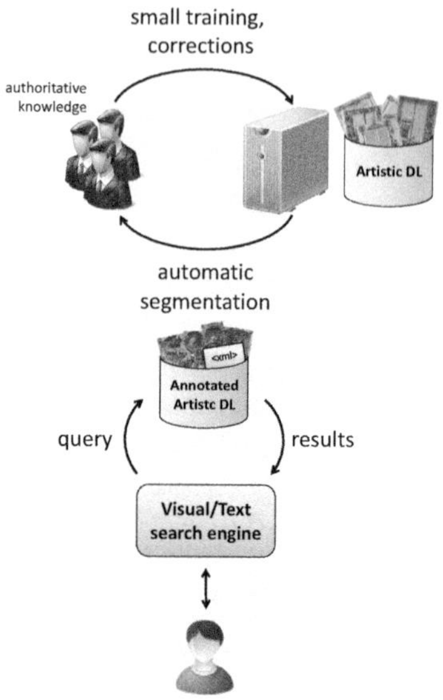

Fig. 1. The standard approach used in information retrieval systems. An expert personnel is required to include information of various nature into the system to allow the user to take advantage of proposed functionalities.

we exploit the search by visual similarity and relevance feedback to assist the process of tagging in a visual fashion, exploiting an engaging user interface.

In this context, Datta *et al.* in [15] proposed a very interesting classification of multimedia systems, based just on the user's intent, distinguishing three categories:

- *Browsing*: when the user's end-goal is not clear, the *browser* performs a set of possibly unrelated searches by jumping across multiple topics;
- *Surfing*: when the end-goal is moderately clear, the *surfer* follows an exploratory path aimed at increasing the clarity of what is asked of the system;
- *Searching*: when the end-goal is very clear, the *searcher* submits a (typically short) set of specific queries, leading to the final results.

In the traditional belief, these three modalities are implemented in a separate approach, which are necessary in order to differentiate the requirements of authoritative and personal experiences. On the contrary, we propose an accommodation of all of them in the same design, allowing surfing on visual and textual contents, without excluding more general browsing functionalities neither more accurate searches. Thus, according with the schema shown in Fig.2, the normal user or expert can begin his analysis by *browsing* the pages of the documents, correcting the automatic segmentation or including a manual one if necessary. Whenever a particularly interesting detail is retrieved, the user can propose a tag to the selected picture and continue the exploration interactively *surfing* by visual similarities. The system automatically answers with a set of similar pictures, which the user

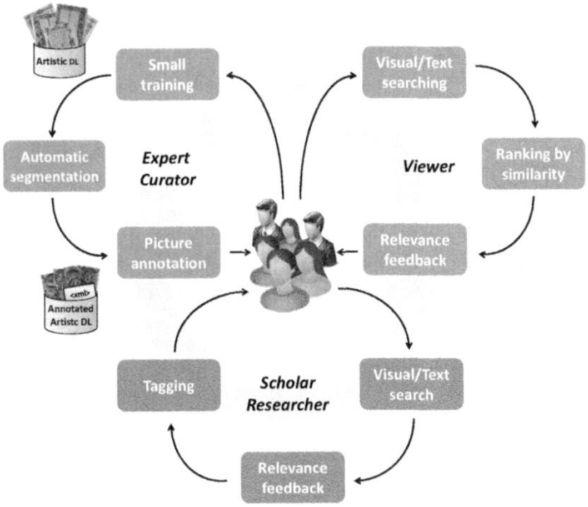

Fig. 2. Our user-centric approach. When the user is an expert, he can add his knowledge without the need of a structured representation (like tags or commentaries), and only a small subset of manually annotated training set (just some pages) is needed by the automatic segmentation [14]. When the user is a scholar or researcher, he can use the visual similarity and the relevance feedback to increase the amount of information of the system. When the user is a tourist, or an art lover, the system can be used as a simple information viewer, using the relevance feedback to improve the query results.

can further provide relevance feedback for. The results, marked by the user as similar, at the end may be given the same tags, so that the user will with minimal effort accomplish the otherwise demanding effort of tagging all pictures in the dataset when sharing the same visual content. In this manner the personal experience is inserted in the system by surfing and by visually assisted tagging. The tags, after a validation task if deemed necessary, become part of the collective experience: any user, art lover or researcher can so keep on analyzing the work by *searching*. Specific and reliable tags can finally give the system the possibility to filter out the visualized dataset, allowing the user to focus his attention on the sections of the work he is mainly interested on.

Basically, this is a virtuous loop in which the surfing through the artistic collection and the similarity search by visual content allows the extraction of similar pictures, i.e. pictures likely sharing the same tags; at the same time, tags will help the system to increase the embedded knowledge, and the user —while enjoying art— is facilitated on searching contents inside the artistic collection or filtering results by topic.

A very powerful analysis tool emerges by expanding this human-centered approach from a single artwork to a complete collection. The visual similarity can find meaningful results across different works. An efficient use of tags can be used to filter and organize documents and pictures across different art works. In this way, the user could have literally the entire collection in his hands (see Fig.3 to get an idea of the variety of pictures available in these collections). That's

Fig. 3. Some examples of pictures available in this collection. Notice that we are dealing with a lot of different visual concepts: symbols with particular iconographic meanings, portraits, animals, group of people depicted in natural environment or court scenes. The pictorial style of these handmade manuscripts increases the difficulty of retrieval.

the reason why we believe this approach may help in the creation of a "smart library", capable to adapt to the user's needs using efficient, yet very simple user interaction approaches.

4 Relevance Feedback for Image Surfing

The first task in image searching on large scale collections is clearly managing the scalability problem. Many techniques for approximated nearest neighbor (ANN) search, starting from the LSH [16] up to the product quantization [17], allow to greatly improve the performance using vocabulary codes (with pre-computed distances) in place of real features. Moreover image search based on contextual information (as done by all search engines) proves to be definitely effective. The real limitation of todays multimedia systems is within the interaction possibilities.

The most important way in which the user can help the system cross the semantic gap and interact with the retrieval results, i.e. the relevance feedback, becomes first of all prohibitive in large scale contexts. Just consider the usual approaches: query point movement, feature space warping or machine learning approaches [18]. The first one is not efficient enough, the second one requires a full space warping (thus a full space re-encoding for ANN, and no proposals at the best of our knowledge takes into account relevance feedback in such a context); finally the learning is notoriously a heavy procedure, often requiring an offline processing and hardly capable of producing real time results. Moreover, the relevance feedback is proposed to the user as a tedious procedure (as well as the annotation) to overcome the limitations of the system itself, which could be considered an admission of poor quality.

Nevertheless, the ability to guide the system towards the desired result needs to be considered as an important feature. The user himself implicitly demands this kind of capability, because visual similarity is mostly helpful when the user does not clearly know or is not capable of expressing the subject of his search: as a matter of facts if he could, he would type the precise query on the search engine. This is even more true when the user is approaching the image collection for fun or curiosity: in this scenario the user is mainly interested in surfing through pictures being guided by his emotional preferences. In the meantime, new and refined results could be suggested by the retrieval system, adjusting his search goal.

In order to satisfy all these requirements, we need to visualize the effect of relevance feedbacks from the original feature space into the two-dimensional mapping. This procedure allows the system to show to the user a real-time feedback of his manipulations, bringing him into the collection itself.

We need to provide the user with a first 2D visualization of his query results. The technique used in this step is FastMap, due to its high performance and the ability to quickly include new points to the map without recomputing the entire mapping. This algorithm briefly works as follows [13]. Firstly, two distant-enough objects are chosen with an heuristic approach. Given a distance function $\mathcal{D}()$ between each pair of objects O_a and O_b in the feature space, each object O_i is projected to object $O_i^{'}$ on the line joining the pivots (O_a, O_b) using the cosine law and obtaining the x coordinates. Then the y coordinate is computed using the distances $\mathcal{D}'$ on the hyperplane perpendicular to the line (O_a, O_b). These may be obtained from the original distance $\mathcal{D}$ by means of Eq.1:

$$\mathcal{D}^{'}\left(O_i^{'}, O_j^{'}\right)^2 = \mathcal{D}\left(O_i, O_j\right)^2 - \left(x_i - x_j\right)^2 \tag{1}$$

When the process is completed, the pictures are visualized on the two-dimensional plane adjusting the scale.

When a query O_q is selected by the user, the points are adjusted in order to support the similarity ranking. In particular the user requires a new projection which better reflects the distances from the query, thus the angle of points from the query is kept fixed, while the distance is scaled along the unit vector proportionally to the ranking itself. In this way, the similar pictures get closer to the query, while the dissimilar ones are moved away. At this point, the user is focused on the query itself (at the center of the screen) and the most similar content within the results is placed nearby, easily gathering his attention.

At this point, the user can provide feedbacks on the results, highlighting what he likes (being more similar to the query he submitted) and what he dislikes (being different from what he expects). For each point O_i in the results set, the system finds the nearest element of both positive and negative feedbacks sets (a process which can be eased up with approximate search) and warps the space. In particular, given f_p the distance from its nearest good feedback (including the query image) and f_n the distance from its nearest bad feedback, the system computes the distance for the projection $\mathcal{P}$ as:

$$\mathcal{P}(O_i, O_q) = \mathcal{D}(O_i, O_q)\left(1 + \frac{f_p - f_n}{\max(f_p, f_n)}\right) \tag{2}$$

The equation states that what is positive should be moved towards the query, while what is negative should be pushed away. The "positiveness" of an image is related to how much more similar to a positive than to a negative the image is. The images may now be ranked according the warped distances and the visualization is updated by moving the images along the line which connects the points to the query in the 2D plane. The new distances are ordered according to the ranking.

Compared with other relevance feedback approaches, this solution may perform worse with respect to the global recall or precision. The real merit, which becomes essential, regards the interface aspect: in fact the changes induced to the ranking are limited to the local neighborhood of the selected feedback element. In other words, only the points for which the feedback is the nearest positive or negative feedback are influenced, therefore a strong connection between the visual mapping and the observed changes appears. Moreover the use of a ranking based projection has the effect of showing the similar images slowly approaching the query, thus the user's attention focus.

The user is still allowed to move the images as he feels like, implicitly asking to prevent the image from being moved by the automatic positioning. Note that the distance calculations are always performed on the original distances, so removing a feedback allows to step back to the previous position: this is an easy way to "undo" the user's choices.

5 Interactive Relevance Feedback on Artistic Image Collections

We employ this technique to improve the browsing capabilities provided in the project "Rerum Novarum" [1], a multimedia application developed to enhance the fruition of artistic image collections, showcased in ACM Multimedia 2010. The system allowed to use visual search and relevance feedback to provide visually assisted tagging. Starting from the original digitalized pages of the Holy Bible of Borso d'Este, the system performs an automatic picture segmentation using the strategy described in [14,19,20], possibly followed by a manual refinement. At this point, we came out with a dataset of 2282 pictures. The visual descriptor used to represent those images was the covariance matrix a simple yet effective second order statistics descriptor, which allows to embed in a very compact form a wide range of visual information: color, texture, spatial distributions and correlations between both color and edge based information.

The user was able to interact with randomly selected images, in order to start exploring the image collection. We chose to follow a different approach: the user is presented with the 2D mapping of the images and allowed to zoom and navigate (Fig. 4(a)). After identifying an interesting image (Fig. 4(b)), the user selects it and the other images are rearranged to convey their distance in

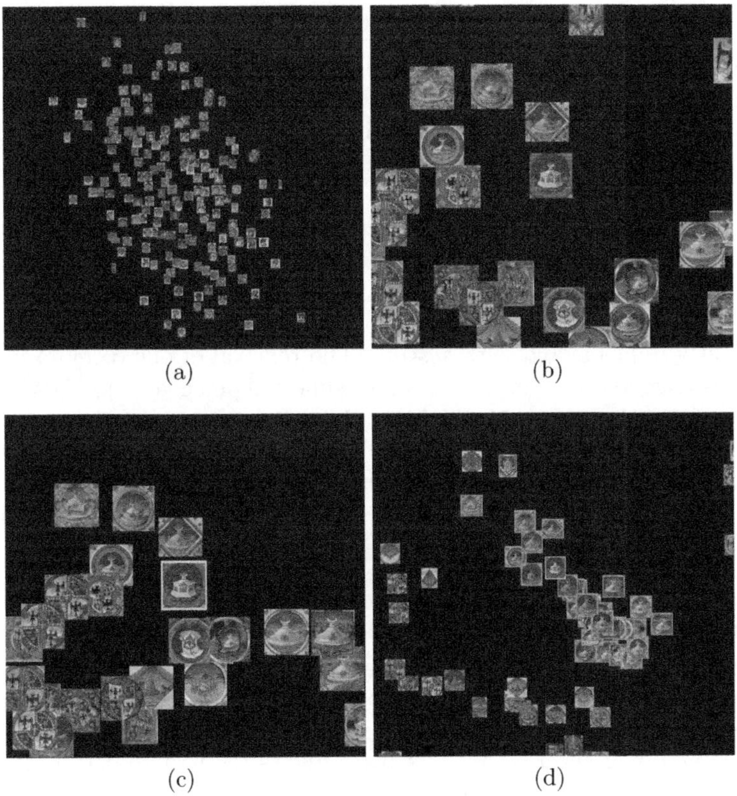

Fig. 4. Application example with the illuminated manuscript historical markings

the feature space from the selected query (Fig. 4(c)). This shows how well the 2D mapping is able to respect the original distance matrix. Now the user may simply select positive or negative samples, getting an immediate feedback of the effect of his choice on the mapping: selecting a negative feedback forces the image and some other neighbors to be pushed away and at the same time all the lower ranked image to be dragged toward the query. The selection of a positive feedback "recalls" images from outside the current view towards the query. A possible state is presented in Fig. 4(d).

6 Towards a Natural Interaction with Image Collections

The term *natural interaction* regards a human-computer interaction modality conveyed with means which are considered natural since they belong to the nature of human beings themselves [21]. The simpler and the more natural the machine interaction is, the less amount of cognitive effort is delegated to humans.

The aim of natural interaction is therefore the design of an interaction system able to getting rid of computer-friendly interaction paradigms (like windows, menus, scrollbars, mouses) towards more human-friendly paradigms. In this context, very important roles are played by concepts like aesthetic beauty, emotions and a playful dimension between the user and the system; moreover, an intensive use of animations and dynamic mathematical models is necessary in order to link the virtual interface with real life metaphors. Finally, the spatial organization of information is fundamental to improve content understanding, for example by clustering similar objects.

This proposal just moves towards this kind of interaction. The image collection is not only a list of images, but becomes a space to explore, reacting dynamically on the user's preferences collected continuously through relevance feedback. By exploiting a multitouch panel, the process of interacting with the system can be conveniently implemented with gesture. The removal of one or more undesired pictures is triggered with swipe gestures, while the pinch gesture allows to zoom the collection to focus on the individual pictures (or groups of pictures). Groups of good or bad feedbacks can be selected drawing circles around them. Once the collection has been filtered, according to the desired predominant visual characteristic, a tag could be associated to the resulting group of pictures, performing a visually assisted tagging.

7 Conclusions

In this paper we introduced a novel proposal for the presentation of image collections, obtained by querying or similarity search. We believe that the combined use of 2D mapping and relevance feedback allows the user to better express his querying intention, therefore easily surf through the results.

This technique, however much simple, could open a wide range of improvements of today's web search engines and image collections management software. For example, new results could be dynamically added to the mapping, based on the already selected images, thus formulating a new query based on the positive and the negative selections. Moreover, the visual similarity search can be exploited also to mine the not indexed content using positive feedbacks as suggested prototypes for the retrieval system. Finally, an interesting possibility is the exploitation of such an interactive experience to collect user provided information and therefore improving the retrieval system itself.

References

1. Grana, C., Borghesani, D., Cucchiara, R.: Surfing on artistic documents with visually assisted tagging. In: ACM Multimed., pp. 1343–1352 (2010)
2. Lowe, D.G.: Distinctive Image Features from Scale-Invariant Keypoints. Int. J. Comput Vision 60(2), 91–110 (2004)
3. Bay, H., Ess, A., Tuytelaars, T., Van Gool, L.: Speeded-Up Robust Features (SURF). Comput. Vis. Image Und. 110(3), 346–359 (2008)
4. Mikolajczyk, K., Schmid, C.: A performance evaluation of local descriptors. IEEE T. Pattern Anal. 27(10), 1615–1630 (2005)

5. Tuzel, O., Porikli, F., Meer, P.: Pedestrian Detection via Classification on Riemannian Manifolds. IEEE T. Pattern Anal. 30(10), 1713–1727 (2008)
6. Oliva, A., Torralba, A.: Building the gist of a scene: The role of global image features in recognition. Visual Perception, Progress in Brain Research 155 (2006)
7. Heesch, D.: A survey of browsing models for content based image retrieval. Multimed. Tools Appl. 40, 261–284 (2008)
8. Sammon, J.W.: A nonlinear mapping for data structure analysis. IEEE T. Comput. 18(5), 401–409 (1969)
9. Walter, J.A.: H-mds: a new approach for interactive visualization with multidimensional scaling in the hyperbolic space. Inform. Syst. 29(4), 273–292 (2004)
10. Tenenbaum, J.B., Silva, V., Langford, J.C.: A Global Geometric Framework for Nonlinear Dimensionality Reduction. Science 290(5500), 2319–2323 (2000)
11. Hinton, G.E., Roweis, S.T.: Stochastic neighbor embedding. Neu. Inf. Pro. Syst., 833–840 (2002)
12. Roweis, S.T., Lawrence, K.: Nonlinear dimensionality reduction by locally linear embedding. Science, 2323–2326 (2000)
13. Faloutsos, C., Lin, K.I.: Fastmap: a fast algorithm for indexing, data-mining and visualization of traditional and multimedia datasets. In: ACM SIGMOD International Conference on Management of Data, pp. 163–174 (1995)
14. Grana, C., Borghesani, D., Cucchiara, R.: Automatic segmentation of digitalized historical manuscripts. Multimedia Tools and Applications, 1–24 (July 2010)
15. Datta, R., Joshi, D., Li, J., Wang, J.Z.: Image retrieval: Ideas, influences, and trends of the new age. ACM Computer Surveys 40(2), 1–60 (2008)
16. Andoni, A., Indyk, P.: Near-optimal hashing algorithms for approximate nearest neighbor in high dimensions. In: IEEE Symposium on Foundations of Computer Science, pp. 459–468 (2006)
17. Jégou, H., Douze, M., Schmid, C.: Product quantization for nearest neighbor search. IEEE T. Pattern Anal. 33(1), 117–128 (2011)
18. Chang, Y., Kamataki, K., Chen, T.: Mean shift feature space warping for relevance feedback. IEEE Image Proc., 1849–1852 (2009)
19. Seidenari, S., Pellacani, G., Grana, C.: Computer description of colours in dermoscopic melanocytic lesion images reproducing clinical assessment. British Journal of Dermatology 149(3), 523–529 (2003)
20. Grana, C., Borghesani, D., Cucchiara, R.: Optimized block-based connected components labeling with decision trees. IEEE Transactions on Image Processing 19(6), 1596–1609 (2010)
21. Baraldi, S., Del Bimbo, A., Landucci, L., Torpei, N.: Natural interaction. In: Encyclopedia of Database Systems, pp. 1880–1885. Springer, US (2009)

Designing Virtual Reality Reconstructions of Etruscan Painted Tombs

Mirko Rao[1], Davide Gadia[1], Stefano Valtolina[1],
Giovanna Bagnasco Gianni[2], and Matilde Marzullo[2]

[1] Dip. Informatica e Comunicazione, Università degli Studi di Milano,
Via Comelico 39, 20135, Milano, Italy
{gadia,valtolin}@dico.unimi.it

[2] Dipartimento di Scienze dell'Antichità, Università degli Studi di Milano,
Via Festa del Perdono 7, 20122, Milano, Italy
giovanna.bagnasco@unimi.it, matilde@infinito.it

Abstract. The application of Virtual Reality technologies is becoming largely widespread in the Cultural Heritage field. Digital restorations, virtual reconstructions, interactive navigations, are just some of the possible applications. In this paper, we present a preliminary Virtual Reality reconstruction of the Etruscan painted Tombs in Tarquinia. Only a part of these tombs are open to the public: using Virtual Reality it could be possible to visit all the Necropolis, with the possibility to interact with the environment, and to visualize additional information.

The application has been designed in order to be modular and flexible. To test the application, we have used the Virtual Theater of the University of Milan, a Virtual Reality installation based on a large semi-cylindrical screen and passive stereoscopic visualization.

Keywords: Virtual Reality, Cultural Heritage, Virtual Reconstruction, Etruscan Tombs.

1 Introduction

The application of Virtual Reality (VR) technologies in the Cultural Heritage (CH) field has shown a relevant growth in the last years. In fact, the flexibility of VR allows archaeologists and historians to experiment with new approaches and validate different theories through simulations and digital reconstructions. The use of VR in the CH needs an intense interdisciplinary collaboration among IT (Information and Technology) and cultural experts for providing attractive environments that are also accurate from a scientific point of view. Each detail of the interactive VR simulations must be validated by the cultural experts, in order to avoid the diffusion of inaccurate and superficial information. On the other side, VR scientists can suggest new possible solutions to CH experts, on the basis of recent technological advances [1].

Archiving, reconstruction, restoration, interpretation, simulation, dissemination are the most used keywords related to the use of VR in the CH field. For

C. Grana and R. Cucchiara (Eds.): MM4CH 2011, CCIS 247, pp. 154–165, 2012.

example, VR has been effectively used for digital reconstruction of existing monuments [2], and for digital restoration of paintings [3]. By means of 3D modeling and animation, different interpretations and theories about the vestiges of the original places or monuments have been investigated [4–6].

By means of VR, it is often possible to offer students, scholars and tourists, an organic presentation of a CH site placed in in locations difficult to reach and hard to visit [7]. From this point of view, VR introduces new interaction patterns in the cultural context increasing its role in conservation, interpretation and dissemination of ancient cultures; however sometimes interaction patterns such as virtual devices are simply meant to assess historic or naturalistic objectives rather than introduce visitors to experience ancient cultures. To develop an environment where to share and exchange knowledge about a specific context of interest, it is crucial to enrich the VR visualization with additional information concerning the context in which the heritage was originally set. VR technologies are particularly useful to fulfil such goals because they make the integration of multifaceted information easy in an interactive and appealing way [8, 9]. Some researches have been already presented [1, 10–14] to investigate efficient integration of database technology for accessing contents from multiple digital archives of CH information.

In this paper, we present a preliminary version of a VR reconstruction of the Etruscan Necropolis of Tarquinia (UNESCO site since 2004), where a relevant number of painted tombs are present; however, not all of them are open to the public at the same time. Using VR, we have designed a modular and flexible application, in order to give an overview of the area with the location of the tombs, and to perform virtual visits enriched by the integration of additional materials currently stored in different cultural institutions.

Section 2 is meant to give some information about the Necropolis, and section 3 to present the details of the VR reconstruction and of the VR installation used to develop and test the application.

2 The Etruscan Necropolis in Tarquinia

The Necropolis of Tarquinia, together with that of Cerveteri, are UNESCO sites since 2004. In particular, Tarquinia is an outstanding testimonial of the Etruscan culture, with its 6.000 unearthed tombs cut in the rock among of which 140 are extraordinary painted. The earliest graves date from the 7th century BC. Most of them are made of a single room, while others are more articulated. Currently, 64 graves are accessible and some of them are protected by glass whereas others are open in rotation for visits.

The perception of the existence of the Necropolis goes back to the Renaissance, but the first findings were documented only in 1699. The most part of the painted tombs were discovered in the second half of 18th century. Across the centuries, many paintings were detached from the walls and were then lost or destroyed, others are currently not visible due to the fading of the original colors. In these cases our knowledge of these paintings is mainly based on descriptions and paintings made by artists and scholars in 17th and 18th centuries

[15]. It must be noticed that these copies present several differences when compared to the original ones: some elements and details were not considered, the overall style was often changed. Some of the differences have been caused by the insufficient knowledge among the artists of the Etruscan culture, some surely are due to the difficulty of painting at the light of fire torches. However, often these changes were introduced with precise reasons, for example to make the copies uniform with the stylistic canons of the current age, more familiar to the public. In fact, it must be considered that often these copies were made to be sold by art merchants.

In the proposed reconstruction of the Necropolis, we have implemented virtual navigations for the Tomb of Pygmies and the Tomb of Shields. 3D models and textures of these two tombs have been created by the archaelogists having access to the graves for research reasons. The 3D modeling of other tombs is currently in progress. The use of 3D models makes it possibile to appreciate and investigate the morphology of the architecture in its completeness, providing an opportunity to see every detail in relation to the rest of the architecture, allowing a full view of the monument in each of its components: walls, ceilings, floors, niches, furniture, dromos. Moreover, it allows to better understand the relationship between different paintings and their spatial context: 3D models give the opportunity to virtually travel within the hypogeum and to perceive visual pathways depending on the use of space in Etruscan times.

The Tomb of the Pygmies was discovered in 1961, and it is dated from 350-325 BC. It is made of only one room, and most of its paintings are currently lost. It is named after one of the few scenes still visible: a battle betweenpygmies and cranes.

The Tomb of the Shields, belonging to the Velcha family, was discovered in 1870, and it is dated from 350-300 BC. It is painted with scenes representing the members of the family and decorated shields that give the tomb its name. Their copies were drawn in 1871 by the painter Gregorio Mariani. Since 1900, watercolor paintings based on these drawings were commissioned to painters working for the Danish art collector and philanthropist Carl Jacobsen [15]. The drawings are currently conserved in Rome, while the paintings are now in the Museum of Art in Boston.

Subsection 3.2 describes the layout of drawings and paintings in the virtual navigation inside the Tomb of the Shields.

3 Virtual Reality Reconstruction of the Necropolis

The VR reconstruction of the Necropolis here implemented is based on a modular and flexible approach using separate modules, in order to handle a site composed by a large number of independent tombs. A main application is dedicated to the choice among currently reconstructed tombs, and independent applications are dedicated to virtual navigation inside selected tombs. Such an environment is already active even with a very limited number of reconstructed tombs. New completed modules can be easily linked at any time to the main application. Moreover, due to the complete independency of the applications, different developers can work to the reconstruction of different tombs at the same time, just relying on a template of the application.

Different choices are less effective, such as a full 3D reconstruction and integration of all the locations inside a unique application, because the necessary stage of measurement and acquisition of textures is not an easy and fast process: it must be performed accurately by personnel having access to the tombs, in accordance with maintenance works and visit hours. Therefore, it may take several months before having a 3D modeling and texturing of all the tombs, even limiting the process to the most relevant ones.

The applications have been developed using the open-source Processing environment [16]. Processing is an environment for the development of Computer Graphics and Multimedia applications, whose programming language is based on Java, extended with higher-level functions and libraries. For the development of the applications, we have used external open-source libraries for the loading of *Bing*™ satellite maps of the Necropolis area, and of the OBJ 3D models of the tombs.

We have decided to include stereoscopic visualization inside the VR reconstruction. Stereoscopic visualization simulates human binocular vision, allowing a more accurate simulation and perception of depth and distances of a virtual environment. If the visualization device used during the navigation has adequate sizes, it is possible to achieve a realistic depiction of measures between the real environment and its visualized simulation. We have developed and tested the applications inside a VR installation available at the University of Milan, characterized by a large projection screen. Therefore, we have implemented a Processing library for stereoscopic visualization using anaglyphic visualization or quad-buffer technology. In subsection 3.3 we will describe the VR installation and we will give some details about the hardware requirements of the applications.

In the following subsection we will give also further details on the applications.

3.1 Main Application

The main application is based on a menu enabling to choose among available reconstructed tombs: it loads a satellite map of the Necropolis area, and shows the reconstructed tombs that are available in blue circles on the map. Moving the mouse cursor over the circles, the names of the tombs appear on the screen. Clicking over a circle, the main application is closed, and the chosen virtual navigation of the tomb is triggered. All of the functionalities of the satellite map website are still available inside the application: it is thus possible to zoom and move around the area. This is important, because the tombs in the Necropolis are very near to each other, and when they will be all reconstructed, the map will be quite crowded of blue circles.

Fig. 1. The interactive map of the Necropolis (left) and loading screen after the selection of a tomb (right)

Besides the above mentioned reasons related to modularity, we decided to use this approach also because it helps in studying the geographical location of painted tombs: by using an interactive map, it is possible to understand the actual spatial location of the tombs over the whole area of the hill used as a necropolis. This helps in assessing the use of space in relation to its history and in investigating the dissemination of tombs according to style of paintings and type of architecture. A screenshot of the main application with the indication of the available tombs is shown on the left in Fig. 1.

Adding a new reconstruction of a tomb to the main application is very easy, and it does not need to change the code of the application. In fact, the main application reads the information about the available tombs from an external configuration file. To add a new tomb, it is only needed to add some lines of text: the name of the tomb, the coordinates of the tomb in the map, and the relative path to the executable file of the new application.

3.2 Virtual Navigation of the Tombs

In a 3D reconstruction of an environment, the first and most important stage is the acquisition of data to be used inside a 3D modeling and texturing tool. The data can be obtained both with laser scanner technology or with traditional measuring systems.

While the laser scanner technology is excellent to retrieve measures and distances, the philological interpretation of the relationship between architectural features of the tombs and paintings can only be assessed through traditional measuring systems that can be better controlled and implemented by the archaeologist's eye [15], in order to enhance the cultural value which is the aim of the present project, as will be explained afterwards. This is the reason why we take advantage of the models and textures of the Etruscan tombs created by the archaeologists having access to the site.

Accurate sessions of photographic acquisition were carried out for the creation of textures used for the reproduction of the paintings. Many samples were acquired of each area that compose the inside of the tombs, to give evidence of the state of conservation not only of the painted walls, but also of the floors and ceilings. The accuracy of this process enriches the virtual navigation, allowing to appreciate the various details of the Etruscan frescoes: brush marks, graffiti, use of cord soaked in color to create the meshes of regular geometric figures, the deterioration of paints, etc... As a consequence, the final result depends mainly on the accuracy of this process, that could be more difficult because of the characteristics of the site, e.g. limited accessibility, presence of maintenance works or rubble, lack of light, etc. Even if experience leads to a more efficient and faster process, this stage is surely time-consuming [17].

In this paper we are focusing on an organized presentation of the tombs inside the Necropolis area, and a fruition of the reconstructed environments. As stated in section 2, currently the 3D models and textures of the Tomb of the Shields and of the Tomb of the Pygmies are available. Other sessions for the acquisition of measures and images of other tombs are currently in progress.

After the selection of a tomb from the main application, the models and textures are loaded. This process may take some time according to the quality of the selected textures. During the loading stage, some information and pictures about the tomb are shown (an example is shown on the right in Fig. 1).

The virtual navigation, based on a first-person point of view approach, starts at the entrance of the tomb. The virtual camera is placed at a height of 1.7 meters from the floor, but this parameter could be changed by editing the external configuration file.

The user can virtually walk inside the environment by using mouse and keyboards (more advanced interaction devices can be supported in the future).

It is possible to enhance the visitors experience and education suggesting a walk-through of the monument including the perception of the architectural structure and of any detail giving information about the ritual use of space in the Etruscan age. This could also help in avoiding the risk of misleading anachronistic and spectacular modern approaches.

In case of visualization in a multi-user environment (like e.g. a theater room), a single user will be in charge of controlling the virtual navigation. It must be considered that her/his personal choice can affect the other users experience. However, in some cases (for example, if this person is an expert or an archaeologist) this situation may be useful for a better presentation of the virtual experience.

In the virtual navigation, to avoid trespassing walls, a map of the floor of the tomb (obtained during the measurement sessions on the site) is used to determine the walkable areas inside the virtual environment. With this technique, the user can move from room to room only through really doors and passages. At the bottom-left corner of the VR visualization, a map is placed to show the user's position in the VR scene.

One problem we had to solve was how to illuminate the virtual tombs. In the real environments there is no natural light: some artificial lights are placed inside the tombs, controlled by a switch timer, during tourists visits. Inside the tombs there are signs of smoke on the walls, and therefore it was suggested that probably fire torches were used when needed to illuminate the environments. Some studies are currently ongoing about the placement of these torches, and whether their use and position might have had some importance during ritual activities.

In our simulation, considering the main purpose of the application, i.e. cultural dissemination, we have decided not to place light sources on the walls of the tombs, leaving this question open for future works and virtual simulations. We have then decided to link the virtual illumination source inside the simulation to the virtual camera. Therefore, while moving inside the tomb, the light changes, following the virtual observer, like if she/he was wearing a hard hat with a light. To have a realistic effect, we have introduced an attenuation parameter in order to decrease the intensity of light when the distance from the virtual camera increases. In Fig. 2 we show two views of the virtual navigations inside the Tomb of the Shields and the Tomb of the Pygmies.

In section 2, we have already mentioned drawings and paintings of the original scenes on the walls of the Tomb of the Shields made by artists during 18th century [15] and nowadays stored in different cultural institutions. In the virtual navigation of this tomb, we have introduced the possibility, by pressing a key, to visualize these additional materials, superimposed on the original walls of the tomb. In Fig. 3 we show some views of the drawings and paintings placed over the original frescos of the Tomb of the Shields.

Therefore the 3D model allows a visual comparison between the ongoing situation of the paintings of the tomb and its copies placed in their right position, produced since the date of the discovery. It is also possible to spatially place objects or documents stored in museums or institutions elsewhere in the world.

These examples show the potentiality of VR as a cultural dissemination tool, allowing a synergy between different sources of information not available in reality. Textual or audio description of the origin of these paintings may be added to enhance the level of the virtual experience. Additional material to be included in the visualization is retrievable from networks of digital archives of information developed in the previous project T.Arc.H.N.A. [1, 10, 11, 14].

Finally, by exiting the virtual navigation, the application will close and the main application will be launched again, making possible to start a tour in another available reconstruction.

Implementing applications for the visit inside other tombs necessarily needs some development and testing, therefore the process will not be as easy and fast as the above mentioned integration of new tombs in the main application menu. However, the implementation process will surely have benefits by using the two currently available simulations as application templates. In fact, the implementation of a virtual navigation of a tomb similar to the Tomb of the Pygmies (characterized by simple geometry, and without additional material to integrate in the visualization) would be very fast: the code used for the Tomb of the Pygmies can simply be adapted by loading the new model and textures, and tuning some visualization parameters. For more complex environments, in which

Fig. 2. A view of the Tomb of the Pygmies (top) and of the Tomb of the Shields (bottom)

it is necessary the integration and visualization of other cultural information, more time will be needed. However, many implementation choices and details from the Tomb of the Shields can be reused in the new applications.

3.3 Hardware Requirements and Flexibility

The application was tested inside the Virtual Theater of the University of Milan [18], a multi-user VR installation, characterized by a semi-cylindrical screen with height 2.70 m, radius 3 m, and arc length 8 m. The projection system of the Virtual Theater is composed by four high resolution Barco Sim 5Plus projectors with built-in *INFITEC*^{TM} filters for passive stereoscopic visualization. The resolution of the projected images is 2416 x 1050 pixels. From an observation distance of 3.5 m, the field of view involved by the visualization is 120° horizontally and 90° vertically. An image of the Virtual Theater is shown on the left in Fig. 4. Real-time rendering in the Virtual Theater is computed on a quad-core HP XW9300 workstation with a *NVIDIA Quadro*^{TM} FX5500 graphic board, equipped with quad-buffer technology.

The characteristics of the Virtual Theater allow a realistic depiction of measures and distances of the original environments, giving as result a very immersive experience in the visualization and navigation inside the virtual reconstruction. An image of the visualization of the Tomb of the Shields reconstruction inside the Virtual Theater is shown on the right in Fig. 4.

Fig. 3. Watercolor paintings and drawings visualized over the original frescos in the Tomb of the Shields

A VR installation with the same characteristics of the Virtual Theater is probably not compatible with a normal museum budget. However, the VR application was designed in order to be as flexible as possible, in order to allow visualization and navigation on different hardware settings. Therefore, it is possible to arrange a visualization and navigation setup on the basis of different available budgets, ranging from a multi-user room to a single-user workstation.

First of all, the application is cross-platform, being the Processing programming language based on Java. As a consequence, it could run on different operating systems (proprietary or non-proprietary).

Fig. 4. The Virtual Theater of the University of Milan (left) and the application projected on the semi-cylindrical screen (right). The user controlling the navigation is not shown in the picture.

Moreover, different versions of the textures were prepared, and it is possible to choose their quality by changing a parameter in the external configuration file. Therefore, by choosing a lower resolution of the final rendering, and an adequate quality of the textures, the application can be adapted to run on machines with different computational power.

From the visualization point of view, the implemented library supports two stereoscopic visualization options: quad-buffer technology, and anaglyphic technique.

The first option needs a high-level, expensive, graphic board, and it is usually adopted in large VR installation like the Virtual Theater. It gives the best visualization quality and resolution, and it is easy to use from the development point of view. The second technique is instead based on the application of color filters to the right and left views of a stereoscopic image, and it does not need any particular technology, but just a standard display and cheap anaglyphic glasses. The visual quality is quite low, with an evident colors distortion. The anaglyphic effect is not difficult to create: it needs some elaborations on the original color signals of the frames. However, other different technologies for stereoscopic visualization are currently available, with different costs and characteristics; thus, it is possible to choose the best solution on the base of the available budget.

In any case, the library allows also to adopt a classic monocular visualization, and it can be extended with other stereoscopic visualization techniques.

4 Conclusions and Future Works

In this paper, we have presented a Virtual Reality reconstruction of the Etruscan Tombs in Tarquinia. The application allows to choose between available reconstructed tombs, whose location is visualized in a satellite map of the Necropolis area. The navigation inside the virtual tombs is based on a first-person point of view approach, using stereoscopic visualization for an immersive perception of the distances and measures. By means of VR technologies, it is possible to integrate in the simulation additional materials such as drawings and paintings made in the 18th century, currently conserved in different places around the world. The application was tested inside the Virtual Theater, a Virtual Reality installation available at the University of Milan.

The VR application presents virtual navigations inside two tombs (Tomb of the Pygmies and Tomb of the Shields), using 3D models of the environments created by the archaeologists having access to the site. The overall design of the VR reconstruction of the Necropolis has been created in order to be modular and flexible, allowing a fast development of new modules.

Currently, 3D modeling of other tombs is in progress, and as soon as this stage will be completed, new virtual navigations will be developed and integrated in the main application.

Moreover, we will also integrate new stereoscopic visualization techniques in the implemented Processing library, in order to allow more flexibility in the possible choices of the visualization setup.

Finally, we will perform an user evaluation of the presented application considering both experts and non-expert users.

Acknowledgements. This work has been partly funded by project T.Arc.H.N.A. (Towards Archaeological Heritage New Accessibility) under the EC-grant No 2004-1488/001-001, CLT-CA22 (CULTURE2000), 2004-2007.

References

1. Bagnasco Gianni, G.: Archaeology as research engine in the field of cultural heritage. In: Bridging Archaeological and Information Technology Culture for Community Accessibility, Milan, pp. 39–45 (2007)
2. Levoy, M., Pulli, K., Curless, B., Rusinkiewicz, S., Koller, D., Pereira, L., Gintzon, M., Anderson, S., David, J., Ginsberg, J., Shade, J., Fulk, D.: The Digital Michelangelo Project: 3D Scanning of Large Statues. In: Proceedings of ACM SIGGRAPH 2000, pp. 131–144. ACM, New York (2000)
3. Barni, M., Pelagotti, A., Piva, A.: Image processing for the analysis and conservation of paintings: opportunities and challenges. IEEE Signal Processing Magazine 22(5), 141–144 (2005)
4. Guidazzoli, A., Delli Ponti, F., Diamanti, T., Sangiorgi, L., Cirifino, F.: Daily Life in the Middle Ages - Parma in the Cathedral Age. In: ACM SIGGRAPH 2007 Posters, p. 125. ACM, New York (2007)
5. Magnenat-Thalmann, N., Foni, A., Papagiannakis, G., Cadi-Yazli, N.: Real Time Animation and Illumination in Ancient Roman Sites. The International Journal of Virtual Reality 6(1), 11–24 (2007)
6. Baracchini, C., Brogi, A., Callieri, M., Capitani, L., Cignoni, P., Fasano, A., Montani, C., Nenci, C., Novello, R.P., Pingi, P., Ponchio, F., Scopigno, R.: Digital reconstruction of the Arrigo VII funerary complex. In: Proceedings of the 5th International Symposium on Virtual Reality, Archaeology and Cultural Heritage (VAST), pp. 145–154 (2004)
7. Ruiz, R., Weghorst, S., Savage, J., Oppenheimer, P., Furness, T.A., Dozal, Y.: Virtual Reality for Archeological Maya Cities. Presented at UNESCO World Heritage Conference, Mexico City (2002)

8. Vlahakis, V., Ioannidis, N., Karigiannis, J., Tsotros, M., Gounaris, M.: Virtual Reality and Information Technology for Archaeological Site Promotion. In: Proceedings of 5th International Conference on Business Information Systems (BIS), Poland, pp. 24–25 (2002)
9. Gaitatzes, A., Christopoulos, D., Roussou, M.: Reviving the past: cultural heritage meets virtual reality. In: Proceedings of the 2nd International Symposium on Virtual Reality, Archaeology and Cultural Heritage (VAST), pp. 103–110 (2001)
10. Valtolina, S.: Design of Knowledge Driven Interfaces in Cultural Contexts. International Journal on Semantic Computing (Special Issue on Human Centric Communications) 2(4), 525–553 (2007)
11. Valtolina, S., Franzoni, S., Mazzoleni, P.: Building Knowledge Networks Using Panoramic Images. International Transactions on Systems Science and Applications 6(4), 317–325 (2010)
12. Bertino, E., Franzoni, S., Mazzoleni, P., Valtolina, S., Mussio, P.: Integration of Virtual Reality and Database Systems for Cultural Heritage Dissemination. International Journal of Computational Science and Engineering (IJCSE) 2(5/6), 307–316 (2006)
13. Valtolina, S.: View What You Want How You Want: Combining Database Systems and Customizable Virtual Reality Techniques in Cultural Context. In: International Conference on Virtual Systems and Multimedia Dedicated to Digital Heritage (VSMM 2008), pp. 317–324 (2008)
14. Valtolina, S.: The T.Arc.H.N.A. System as a Model of Accessibility to Cultural Heritage. T.Arc.H.N.A.: Bridging Archaeological and IT Culture for Community Accessibility, pp. 61–69. L'Erma di Bretschneider, Milan (2007)
15. Bagnasco Gianni, G., Marzullo, M., Perego, L.: La tomba del Tifone: effetti speciali etruschi. In: Atti del Convegno Diavoli goffi con bizzarre streghe (2009) (in press)
16. Processing homepage (April 2011), `http://www.processing.org`
17. Stinson, P.: Technical and Methodological Problems in Digital Reconstructions of Archaeological Sites: the Studiolo in the House of Augustus and cubiculum 16 in the Villa of the Mysteries. In: UT NATURA ARS. Virtual Reality e archeologia. Studi e Scavi, vol. 22, pp. 71–79. University Press, Bologna (2001)
18. Virtual Theater homepage (April 2011),
`http://eidomatica.dico.unimi.it/theather.php`

A Case Study for the Development of Methods to Improve User Engagement with Digital Cultural Heritage Collections

Maristella Agosti, Giordana Mariani Canova,
Nicola Orio, and Chiara Ponchia

University of Padua, Italy
{maristella.agosti,giordana.mariani.canova,nicola.orio}@unipd.it,
chiara.ponchia.1@studenti.unipd.it

Abstract. The aim of this paper is to report the results of an ongoing project that deals with the exploitation of a digital archive of drawings and illustrations of historic documents for research and educational purposes. A prototype system, called IPSA (Imaginum Patavinae Scientiae Archivum), has been developed and is currently used as a case study to provide innovative tools for researchers and scholars active in the preservation and dissemination of cultural heritage. After describing the initial user requirements that motivated the development of IPSA, we focus on the research questions that can be addressed by new system functions and on its extension to additional user groups, including students, experts in other domains, and the general public.

1 Introduction

The ideas and concepts reported in this paper build upon our experience on the analysis of the user requirements, the design of a methodology, the development of a prototype system, and the analysis of the feedback from real users of a digital archive of historical material. The archive aims at the study and research on *illuminated manuscripts*, i.e. usually handwritten books which include illustrations and which in past centuries were manually and artistically decorated. Illuminated manuscripts are the subject of scientific research in different areas, namely the history of art and the history of science, and all disciplines related to the subject of the book – e.g. botany, astronomy, medicine [1]. Before the invention of photography, illuminated manuscripts played a central role in the dissemination of scientific culture, and to this end they bear witness to the heritage of different cultures, in Europe, Asia, and in the countries under the influence of Arab culture.

The digital archive of illuminated manuscripts that has been developed within our research activities is called *IPSA*, which stands for *Imaginum Patavinae Scientiae Archivum* (archive of images of the Paduan science) [2,3]. This is because the main focus of our initial project was to provide a tool for the analysis of the role played by the Paduan school during the Middle Ages and the Renaissance

C. Grana and R. Cucchiara (Eds.): MM4CH 2011, CCIS 247, pp. 166–175, 2012.

in the spread of the new scientific method in difference sciences, from medicine to astronomy to botany.

IPSA can also be considered as a case study for our research on methodologies and tools for researchers and scholars working on the analysis, preservation and dissemination of cultural heritage. After a number of years of usage by scholars and students, we started a new phase of recollection of user requirements, with a focus on the *research questions* that can be addressed by an improved systems. To this end, our aim is to provide innovative services to improve user engagement with digital cultural heritage collections.

The final goal of this new phase of our work is to exploit the experience gained over the years both in the design and development of systems that manage digital cultural heritage metadata [4,5] and collections [6,7], and in the usage of multimedia digital archives in order to address new requirements that become evident only after the system has been extensively used as a research tool.

The paper is divided in two parts. The first part describes the initial requirements and development of the actual working system that meets them. The second part introduces our ongoing research on additional user requirements, in the form of research questions related to the disciplines involved in the study of illuminated manuscripts.

2 IPSA Motivations and Objectives

The development of models and tools for researchers and scholars in the area of illuminated manuscripts requires a careful analysis of user requirements [8]. As it turned out from the analyses, the requirements for carrying out scientific research will be more complex and articulated than requirements for final users. Final users access an image digital archive to acquire information in a given field, researchers access the archive to disclose knowledge and discover new relationships between digital objects.

Instead of limiting the analysis to a number of interviews, our approach was to create a research team, where computer scientists and scholars in history of art collaborate. Additional contributions from scholars in related disciplines, such as history of science, botany, astronomy, have been integrated as well and formalized in a draft proposal that has been presented and discussed with research users. A similar approach has been maintained during the development of the prototype system, because all the novel functionalities have been directly tested by members of the research team.

Main results of this initial study are summarized in the following sections. The interested reader can gain further and general information by accessing the Web site that has been developed to document both the projects which have made possible the design and development of IPSA and the managed digital cultural heritage collection[1].

[1] URL: `http://www.ipsa-project.org/`

2.1 Disclosure of Relations between Images and Manuscripts

Scholars in history of miniature are mostly interested in analyzing images, their style, their elements and possible relations with other images belonging to different manuscripts. In particular, it is of primary importance for researchers to discover whether illustrations have been copied from images of other manuscripts, merely inspired by previous works, or directly inspired by nature. A major requirement thus regards the possibility of enriching the digital archive by highlighting explicit relations that have been discovered by a researcher. The analysis of user requirements highlighted a number of issues that are of particular relevance.

- *Authorship*: The definition of a relation between two or more images depends on the scientific results of a researcher, who owns the intellectual rights of this additional knowledge.
- *Typology*: Since two images or two manuscripts can be related for a number of different reasons, the kind of relations should be explicitly expressed.
- *Paths*: Relations may form *historical paths* among images, because images in a manuscript can be copies of another one which in turn are copies themselves of previous illustrations.

These requirements suggested the use of annotations that allow the scholars to connect two manuscripts or two images. These annotations, which have been called *linking annotations*, have a type which describes the kind of relations between the two objects and provides a semantic to the link. We proposed a taxonomy for linking annotations [2] which is divided in two classes, including annotations that express either hierarchical or relatedness links. Annotations have been developed and integrated within the digital archive according to the formal model described in [9].

2.2 Personalization and Collaboration

Almost every digital archive dynamically changes over the years, because of new acquisitions that increase the number of documents and because of changes or redefinition of the descriptive records. In particular, the study of the digital archive content produces new knowledge that, apart from being disseminated through scientific publications, can be represented within the archive itself.

This novel information, which is due to original results, should be stored in the digital archive at a different level than the information based on a general consensus. To this end, both classical textual annotations and the proposed linking annotations can be a viable tool providing that a user is able to state which annotations can be shared with the community or his research group, and which ones have to remain private. Such a mechanism allows scholars to use the digital archive as an advanced research tool, which reflects their personal view of the collection of manuscripts, as well as protect their intellectual rights.

Scholars' annotations on the archive, besides being a means of personalization, can be exploited to foster collaboration. It has to be noted that illuminated manuscripts are of interest to both the historian of art and the historian of science, but at the same time, a herbal is of interest to the botanist because they represent plants and their possible variations through the centuries, a codex is useful for researchers on the evolution of civil and criminal laws, an astrological book may give insights to researchers in medicine on the way stars where perceived to influence the health of people and to astronomers on how constellations where seen and represented. Hence, the scientific research on illuminated manuscripts involves a number of persons with different expertise, which should be able to cooperate in order to share their different knowledge and background.

A digital archive of illuminated manuscripts has to provide a collaborative environment, such as in [10], where researchers should be able to interact and give different contributions to the definitions and redefinitions of objects in the manuscript. For this reason, different levels of users of the archive need to be considered. Apart from the administrators, the group of research users should be able to modify the records of the underlying database when new features of the stored objects are discovered.

3 Development of IPSA

A prototype implementing the proposed methodology has been developed. The close collaboration within a single team of researchers and scholars of all the disciplines involved allowed us to create a closed loop for evaluation, testing and refinement of the different functionalities. Once the underlying database structure had been designed and developed, the organization of the user interface and the development of the novel functionalities highlighted by the user requirements were done incrementally, with scholars in history of art starting to populate the archive and studying the collection of images during the refinement of the software tools.

Figure 1 shows the search page of the IPSA prototype, which is text-based using available metadata, because content-based search was not part of the user requirements. This means that metadata, especially in the form of annotations, should provide information about the visual similarity of the images as well, which – according to the interviewed scholars – can be stated only by an expert.

Figure 2 shows the selection of an image from the results. As usual, information and metadata about the image are reported. Moreover, the image can be explored and navigated. Only a small part of the complete image can be visualized at high resolution, and this is done through a proprietary Java application. Finally, the user is also presented with the annotations of the link the retrieved image to other images.

The prototype of IPSA has been used as a research tool by scholars in the history of art in our team. An effort of dissemination has been made to present it to other researchers in Italy and Europe, through a number workshops and presentations in the research area of illuminated manuscripts.

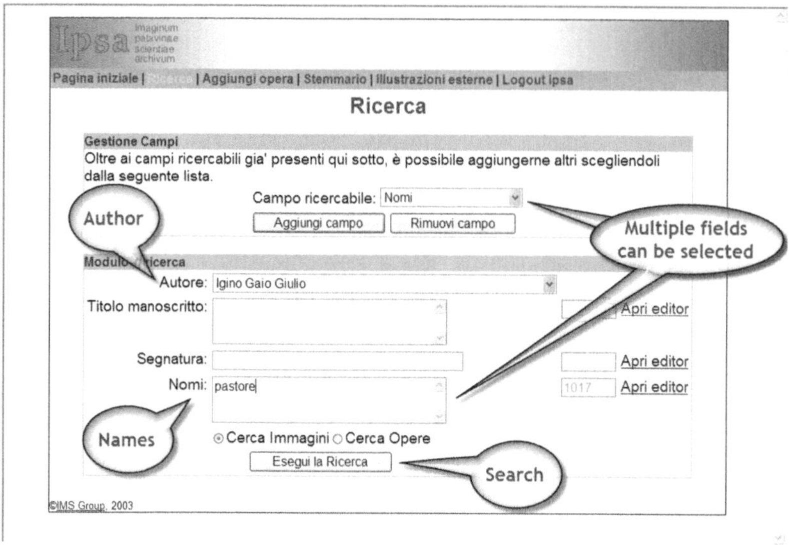

Fig. 1. Search functionalities in IPSA

4 Improving User Engagement

Building from the experience in using the actual version of the prototype, the next step in our ongoing project was to study how to extend its functions to develop it as an education and dissemination tool. At the same time, we wanted to elaborate on actual functionalities to address a number of *research questions*, which can be addressed by automatic tasks to help scholars to discover new knowledge. In this study process, IPSA can be considered as a sort of *case study* to be used to learn new ways of using and extracting information of interest from new categories of users. A further step will be to generalize the findings of this case study to similar digital cultural heritage collections and applications.

5 Research Questions

Using IPSA as a new starting point to develop tools for researchers in illuminated manuscripts, we begun a new analysis of requirement on the *research questions* that should be addressed by a digital archive. The analysis has been carried out on a focused group of scholars and professional users, including professors in the history of illumination, in the history of medieval art, and experts in digitized manuscripts.

The initial results of this ongoing study highlighted some priorities. The research questions described in Section 5.1 confirm the results of our initial analysis of requirements, introducing additional concepts to refine the existing tools.

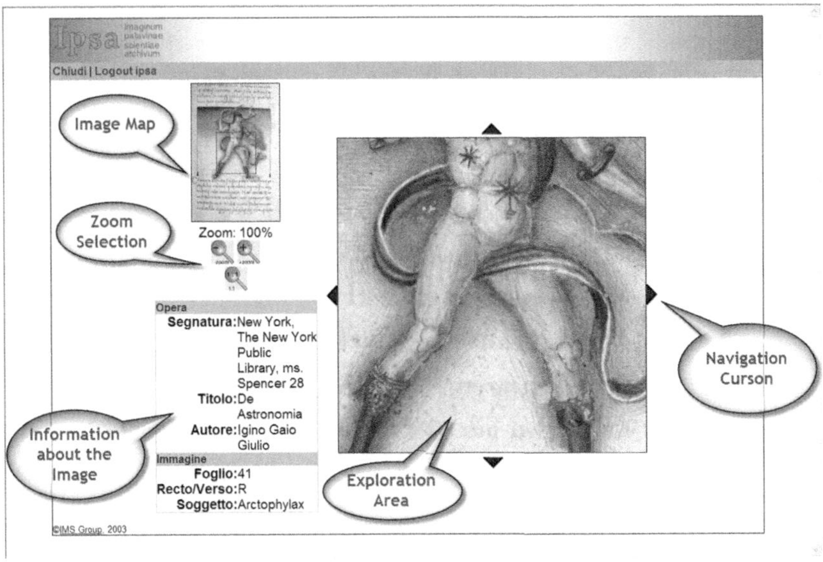

Fig. 2. User interface of IPSA for the analysis of images

The research questions that are described in the subsequent sections are novel, and we believe that the possibility of using IPSA as a research prototype helped the user group to highlight them more clearly.

5.1 Relations between Images

The user group underlined that images are the main subject of scientific research on illuminated manuscripts. Text surrounding the image is important as well, as described in Section 5.3, yet it has to be noted that in many cases the author of a manuscript copied the text of pre-existing manuscripts, while the illustrator added original drawings. These drawings can be copied, with some modifications, from previous images, or just be inspired by them.

Thus an image, besides being relevant because of its intrinsic artistic value, becomes of particular interest because of its relations with other images. The first research question regards the possibility of *following the development of illustrations of a specific text*, that is to track the evolution of iconography of the subjects described in a text, stating where changes have been applied by illustrators and which were their references while drawing images for a text.

At the same time, it is of interest the study on the representation of a specific subject, leading to a second research question that regards the possibility of *following the evolution of the images describing a specific subject*. Also in this case, it is important to state which were the references for illustrators and whether they copied or be inspired by previous drawings, which may be surrounded by different text.

The actual version of IPSA already supports an annotation mechanism that partially addresses these questions. In particular, linking annotations can be used to represent relations between images, while their type describes the kind of relations. Yet, a third research question regards the possibility of *expressing in detail the research results that motivate a relation.* This additional requirement regards the possibility of including textual annotations that describe the considerations for expressing a relation between images.

It is interesting to note that, although most of the research is carried out by analyzing images, also in this case the user requirements did not highlight the need of tools for the automatic computation of visual similarity. It has to be noted that scholars normally have a complete knowledge of the domain they are studying, and they are not used to count on automatic tools to discover relations between images. It is likely that non expert users could take advantage from automatic tools, although the extension to other user categories will be part of future work and it is not covered by this contribution.

5.2 Exploitation of External Resources

A second group of research questions regarded the relations between the content of the archive and external collections. Illustrators could be inspired by manuscripts that are part of other collections but also by other art forms of the same historical period. For example, a drawing can be derived from a painting, a fresco or from illuminated manuscripts with a different subject (for instance religious manuscripts are not included in the collection managed by IPSA). It is important to note that, in a period where traveling was difficult, illuminated manuscripts gave an important contribution to the spread visual representation styles across Europe and the Mediterranean area.

The main research question related to this point can be expressed in two main forms, regarding either the possibility of *finding relations with other digital archives* or the possibility of *querying the archive using external information.* From the analysis of requirements it seems that automatic tools that mine the content of online collections can be a valuable tool for researchers. In particular, scholars find particularly useful the automatic mining of metadata, including authorship, subject, iconography, and geographical area of production. At the same time, the scientific research on illuminated manuscripts can take advantage for any kind of documentation that can be related to the content of the manuscripts. The possibility of having this information available when studying an image is considered of great importance.

5.3 Relevance of Textual Information

As mentioned above, scholars in the history of miniature are mainly interested in images. For this reason, the user requirements for the development of the actual version of IPSA did not highlight the need of including the text of the manuscripts in the archive. In many cases, the text was directly copied with only few variations mainly due to errors made by the copyist. The analysis of text is of interest for philologists, which were not included in the focused group.

Yet new requirements highlight the importance of the text surrounding the images, especially in relationship with the possibility of using external information to query the archive, as described in Section 5.2. In this case, the main research question regards the possibility of *segmenting the text of the manuscript and linking segments to images*. Information retrieval techniques can be applied to a focused crawling of external resources, integrating the results obtained with metadata. Textual information is considered by scholar a more important evidence of the relations between images than the ones obtained by visual features that can be extracted automatically from images.

The inclusion of textual information poses challenging problems, because text is hand written (and thus very difficult to parse automatically) and usually in Latin. Automatic translations, to English and other languages, should be used to find similar content outside the collection. Moreover, language processing techniques should be tailored to the particular application domain, where terms are not normalized and the writing style is not comparable to the one of modern languages.

5.4 Graphical Representation

A final set of research questions regards the visual organization of the archive content and of the results of a search. Scholars need to compare different images, that have to be presented on the screen at the same time, with high resolution and the possibility of zooming on details. The kind of relations between images have to be represented as well, with simple visual cues that represent it. At the same time, the presence of relations induce a hypertextual structure to the collection of images, which should be represented effectively. An example of the possible relations of a given image is depicted in Figure 3.

The research questions on the graphical representation regard both the possibility of *expressing graphically the kind of relation between two images* and the possibility of *changing the focus of the representation*, highlighting the image of interest inside the graphical representation. A number of possible representations has been designed and are currently taken into account by scholars. The hierarchical relations between images is of paramount importance for the scholars, who are interested in the spread of a given iconography across the century and are used to represent it with a *stemma codicum* (a tree-like representation of the hierarchical relations). To this end, an additional research question regards the possibility of *automatically building a stemma codicum for each image*, from an archetype to the image under analysis.

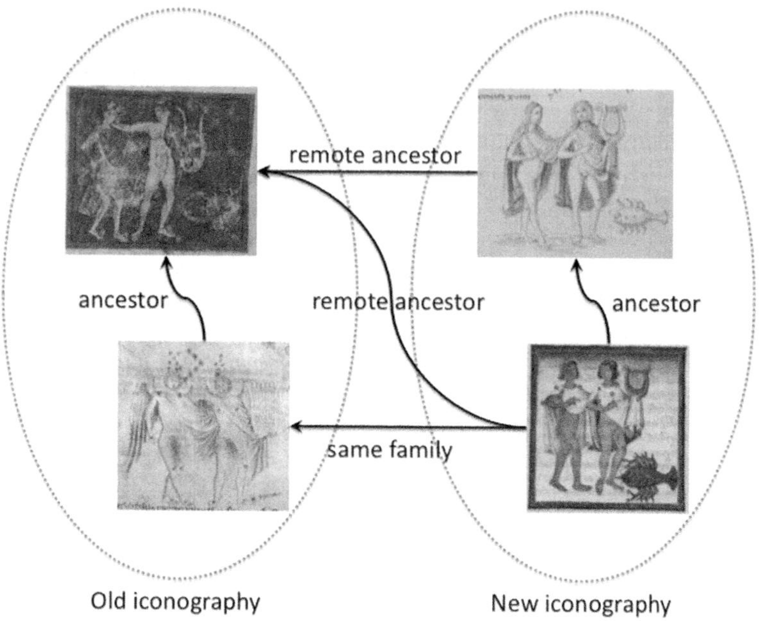

Fig. 3. Example of a personalized view on some linked images of the same subject, belonging to two different iconographies

Acknowledgements. The work reported has been partially supported by the CULTURA project[2], as part of the Seventh Framework Programme of the European Commission, Area "Digital Libraries and Digital Preservation" (ICT-2009.4.1), grant agreement no. 269973.

References

1. Mariani Canova, G.: Hyginus De Astronomia. In: The Splendor of the Word. Medieval and Renaissance Illuminated Manuscripts at the New York Public Library, pp. 337–339. Harvey Miller, New York (2006)
2. Agosti, M., Ferro, N., Orio, N.: Annotating Illuminated Manuscripts: an Effective Tool for Research and Education. In: Marlino, M., Sumner, T., Shipman III, F.M. (eds.) Proc. 5th ACM/IEEE Joint Conference on Digital Libraries (JCDL 2005), pp. 121–130. ACM Press, New York (2005)
3. Agosti, M., Ferro, N., Orio, N.: Graph-based Automatic Suggestion of Relationships among Images of Illuminated Manuscripts. In: Haddad, H. (ed.) SAC, pp. 1063–1067. ACM (2006)
4. Agosti, M., Masotti, M.: Design and functions of DUO: the first Italian academic OPAC. In: Berghel, H., Deaton, E., Hedrick, G., Roach, D., Wainwright, R. (eds.) SAC 1992: Proceedings of the 1992 ACM/SIGAPP Symposium on Applied Computing: Technological Challenges of the 1990's, pp. 308–313. ACM, New York (1992)

[2] CULTURA Project Website, URL: `http://www.cultura-strep.eu/`

5. Agosti, M., Ferro, N., Silvello, G.: An Architecture for Sharing Metadata Among Geographically Distributed Archives. In: Thanos, C., Borri, F., Candela, L. (eds.) Digital Libraries: Research and Development. LNCS, vol. 4877, pp. 56–65. Springer, Heidelberg (2007)
6. Agosti, M., Bombi, F., Melucci, M., Mian, G.A.: Towards a digital library for the venetian music of the eighteenth century. In: Proc. of Third International Conference on Digital Resources in the Humanities (DRH 1998), pp. 75–77. The Humanities Advanced Technology and Information Institute, Glasgow (1998)
7. Agosti, M., Benfante, L., Orio, N.: IPSA: A Digital Archive of Herbals to Support Scientific Research. In: Sembok, T.M.T., Zaman, H.B., Chen, H., Urs, S.R., Myaeng, S.-H. (eds.) ICADL 2003. LNCS, vol. 2911, pp. 253–264. Springer, Heidelberg (2003)
8. Crane, G.: Cultural Heritage Digital Libraries: Needs and Components. In: Agosti, M., Thanos, C. (eds.) ECDL 2002. LNCS, vol. 2458, pp. 626–637. Springer, Heidelberg (2002)
9. Agosti, M., Ferro, N.: A Formal Model of Annotations of Digital Content. ACM Transactions on Information Systems (TOIS) 26, 3–57 (2008)
10. Thiel, U., Brocks, H., Frommholz, I., Dirsch-Weigand, A., Keiper, J., Stein, A., Neuhold, E.J.: COLLATE - A collaboratory supporting research on historic European films. International Journal on Digital Libraries 4, 8–12 (2004)

The Multimedia Archive of the Fondazione Isabella Scelsi

Nicola Bernardini[1] and Alessandra Carlotta Pellegrini[2]

[1] Conservatorio "C.Pollini" Padova, Italy
nicb@sme-ccppd.org
[2] Fondazione Isabella Scelsi Rome, Italy
direzionescientifica@scelsi.it

Abstract. This paper documents and summarizes the (still ongoing) work concerning the digital recovery of the complete archive of documents which constitute the legacy of the late composer Giacinto Scelsi (1905-1988). This recovery has a number of peculiarities which are mostly related to the variety of document typologies which constitute the archive. In particular, the archive contains several hundred tapes and just short of 80 aluminum-lacquer discs which have been used directly by the composer in his compositional processes. These audio documents constitute an extremely important source of musicological investigation to discover the compositional methodologies used by Scelsi, most of which are not quite understood today. The specific archival procedure and model used are then described and future work is outlined at the end.

1 Introduction

Italian composer Giacinto Scelsi (1905-1988) lived a very peculiar and interesting life and – as it is often the case – these characteristics are indeed fully reflected in his music [2]. He grew up during the dodecaphonic turmoil while entertaining very close acquaintances with the buzzing intellectual world in Paris in the thirties. He was attracted by the United States as well as the exotic Egyptian and Japanese worlds while being strongly rooted in Rome, the city that he elected as his permanent residence. At the beginning of the fifties, Scelsi experienced a long and deep creative crisis which reduced him to silence for a few years. He came out of that crisis with a renovated composing spirit - and with the strong resolution to resolve the gap between the "zen spontaneity" of improvisation and the long and detailed table-work of occidental composition. He developed a technique which consisted in recording long piano improvisations engraving them on wax discs first, then on magnetic tape as soon as it became widely available. Remaining coherent with the idea of being just a mediator (and being quite wealthy) he decided to delegate to others – usually young composers in need of a job – the chore of transcribing these improvisations to (fairly) standard notation, collaborating with them only in indicating the instrumental combination he had in mind at the beginning and in the finishing touches at the end.

C. Grana and R. Cucchiara (Eds.): MM4CH 2011, CCIS 247, pp. 176–191, 2012.

Fig. 1. One of the two *Ondiolas* belonging to Scelsi

As the time went by, he added to its instrumental palette a couple of *Ondiolines* [4], one of the first electronic synthesizers, because he was interested in its micro-tonal capabilities (cf.Fig.1).

Of course, this compositional methodology caused huge scandals in the academic entourages, where on the contrary the focus was entirely devoted to the abilities of composers to control their activities down to the most minute detail. Particularly in Italy where he lived, Scelsi was considered a fake composer and was isolated for some thirty years [5]. At the end of the seventies, German and French musicologists and music critics re-discovered the modernity of his compositions – which may be placed half way between Varèse and Xenakis, so to speak – and Scelsi was finally recognized and hailed, albeit outside of his country, as one of the most prominent figures of the second half of the twentieth century (cf. for ex. [7]).

Today, the Fondazione Isabella Scelsi, created by Scelsi's himself some time before his death, is actively promoting the composer's work organizing and coordinating research and performance activities in cooperation with other institutions in Italy and abroad.

2 Outline of the Archive

2.1 Foreword

"The establishment of an archive which is intended to document anything that relates to contemporary music - and in particular to the work of Maestro Scelsi" [1] is among the main objectives of the Fondazione Isabella Scelsi. The constitution act further specifies that the archive should be "open to scholars for reference" and should also pursue "the creation of collections related to musical instruments, sound recordings and any other collectible". Thus, the Historical Archive constitutes the main tool for the real and deep knowledge of the music and life of Giacinto Scelsi. Currently the archive includes more than 16,000 documents, disclosing a wealth of multimedia information of considerable importance in contemporary music.

In July 2000, an official Act of the Archive Superintendence of the Lazio region declared this Archive "of great historical interest". Based in the headquarters of the Fondazione Isabella Scelsi, the archive is currently undergoing a complex reorganization of assets and inventory which is carried out in parallel to a digital transfer of all sound documents (cf.Sect.3). The main objective of this work is to grant access to the archive to scholars and to present them with an easy computational access to documentation. The public opening took place on May 6th 2009, and after that date the archive has been regularly visited and consulted by a variety of national and international users mainly constituted by musicologists and performers.

2.2 Similar Experiences

Before and while undertaking the demanding task of archiving Scelsi's materials several similar or reference experiences were investigated and analyzed to "learn how to do it right". We still look at these and other experiences with great curiosity because the comparison between the solutions adopted by the Fondazione Isabella Scelsi versus other solutions is always stimulating.

Important prior models for the Fondazione Isabella Scelsi archive were:

1. the Arnold Schönberg Center Archive indeed was the most inspiring model: completely realized using Free Software (the archive web services and database are based on the *Joomla* content management system), this archive was the best and clearest example of integration between a pure content management system and a full–fledged archiving and indexing engine that was available at the time;
2. the Archive of the Santa Cecilia Academy in Rome, a very large music archiving endeavor encompassing the works and documents of several hundred composers and the activity of the over–hundred years old Academy, based on a proprietary archiving system (*Gea*). This archive stands indeed as a model for very large multimedia archives;
3. the Archive of the Fondazione Archivio Luigi Nono, based on another Free Software content management system (*drupal*) interfaced with a *Framemaker* database back-end, was closely investigated because of the similarities of materials and logistic situation between the Fondazione Luigi Nono and the Fondazione Isabella Scelsi;

In addition to these models, the participation of the Fondazione Isabella Scelsi to the "Archivi del Novecento" project (an aggregation of archives based on the aforementioned proprietary software *Gea*) has been essential in acquiring the necessary knowledge of standards and canonic record structures, since this project is an attempt to integrate multiple archives using the *MAG–XML* standard as an exporting data aggregator.

However, in the end the Fondazione Isabella Scelsi decided to take yet another route to create its own information system. This was a hard decision to take, but there were many elements that led up to it as an inevitable choice. These will be synthetically summarized here:

- adopting an existing stock content management system (such as *Joomla* or *drupal*) would have required an important amount of extension work to accommodate the multimedia documents that are at the core of the archive. Furthermore, all this work would have resulted in a half–baked situation exposing the archive to potential failures in the long run;
- adopting the proprietary software *Gea* was out of the question for three essential reasons: a) first and foremost, its TCO (Total Cost of Operation) was far from the possibilities of the Fondazione Isabella Scelsi: the price tag of a basic *Gea* system in 2006 was over a 15 kEuro range; b) given the specific document set of the Fondazione Isabella Scelsi, this software would have required a consistent set of extensions which would have certainly doubled (if not more) its TCO, and c) the software would have been forever out of the direct control of the Foundation, thus exposing the stored data to the risk of being unreadable due to the disappearance of the privately-owned software house (ElsagDatamat);
- the integration between a content management system and an archive back-end realized with either proprietary (*Framemaker*) or Free Software (*tomcat*) components was deemed unsatisfactory in its cost effectiveness: the effort would have been considerable for the kind of results that were foreseen.

Other considerations were: i) one of the authors of this paper had already accumulated in 2006 considerable experience in building web–based archival and indexing systems using the latest generation frameworks and languages (such as *Rails*, *Django* or *CakePHP*); ii) he was amenable to the idea of creating a brand new system at no extra cost for the Foundation at the condition that he would be allowed to license it under a Free Software license; iii) the semantic links between the different typologies of document (such as music scores, magnetic tapes, letters, photographs, etc.) were completely unknown at the time and they still remain mysterious to a large extent; this situation required an information system completely open and under the strict control of the experts; iv) while not setting any formal time requirements, the Fondazione Isabella Scelsi needed the system as quickly as possible, because the opening of the archive to a specialized public was a very important objective of its board of directors.

So in the end it was decided that a new information system based on an *agile* programming paradigm[3], including thus test–based development and fast release turnaround time. A few months later `FIShrdb` (cf.Sec.2.5), an information system based on the *Ruby–on–Rails* framework, was born and functional. A year later, the archive opened its doors to the public sporting this multimedia system already storing several thousand records of all kinds.

Lately, in a joint research project with IRCAM the Fondazione Isabella Scelsi was exposed to a new kind of software for genetic analysis of musical works (`MuTEC`), basically constructed with the same *agile* principles as `FIShrdb`. While a close integration between `FIShrdb` and `MuTEC` is currently under scrutiny, it is clear that such a thing is possible only because both systems are built with flexibility and adaptation to change in mind - thus reinforcing the idea that the strategic choice carried out by the Fondazione Isabella Scelsi has been the right one.

2.3 Reorganization and Inventory

The re-ordering of documentation took off from the creation of a framework within which all documents have been organized following a number systematic coherence criteria. In the first place, a sharp distinction between a private archive and a proper music archive was created. The private archive includes correspondence, poetry and philosophical writings, notes, press clips, printed matter, drawings and photographs, administrative and family paperwork, relationships with agencies and institutions (cf. Fig.2). The music archive is subdivided instead into scores, tapes and disks. Two additional sections have been added to this early kernel: the first is a bibliographic section which carries collected essays, studies and articles on Giacinto Scelsi, in order to provide scholars with initial orientation and support of their research; the second section collects and documents the activities of the Fondazione Isabella Scelsi in recent years. Furthermore, an inventory of the personal library of Giacinto Scelsi was created. The books which constitute this library contain many hand-written annotations by Scelsi himself; many of them – especially those related to Eastern philosophies – were very influential on the creative activity of the composer. Therefore, this library is a particularly interesting source of insight of Scelsi's creative processes.

2.4 The Documents

Within the private archive, the documents were aggregated to form organic folders which have been organized in turn into eight archival series in order to constitute the typical hierarchical tree structure. The *correspondence* series stands out documenting the extraordinary breadth of Scelsi's contacts with many personalities from the worlds of music and art.

In the musical archive, significant documents include manuscripts, printed editions, blueprints, sheets, transparencies, drafts hand-annotated by the author. To catalog this series a specific record model was adopted. While respecting the indications provided by the catalog rules for musical manuscripts and prints, this record simplifies its layout allowing an easier user access to information. A folder was created for each composition by Scelsi gathering all related material together (manuscripts, printed music, blueprints, transparencies), thus providing the user with a complete picture of all the documentation related to a specific work.

Fig. 2. A sample from the printed matter section of the Archive

Fig. 3. A sample from the manuscript score section of the Archive

This unique set constitutes the main core of the entire archive and has led to the need of a thorough review of Scelsi's production catalog as it was known so far, opening up new and stimulating perspectives on the evolution of the style of the author. A careful analysis of the scores has led to the discovery of a considerable number of unpublished compositions as well as incomplete ones or fragments merged later on into larger-scale works: a still ongoing detailed analysis and comparison work is giving interesting as well as surprising results.

The archive also holds scores by classical composers which where inherited from the composer's family (especially from his mother). Finally, there are scores of contemporary compositions, many of which carry a signature and a manuscript dedication to Scelsi.

Through the peculiarity and interest of these documents, along with the multimedia tools that allow their access and identification, the Archive of the Fondazione Isabella Scelsi has spun off a number of research projects carried out in collaboration with leading research institutions in Italy and abroad.

2.5 The Software

The cataloging and inventory of all this material was done through an *ad hoc* software: `FIShrdb`[1], fully released under Free Software licences (GNU GPL 2.0). This software meets the strict criteria and international standards ISAD archival and ISAAR. In particular, `FIShrdb` (cf. Fig.4) integrates the characteristics of a hierarchical database (based on a tree representation of documents) with those typical of relational ones. It was designed with extensibility and scalability in mind in order to manage the entire taxonomy of documents which can be found in the archive of the Fondazione Isabella Scelsi (paper documents, music scores, tapes, photographs, etc.). It is particularly easy to develop specialized records for each type and the different data types are linked through a sophisticated system of authority files that allow users to search transversally through access keywords of names, places, organizations and composition titles (with the added possibility of searching also the transcriber, the author of lyrics and the instrument set). A user-friendly interface has been designed and added allowing the user to search the entire archive performing free-form or qualified and constrained searches, showing search results side by side with their location in the hierarchical tree of the archive.

Fig. 4. A snapshot of the `fishrdb` application

2.6 Future Work

Upcoming objectives of this work include the digital transfer of all main series (scores, reviews, correspondence) in order to create an integrated service for research, browsing and access to sources of various types, allowing

---

[1] `http://trac.sme-ccppd.org/fishrdb`

seamless navigation, for example, from a bibliographic record to a particular score to a specific scanned image, and further on to the letters and documents that describe its developments, to the reviews in the press, up to the listening to a related audio recording outlining the compositional processes of the author. The development of a connection and integration processing of digital data coming from very different types of source documents (letter evidences, reviews, scores, tapes) was designed with the needs of a specialized or otherwise interested audience in mind, presenting the latter with an extensive information set tightly organized and integrated. All these developments will be carried out following standards and procedures which will allow the Fondazione Isabella Scelsi to join the Italian Music Network (*ReMI*) which is currently being developed by the Italian ministry of cultural assets and activities within the *InternetCulturale* portal. This will allow in turn to be part of an extended multiple-source relational database which will allow to navigate through an entire vertical network of digital music collections connected with each other through common logic and structure.

3 The Tape Collection

While paper documents lend themselves naturally to standard archival techniques, the archiving of Scelsi's tape collection presents a number of difficulties which exceed the usual problem of archiving of multimedia data.

3.1 The Recordings

The tape collection has been divided in two large groups: a) 287 tapes of improvisations and other compositional material by the composer and b) a still unknown number, probably in the 400–500 range, of recordings by Scelsi of other composers' music (from the radio and from other sources, such as vinyl discs etc.). This division was operated by the Fondazione Isabella Scelsi at an early stage right after Scelsi's death and has been adopted later on for convenience in determining a recovery strategy. However, four years of systematic recovery work of the collection (digitizing the first 287 "primary" tapes over a total of ca. 700 tapes) have already shown that this division is somewhat artificial, since many tapes contain a mixture of improvisations, original compositions and works from other composers. It is highly probable that Scelsi considered tapes as sketchpads where anything valuable could be recorded for future memory – a sharp division between his music and that of other composers was not particularly important to him. At any rate, group a has been termed *tapes of primary interest* while group b became the *tapes of secondary interest.* The digitization of tapes has begun with group a and this process was recently completed in April 2011. After the end of the digitization of group a, group b will be digitized and archived.

Furthermore, a small set of 76 instantaneous recording discs (lacquer-coated aluminum discs which could be singularly engraved with a domestic equipment) belonging to Scelsi was recently uncovered along with the engraving equipment

Fig. 5. Scelsi's disc–engraving recording device

itself (cf. Fig.5) – thus confirming the hypothesis that Scelsi changed his composing techniques way before a magnetic tape recorder was available to him. These discs will also be transferred digitally in the near future.

3.2 Peculiarities

Right from the start it was clear that this would not have been the classical audio recover-and-restore job. Scelsi had just about the same consideration for his tapes as he would have for old sketches hastily jotted down on recycled paper. Tapes were recorded using several tape recorders but always through microphone capture. Most of the time, Scelsi was operating the tape recorders while simultaneously improvising, and the resulting technical quality of the recordings is mediocre at best. All recordings carry a considerable amount of electrical noise as well as abundant environmental noise (cars from the street below, birds, telephone, etc.). Furthermore, while many inscriptions appear on the tapes' container boxes (cf. for ex.Fig.6), the fact that any of these notes may apply to the tape contained therein cannot be taken for granted: Scelsi was known to recycle tapes and boxes, and their misplacement is a common casualty.

Given these initial conditions, two main considerations have driven the recovery of Scelsi's tapes: 1. the electrical noise added by time degradation the tapes is insignificant compared to the large amount of other noise; 2. on the other hand, the identification of very basic properties (such as tape speed or direction) was often found to be quite difficult. In such a situation, the environmental noises proved to be extremely useful (cf.Sect.3.3). Therefore, it was decided early on to transfer the tapes *as they were*; no restoration nor filtering was attempted or desired.

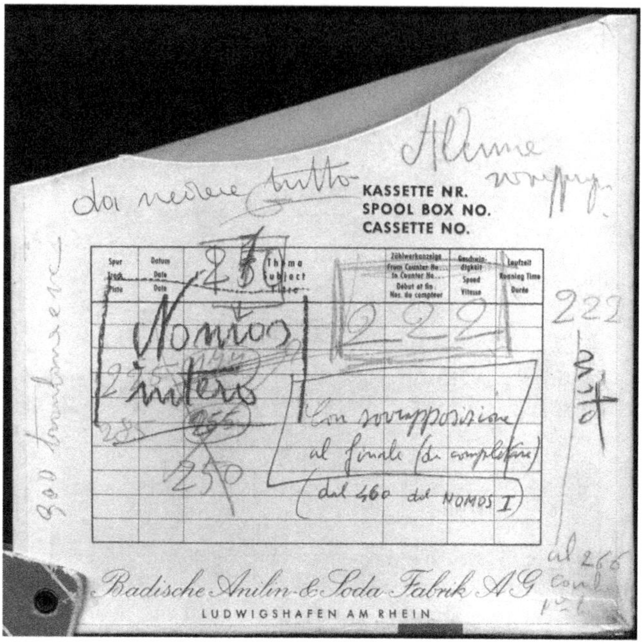

Fig. 6. An example of tape container (591–002)

3.3 Identification Techniques

Yes, strange as it may seem, even the rolling direction and speed of tapes was very often difficult to assess and deceiving. Ondiolas may play synthetic waveforms with slow attacks and very long tones in mid ranges, thus providing no clue related to tape speed and direction. And the recording quality is so bad, and the music so peculiar and experimental, that even piano sounds can often be deceiving in assessing the recording conditions. After tape speed and direction information, which is needed for proper digital transfer, other information could prove to be very useful. Any information on the date of recording, for one, could provide valuable insight in comparison with the date of composition of the second half of Scelsi's production to say the least. Unfortunately, this information is almost completely absent in explicit form. Information concerning the mapping between tape materials and scores is essential to understand in full the actual compositional process of Scelsi's music – assigning proper roles to the composer himself, his copyists, the post-writing editing work, etc. The retrieval of this information constitutes an even more complicated and (so far) ill-defined problem (cf.Sect.5).

Therefore, identification techniques had to be put into place very early on – and this is where all the noise that is present in all tapes constituted a great help.

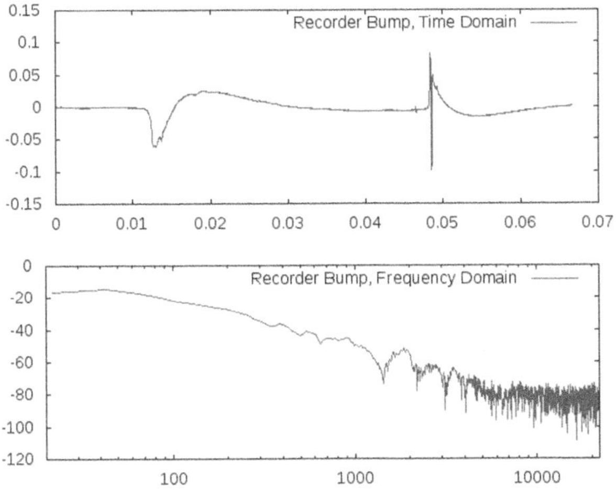

Fig. 7. An example of tape recorder *bump*

Currently, these techniques are still quite empirical and they certainly could use stronger scientific evidence (cf.Sect.5).

The strongest grounds for tape speed and direction are currently given by the so-called *ancillary sounds* provided by the tape recorders themselves. Scelsi never performed any editing on his tapes, so all the record drop in/drop out noises are there. Therefore, most of the tapes carry interesting information precisely in these ancillary sounds (cf.Fig.7). These can be correlated with template sounds recorded *a posteriori*, and the results can give valuable information to identify a) speed and tape rolling direction, and b) the machine that performed the recording. Consequently, item b can provide valuable insight about the date of recording, or at least about a potential range of dates, since it is possible, in some cases, to reconstruct the date of acquisition a given tape recorder out of the administrative documents present in the archive.

Another interesting information is the room's impulse response present in the recordings, which can be correlated too with an *a posteriori* template (cf. Fig.8): Scelsi lived and recorded his improvisations in at least two different houses in Rome, in different periods. Identifying the room could lead to the specific time of recording.

Finally, environmental sounds can sometime come to the rescue: bird sounds allow to identify broadly season/hour of recording, car noise allow to identify tape direction because Via S.Teodoro is a one-way street[2],etc.

In some very rare lucky cases, fragments of radio recordings allow to identify very precisely the date of recording.

---

[2] Though this detail is somewhat complicated by the fact that street direction changed around the beginning of the eighties.

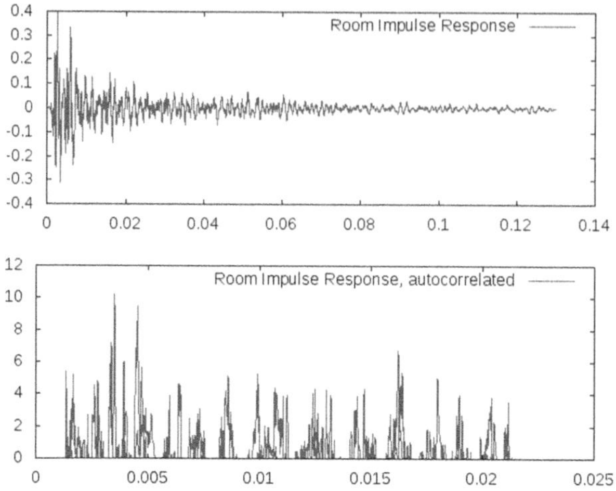

Fig. 8. The impulse response of Scelsi's living room in Via S.Teodoro 8, Rome

4 Transfer Procedures

Up to the date of this writing, all tapes have been transferred to digital files using a Studer A810 tape recorder connected to a Digidesign ProTools workstation using a 96 kHz sample rate and 24-bit samples. The digital files have been saved on a an array of Firewire 800 disks in RAID-1 configuration (plus 1 disk for a running backup).

Each transfer to date was carried out respecting the following protocol:

1. the tape material (acetate or polyester) is identified along with possible rolling difficulties (mildew presence, etc.);
2. the effective length is measured with a first run at moderate speed (not touching the tape heads);
3. existing splices and corruptions are photographed and their position is logged;
4. an order number is created combining a progressive indexing number along with the numbers of two previous numbering attempts;
5. the following data get archived:

   a) order number
   b) manufacturer and type of Magnetic tape (as it appears on the container box)
   c) flange diameter
   d) measured tape length (in m)
   e) measured tape length (in feet)
   f) tape material
   g) tape speeds
   h) audio positioning (head, tail)
   i) recording typology (stereo, mono A/B, etc.)

j) transfer software version
k) file format
l) sample rate
m) sample bit width
n) transfer start date
o) transfer end date
p) notes

6. a "ProTools session" is created along the following lines:

   i) the top tracks hold the uninterrupted transfer at different speeds (as required by the speed identification – cf. Sect.3.3);
   ii) two mono tracks follow, carrying out the tape "layout"
   iii) one (mono) or two (stereo) tracks follow containing the full audio sequence in the identified order, starting from side A and following on side B, with all the identified reading speeds; these are the only active playback tracks (while the others are muted).

7. the transfer is subdivided in "regions" which get numbered progressively; the regions are detected identifying all recording punch in/out performed by the composer; an example of this sectioning work is shown in Fig.9;
8. all regions, splices and stretches are identified and logged on an ASCII text file;

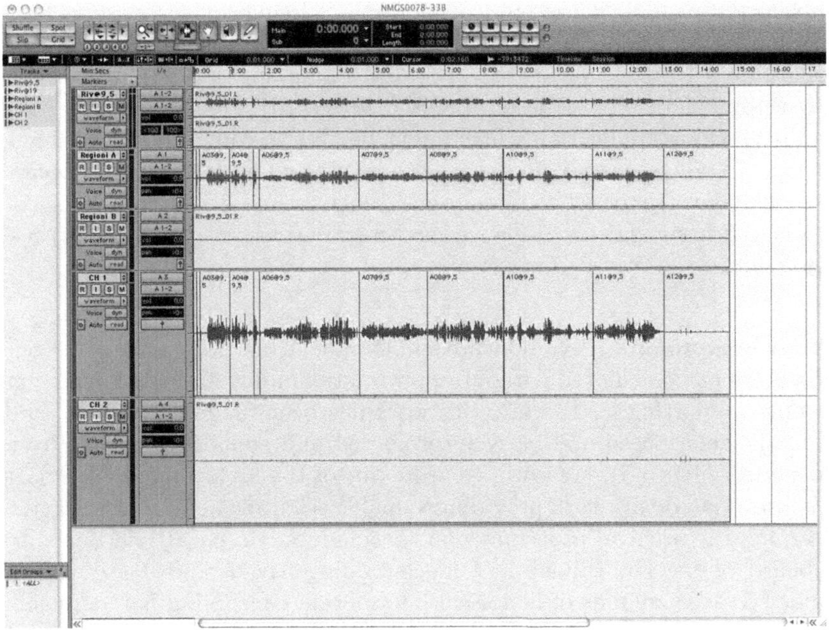

Fig. 9. An example "ProTools" transfer session

9. all other peculiarities (tape content, spoken fragments, container notes, rough calligraphic analysis, etc.) get logged on an ASCII text file;
10. a snapshot (image) of the session is performed;
11. the container is photographed and scanned.

A the end of each session a disk backup is performed. All data is saved using well-known open standards (*AIFF-big-endian* `.aiff` for the audio files, *TIFF* for the *ProTools* session snapshots, *ASCII* for the text logs). Proprietary files (such as the *ProTools* sessions themselves) are exported on open standard files (*ASCII*).

5 Future Work

Even if the digitization work has begun over four years ago, it has still a long way to go to be completed (only the complete set of "primary" tapes have been archived to date – about 40% of the total number). However, this just the beginning of the work to be done on Scelsi's legacy: a complete and detailed archive of Scelsi's is an essential pre-condition in order to start a wide range of investigations on the music and on the compositional methods of this still very mysterious case in contemporary music.

Some of this research is already being planned. It concerns: a) a mapping of Scelsi's tape recorders equipped with a detailed analysis of their *machine fingerprinting* (ancillary noises, background noise, frequency response, etc.); such a mapping would constitute the solid grounds for a scientific analysis of the ancillary noises present on many tapes; b) a mapping of Scelsi's recording environments (i.e. the rooms where he used to record); c) the development of a software tracking application which might be able to compare moderately large corpuses of audio material along with scores in symbolic format to propose evidence of similarities to scholars and musicologists; and d) a full analysis of the Ondiola synthesis and performance modes to derive (and reconstruct) Scelsi's playing out of the recorded material.

Acknowledgements. A complicate and long-term endeavor such as the one described cannot be achieved without appropriate funding and a motivated group of people supporting it. To date, this work has been funded in full by the Fondazione Isabella Scelsi and actively promoted and supported by its President Nicola Sani. Mauro Tosti Croce, Coordinator of the archive of the Fondazione, has substantiated this work providing valuable scientific insight and suggestions concerning the archival procedures and techniques. Barbara Boido, member of the board of the Fondazione and long-standing friend of the late Scelsi, has provided a large amount of historical information concerning habits, machines, locations, and much more which proved to be extremely useful even at such an early stage.

Considerable initial help was provided by Prof. Sergio Canazza from the University of Padova. The first year of this digitization work has been carried out in close collaboration with Piero Schiavoni (Studio Coltempo, Rome), to whom this report owes most of the transfer procedure described above (cf.4) and much more. Besides his universally acclaimed technical excellence and virtuosity, Piero has been an integral part of most contemporary music recordings in Rome and abroad since the 70s (including some of Scelsi's own recordings in his late period) and as such he is also a living memory of many situations and cultural passages which are difficult to reconstruct nowadays.

Since the beginning of 2007, the Fondazione Isabella Scelsi has been closely collaborating with the *Istituto Centrale dei Beni Sonori e Audiovisivi* (ICBSA – the Italian National Sound Archive) and this specific project has been strongly supported by its Director Massimo Pistacchi. The archival work is being carried out under the expert and attentive supervision of Bruno Quaresima and Carlo Cursi.

References

1. Fondazione Isabella Scelsi, Atto Costitutivo (21 gennaio 1987)
2. Castanet, P.A., Cisternino, N. (eds.): Giacinto Scelsi, Viaggio al centro del suono. Luna Editore, La Spezia, 2nd edn. (2001)
3. Dingsøyr, T., Dybå, T., Moe, N.B. (eds.): Agile Software Development: Current Research and Future Directions. Springer, Heidelberg (2010)
4. Fourier, L.: Jean–Jacques Perrey and the Ondioline. Computer Music Journal 18(4) (Winter 1994)
5. Freeman, R.: Tanmatras: The Life and Work of Giacinto Scelsi. Tempo (176), 8–18 (March 1991)
6. Martinis, L., Pellegrini, A.C. (eds.): Giacinto Scelsi: Il sogno 101. Quodlibet, Macerata (2010)
7. Metzger, H.K.: Das Unbekannte in der Musik. Musik–Konzepte 10(31) (May 1983)

RFID-Enhanced Museum for Interactive Experience

Rasoul Karimi, Alexandros Nanopoulos, and Lars Schmidt-Thieme

Information Systems and Machine Learning Lab (ISMLL),
University of Hildesheim, 31141 Hildesheim, Germany
{karimi,nanopoulos,schmidt-thieme}@uni-hildesheim.ismll.de

Abstract. Visitors to physical museums are often overwhelmed by the vast amount of information available in the space they are exploring, making it difficult to select personally interesting content. Personalization solutions can provide the required user-centered interactivity between the visitors and the museum websites or museum guide systems. Recommender systems are among the most successful personalization technologies, as they have already been incorporated to solve similar problems in e-commerce, where users have a lot of choices to select a product. However, developing recommender system for museums is more challenging, because in contrast to e-commerce, museums and their exhibits exist in a physical world. Therefore, we need a hardware technology to provide us the required infrastructure to observe and model the environment and user activities. Radio-frequency identification (RFID) technology is among the best solutions for this issue, because it is cheap, fast, robust, and available everywhere. In this paper, we describe the vision of our project called RFID-Enhanced Museum for Interactive Experience (REMIX), which aims to developing a personalization platform for museums based on RFID technology and advanced recommender-systems algorithms.

Keywords: Recommender System, Museum, RFID, Web application.

1 Introduction

Visitors to physical museums are often overwhelmed by the vast amount of information available in the space they are exploring, making it difficult to select personally interesting content. To address this problem, personalization solutions are required in order to provide user-centered interactivity between the visitors and the museum exhibits. Such personalized solutions can be involved to assist visitors during their visit (online case) as well as to enhance their post-museum exploration (offline case), e.g., the interaction that visitors have *after* their visit when they can explore the museum's web site and find additional information for the exhibits they are interested for. The advantages of personalization solutions of this form, compared to the involvement of human guides, are their feasibility, efficiency, and lower cost.

C. Grana and R. Cucchiara (Eds.): MM4CH 2011, CCIS 247, pp. 192–205, 2012.

Recommender systems (RS) are among the most successful personalization technologies, as they have already been incorporated to solve similar problems in e-commerce. Recommender systems guide users in a personalized way to interesting or useful objects in a large space of possible options [16]. For example, to provide answers to questions, such as "which movie should I see?" or "what book should I read?". We have too many choices and too little time to explore them all and the exploding availability of information makes this problem even tougher. Therefore, RS is today an essential part of any electronic shop, such as Amazon, eBay, and Netflix.

Developing recommender system for museums is, however, more challenging than in the case of e-commerce, because in contrast to e-commerce, museums and their exhibits exist in a physical world. The application of recommender systems in the context of *artificial* museums guides can be performed in several ways depending on the nature of an artificial guide, which may vary from a sophisticated robot to a common mobile device (e.g., smart phone). Moreover, we need a hardware technology to provide us the required infrastructure to observe and model the environment and user activities. Radio-frequency identification (RFID) technology is among the best solutions for this issue, because it is cheap, fast, robust, and available everywhere. Finally, algorithms for the generation of recommendations should take into account the location of exhibits and the physical distance between them.

In this paper, we describe the vision of our project called RFID-Enhanced Museum for Interactive Experience (REMIX), which aims to developing a personalization platform for museums based on RFID technology and advanced recommender-systems algorithms. Our emphasis is on explaining the novel features of the REMIX architecture, which significantly differentiate it from other applications with similar objectives. We also provide details about the challenges faced by RS algorithms in this new context. We examine two major cases: i) the online and the ii) offline case. In the online case, visitors are able to get recommendation for exhibits during their visit. Meanwhile, their movements are tracked non-intrusively[1] by RFID sensors placed on exhibits. In the offline case, after leaving the museum, the visitors can connect to a personalized web-based application which provides additional information about their actions inside the museum, about the exhibits they have been interested for, and recommendations for potentially interesting exhibits that they can see in future visits. Moreover, the tracked information can help the museum's management to understand the behavior and preferences of its visitors and shape evaluation metrics for, e.g., the popularity of exhibits according to their position in the museum, in order to reshape policies or design effective campaigns for the future.

The general aim of the ongoing REMIX project is the development of a system that will advance state-of-the-art research results from the emerging and increasingly affordable field of wireless RFID [1] technologies and from the field of recommender systems in the application area of museums. Based on the expected results of REMIX, museums will be able to provide to each visitor a

[1] Preserving all aspects of visitors' privacy.

personalized learning experience and the sense of belonging to the museum's community, which can be extended over multiple visits and between visits via a Web application that will be developed by the REMIX project. All these factors can significantly help to increase both the number of visitors and the quality of services they are provided by the museum.

2 Related Work

In this section, we provide a brief summary of existing applications of personalized solutions for museums, and we detail the innovative aspects of the proposed REMIX system.

The Exploratorium [2] is a hands-on science museum in San Francisco that uses the eXspot system, developed in cooperation with the University of Washington's Computer Science and Engineering Department and Intel Labs Seattle. It is intended to support, record, and extend exhibit-based, informal science learning. Its users can bookmark their exhibits of preference, create photographs (use their RFID tags to activate cameras), and access them later via the museum's kiosk or via the internet.

The Museum of Science and Industry in Chicago [3] opened a new 5,000-square foot permanent exhibition called "NetWorld" where visitors use RFID technology to learn about the Internet. First, they design personal avatars that are stored in the exhibition's network. Then, using their NetPass cards (with embedded RFID chips), the avatars accompany them throughout the exhibition, interacting with them as they learn about bits, packets, and bandwidth. With each new exhibit, the network stores visitors' ID numbers and displays their avatars to help them through new experiences. To avoid issues of personal data privacy, no personally identifiable information is collected when the cards are issued.

At the Vienna Museum of Technology [4], RFID has been used in an exhibition on the future of virtual reality. Visitors purchase a card at an admissions desk, take it to a card-reader terminal, and create a personal profile that includes preferred language, favorite color, nicknames, and other low-security identifiers. The interaction metaphor represents a digital backpack for collecting multimedia clips. Visitors take their cards to any number of card-reader terminals in the museum.

The Museum of Natural History in Aarhus [5] in Denmark, uses RFID technology in an exhibit called "Flying," which includes birds tagged with RFID chips. In this exhibit, visitors carry RFID readers and scan tags attached to birds. Scanning a bird results in the presentation of associated text, quizzes, audio, and video to the visitor.

The Tech Museum in San Jose [6], implemented RFID technologies in "Genetics: Technology with a Twist" exhibition in 2004. Earlier this year, it launched the "NetP1@net Gallery" where visitors create personalized Web pages with photographs and images from their visits to the museum, then use their RFID numbers to retrieve the page anytime on the Web.

2.1 Innovative Aspects of the REMIX Project

Similar to the aforementioned existing approaches, REMIX project involves RFID technology for monitoring visitors. However, the it contains several innovative aspects, which differentiate it from existing approaches. These innovative aspects are analyzed as follows:

1. The information system of REMIX monitors visitors not only for the purpose of retrieving this information but also for analyzing it using data mining technologies. As explained, the transfer of state-of-the-art algorithms from the research field of data mining will allow the museum to better capture the preference of users and provide advanced functionalities, such as the recommendation of exhibits for forthcoming visits.
2. The monitored information will be personalized via a Web application that will provide to each visitor data about the visits and also will encapsulate the data mining results, such as the recommendations.

3 The Architecture of REMIX

In this section we describe the overall architecture of the REMIX system, whereas the main component, i.e., the recommender system, will be explained in the following section.

3.1 The RFID Monitoring System

Radio-frequency identification (RFID) is a generic term for technologies that use radio waves to automatically identify people or objects. There are several methods of identification, but the most common is to store a serial number that identifies a person or object, and perhaps other information, on a microchip that is attached to an antenna (the chip and the antenna together are called an RFID transponder or an RFID tag). The antenna enables the chip to transmit the identification information to a reader. The reader converts the radio waves reflected back from the RFID tag into digital information that can then be passed on to computers that can make use of it [17].

An RFID system consists of a tag made up of a microchip with an antenna, and an interrogator or reader with an antenna. The reader sends out electromagnetic waves. The tag antenna is tuned to receive these waves. A passive RFID tag draws power from the field created by the reader and uses it to power the microchip's circuits. The chip then modulates the waves that the tag sends back to the reader, which converts the new waves into digital data [18]. This mechanism is shown in Fig.1.

There are two kinds of RFID tags: active and passive. Active tags have a transmitter and their own power source (typically a battery). The power source is used to run the microchip's circuitry and to broadcast a signal to a reader (the way a cell phone transmits signals to a base station). Passive tags have no battery. Instead, they draw power from the reader, which sends out electromagnetic waves that induce a current in the tag's antenna. Semi-passive tags use a battery to run the chip's circuitry, but communicate by drawing power from the reader. Active and semi-passive tags are useful for tracking high-value goods that need to be scanned over long ranges, such as railway cars on a track, but they cost more than passive tags, which means they can't be used on low-cost items. (There are companies developing technology that could make active tags far less expensive than they are today.) End-users are focusing on passive UHF tags, which cost less than 40 cents today in volumes of 1 million tags or more. Their read range isn't as fartypically less than 20 feet vs. 100 feet or more for active tagsbut they are far less expensive than active tags and can be disposed of with the product packaging [19].

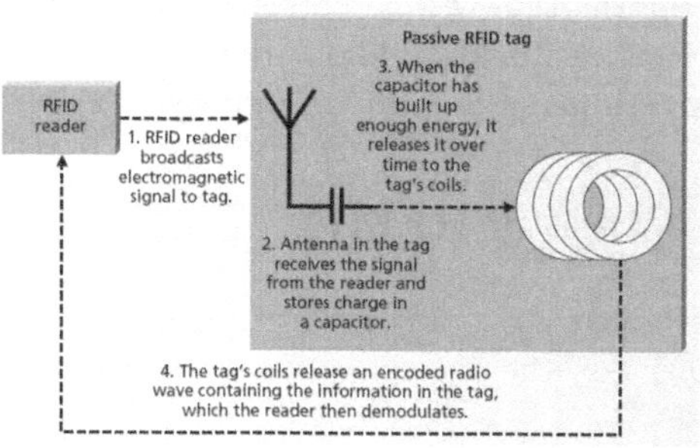

Fig. 1. Simplified view of data transfer in passive RFID tags

The proposed RFID subsystem in the REMIX architecture will monitor the interaction of visitors with exhibits, will consist of three main components:

1. The RFID reader package mounted on the exhibits: A plastic-molded package containing a mote for control and radio connectivity, a low-power RFID reader with range of few centimeters (e.g., 20 cm), and some indicators (e.g., LED) to allow visitors understand the state of the package. For power supply, there exist two main options. The first is to have each RFID reader package powered by rechargeable batteries and the second is to have it connected to constant power supply. The first option allows more flexible installation and relocation of the RFID reader package, whereas the second comprises a cheaper solution. In any case, the size of the RFID reader package will be small in order to be portable and easy to mount on the exhibits.
2. The RFID tags carried by visitors: Visitors can obtain and carry an RFID tag that will allow them to interact with the RFID reader packages mounted on the exhibits. To help visitors easy carry them, the RFID tags can be contained within laminated cards that are ease to wear around the neck. Other solutions will also be examined, like enclosing the RFID tags within bracelets. Whenever visitors want to "bookmark" an exhibit, i.e., record it as visited, they can swipe their RFID tag at the vicinity of the corresponding RFID reader that will perform the recording.

3. The wireless network connecting the RFID readers: The RFID reader packages are connected through a wireless network with a base station. Transmitted information will be sent over mote radio (operating at specific frequency, e.g., 433 MHz). The base station will contain a server that maintains the database where transmitted information is recorded.

The functionality of the proposed RFID monitoring system is explained as follows: The RFID reader packages that are mounted on the exhibits continuously monitor their vicinity for the presence of RFID tags. When a visitor approaches an exhibit at close distance (e.g., 20 cm) , then its RFID reader package reads the RFID tag of the visitor and sends the ID of the tag to the base station via the wireless network. Along with the ID of the tag, the RFID reader package also transmits the ID of the exhibit and the current time. This constitutes the "bookmarking" information that will record the view of the exhibit by the visitor (Figure 2).

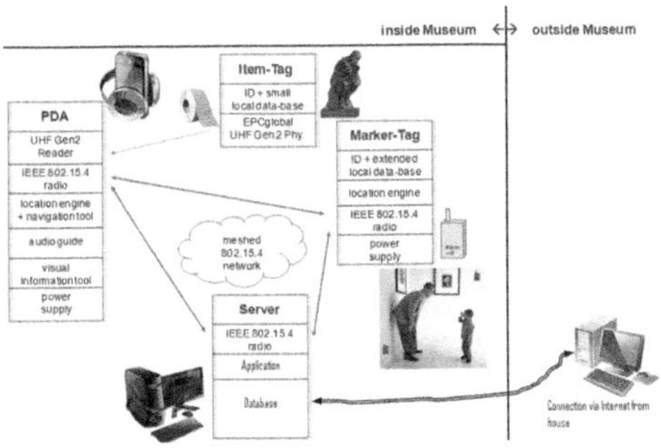

Fig. 2. The functionality of the proposed monitoring system

Visitors can obtain their RFID tags at a kiosk at the museum's entrance. They may perform a simple registration procedure, by providing some additional low privacy information (like email address or favorite color, pet name, etc.), which will increase the security in case the RFID tag is lost, and by receiving some guidelines about the use of their RFID tags. It has to be noticed that the use of RFID tags by the REMIX project offers several advantages compared to alternative solutions. RFID tags offer a low-cost and lightweight solution that permits the unobtrusive view of the exhibits.

3.2 Information System for Recording and Analyzing the Monitored Information

Information that is going to be transmitted by the RFID monitoring system through the wireless network has to be recorded at the base station. One of the main components of the information system that will be developed by the REMIX project is a database in the base station that will contain the following information:

1. Data about the exhibits: Each exhibit that has a mounted RFID reader package will be represented in the database. The recorded fields will be the ID of the exhibit (unique identifier for each exhibit that will serve as the primary key), the name of the exhibit, and additional description, like historical and geographical information pertinent to the exhibit. Moreover, for each exhibit in the database there will be maintained a corresponding amount of information that will be delivered through the web application for post-museum exploration. This information may contain multimedia material, such as photographs or video, hypertext, and links to outside articles, such as Web encyclopedias.
2. Data about the visitors: After each visitor is registered and receives an RFID tag, the database will store the ID of the RFID tag and possibly additional information about the visitor. This additional information may be the email address of the visitor, or other low-privacy information, such as a question and answer that the visitor will propose ("what is your favorite color?"). Such low-privacy information will serve to protect visitors' privacy, because by using only the ID that is written on the RFID tag for accessing the information stored for each visitor may present a risk in case the RFID tag is lost (the ID will be clearly written on the RFID tag). The REMIX project intends to perform a user-study through which the optimal policy (i.e., selection of the type of complementary low-privacy information) for preserving the privacy of stored information will be decided. In any case, it has to be clarified, that no information that violates visitors' privacy (such as names, place of residence, telephone numbers, etc.) will be maintained.
3. Data about the interaction of visitors with exhibits: The information about the exhibits that each visitor interacts with during a visit will comprise a relationship between the two aforementioned data types, i.e., the data about exhibits and the data about the visitors. More precisely, for each interaction the database will store the ID of the exhibit, the ID of the RFID tag, and the date and time of day that this interaction happened. Please notice that these pieces of information are going to be available to the database at the base station, because the will be transmitted through the wireless network by the RFID reader packages on the exhibits. It is important to note that the aforementioned design at the conceptual level follows the principles of relational database development. However, due to the expected rapid flow of information about interactions in the database, the REMIX project will consider special design options at the physical level of the database, to cope with the requirement for fast updating due to the streaming information entering the database as the visitors continuously interact with the exhibits.

The recording of the monitored information about the interactions between visitors and exhibits will be valuable for retrieval purposes. Through a Web application that will be developed by the REMIX project, the visitors will be able to retrieve information about the exhibits they visited and "bookmarked" with the use of their RFID tags. Nevertheless, the information that is recorded about the interactions between visitors and exhibits can serve an additional purpose that is valuable for the museum. Thus, the museum can apply data mining techniques over the database contents and analyze the nature of repeat visits and visitors preferences. For the information system of the REMIX project, we will consider the development of an analysis module that will provide personalization services through a system that will generate recommendations for further visits [10,11] both for the online and the offline case.

Providing recommendations during the current visit (online case) or for future visits (offline case) deepens visitors' experience beyond a single visit, increase their satisfaction, and provide them motivation for multiple visits. The information system of the REMIX project will perform the analysis of visitors' preference and provide recommendations for exhibits that can be visited in further visits. The functionality of the involved recommender systems and the prediction algorithms for identifying exhibits that have not been visited so far but may interest the visitor in future visits, will be analyzed in more detail in the following section.

Besides providing recommendations to visitors, the information system of REMIX will process the tracked information for providing the following services to museum's management:

1. Mining sequential patterns [7,8]: The exhibits with which a visitor interacts during one visit can be represented as a sequence, ordered by the time of interaction. By transforming the information about all interactions into a collection of sequences, the REMIX project will discover sequences of interactions that tend appear more frequently that the rest sequences. Such discovered sequences, which are called sequential patterns, reveal correlations between the exhibits and disclose information about visitors' preferences. For example, a sequential pattern can be the following: "The sequence of visits Egyptian golden mask (1000 B.C) Egyptian sculpture of young woman (1500 B.C) Egyptian papyrus fragment (1200 B.C.) is performed by the 35 of visitors". From such a sequential pattern the museum can understand that these 3 exhibits are preferred to be visited by a significant amount of visitors. Therefore, the museum may relocate these exhibits and put them, e.g., in the same corridor and in the indicated order starting from the entrance of the corridor. Moreover, the correlation between these exhibits can be further exploited by the museum to promote new exhibits. For instance, assuming that the museum has recently acquired a new related exhibit (e.g., an Egyptian weapon), it can place it between the aforementioned exhibits, with the motivation that visitors will often tend to follow the route between these exhibits and, thus, to visit the new exhibit that is promoted by the museum.
2. Mining temporal patterns [9,14]: When analyzing information about interactions between visitors and exhibits, valuable information can be revealed from time-related information that is stored in the database along with each interaction. In the information system of the REMIX project we will develop data mining technology to discover temporal patterns. For instance, the system can discover the "life-cycle" of new exhibits, e.g., that they visitors pick their interest about a new exhibit 3 weeks after its first appearance, and that it is kept to be visited more frequently than older exhibits for about

3 additional months. Another type of interesting temporal pattern is the discovery of trends. The information system of the REMIX project will provide the data mining functionality of exploring information about visits with respect to time at different granularities (e.g., per week, month, season, etc.) and allow the analysts (users of the information system) to discover temporal patterns. For example, after the presentation of the new collection with Roman frescos, the total number of visits to the exhibits of this collection was increased by a factor of 55 compared to the average number of visits to other permanent exhibits one week before. With such patterns the museum can directly evaluate the reaction of visitors to its policies.

3.3 Personalized Web Application for Post-Museum Learning Experience

Among the main goals of a museum is the designing of learning experiences for its visitors by enlightening them about subjects like nature, history, art, or science. A key aspect to enhance the learning process of visitors is the involvement of Web activities,. This will link the exhibits in the museum with further concepts that can be found in the personalized Web pages. These pages match the preferences of each visitor and offer post-museum learning experience, i.e., extended beyond the visits to the museum.

For the aforementioned reasons, the REMIX project will develop a personalized Web application that will retrieve information stored in the database of the base station and create personalized Web pages for each visitor. A visitor can logon to the personalized Web pages by using as user-name the ID of the RFID tag (the ID will be written on the tag) and as password other provided information, like an email address. In the personalized Web pages, a user can see information about the visits, such as dates, hours, etc., the exhibits visited at each visit, and additional teaching material, like Web links to online encyclopedia articles related to the visited exhibits and further descriptions of the exhibits (e.g., detailed historical context). All these additional pieces of information will be maintained for each exhibit in the database. For an example of such a personalized page, please refer to Figure 3.

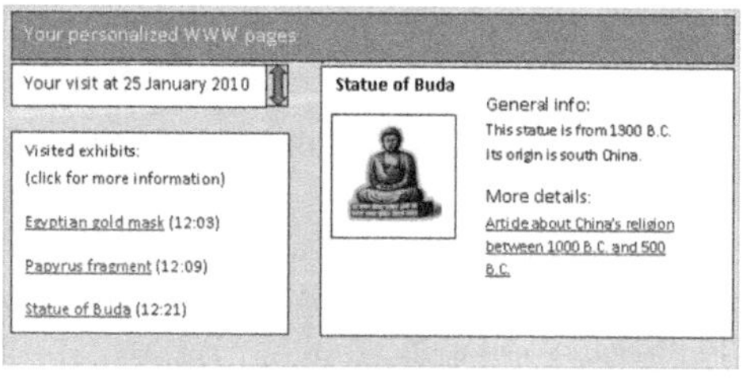

Fig. 3. A personalized web page

The proposed Web application will offer significant advantages to visitors that want to elaborate further the knowledge they acquire from the museum's exhibits. It is ideal for pedagogical activities, like a class visiting the museum. As the teacher of the class will not have adequate time during the visit to analyze all visited exhibits, the proposed Web application will allow the teacher in the following days in the class to continue the discussion and exploration of their visit, to assign home works based on the exploitation of additional information, etc.

Finally, the personalized Web pages will accommodate the recommendations of exhibits that can be viewed in forthcoming visits. This way, the visitors are motivated to visit the museum often and each time they can adjust their preferences according to their available time, knowing that they can continue the exploration of the museum in following visits by planning them ahead through the use of recommendations.

4 Recommender Systems for Museums

In this section, we first describe the main methods that are used by recommender systems, and next we describe how the consideration of spatial processes addresses the new challenges that are introduced when applying recommender systems in museums.

4.1 Recommendation Algorithms

Most recommendation methods fall into two categories: Memory-based algorithms and Model-based algorithms [16]. Memory-based algorithms store rating examples of users in a training database. In the predicating phase, they predict the ratings of an active user based on the corresponding ratings of the users in the training database that are similar to the active user. In contrast, model-based algorithms construct models that well explain the rating examples from the training database and apply the estimated model to predict the ratings for active users. Both types of approaches have been shown to be effective for collaborative filtering. In this subsection, we introduce Aspect Model (AM) and Matrix Factorization (MF) from model-based algorithms and nearest-neighbor as a memory-based approach.

Nearest-Neighbor. Nearest-Neighbor method is centered on computing the relationships between items or, alternatively, between users. The item-oriented approach evaluates a users preference for an item based on ratings of neighboring items by the same user. A products neighbors are other products that tend to get similar ratings when rated by the same user. For example, consider the movie Saving Private Ryan. Its neighbors might include war movies, Spielberg movies, and Tom Hanks movies, among others. To predict a particular users rating for Saving Private Ryan, we would look for the movies nearest neighbors that this user actually rated [23].

Aspect Model. Aspect model is a probabilistic latent space model, which models individual preferences as a convex combination of preference factors [20,21]. The latent factors $z \in Z = \{z_1, z_2, ..., z_k\}$ is associated with each pair of a user and an item. The aspect model supposes that users and items are independent from each other given the latent factor. Therefore, the probability for each rating tuple (m, u, r) is computed as following:

$$p(r|m,u) = \sum_{z \in Z} p(r|z,m)p(z|u) \tag{1}$$

in which $p(z|u)$ stands for the likelihood for user u to be in class z and $p(r|z,m)$ stands for the likelihood of assigning item m with rating r by users in class z. In order to achieve better performance, the ratings of each user are normalized to be a normal distribution with zero mean and variance as 1 [21]. The parameter $p(r|z,m)$ is approximated as a Gaussian distribution $N(m_z, s_z)$ and $p(z|u)$ as a multinomial distribution.

Matrix Factorization. Matrix factorization is the task of approximating the true, unobserved ratings-matrix R by $\hat{R} : |U| \times |I|$. With $\hat{R}$ being the product of two feature matrices $W : |U| \times f$ and $H : |I| \times f$, where the u-th row w_u of W contains the f features that describe the u-th user and the i-th row h_i of H contains f corresponding features for the i-th item.

Matrix factorization models map both users and items to a latent space of dimensionality f [22]. In this space, user-item interactions are modeled as inner products. In the latent space, each item i is represented with a vector $h_i \in R^f$. The elements of h_i indicate the importance of factors in rating item i by users. Some factors might have higher effect and vice versa. In the same way, each user u is represented with a vector $w_u \in R^f$ in the latent space. For a given user the element of w_u measure the influence of the factors on user preferences. Different applications of matrix factorization differ in the constraints that are sometimes imposed on the factorization. The most common form of matrix factorization is finding a low-rank approximation (unconstrained factorization) to a fully observed data matrix minimizing the sum-squared difference to it.

The resulting dot product, $h_i^T w_u$, captures the interaction between user u and item i. This approximates user u's rating of item i, which is denoted by r_{ui}, leading to the estimate:

$$min \sum_{(u,i) \in k} (r_{ui} - h_i^T w_u)^2 + \lambda(\|h_i\|^2 + \|w_u\|^2) \tag{2}$$

in witch λ is the regularization factor, and k is the set of the (u, i) pairs for which r_{ui} is known (the training set).

4.2 Spatial Process

There is an essintial diffrence between recommender system for museum and web-based recommender systems. While web works in a virtual web environment, museum exist in the real world. This diiference could have advantage and disadvantage. In the physical world, there are constraints that do not exist in the virtual world. This issue, might restrict the recommendation algorithms. For example, visitor might not willing to vist an exhibit which is far from his current position in the museum specially in the last of his vistit because he is tired. In the other hand, the physical environment provides additional information which enables us to explore new methods which are not applicable for a recommender system working in a virtual environment.For example, in web-based recommender systems, in order to measure the similarity between items, the Euclidean distance is calculated. However, in a museum, physical distance between items have a meaning and there is no need to use other measurements such as Euclidean distance. Similar items could be grouped together is a same room or floor.

To address this issue, spatial process technique [12] is a suitable method which has recently been suggested for recommender systems in museums [13]. In addition to methods such as Matrix factorization [22], Aspect model [20,21], and Nearest-Neighbor [23],we intend to investigate spacial process technique as well.

5 Conclusions

In this paper, we described our vision for the ongoing REMIX project. REMIX aims to developing a personalization platform for museums based on RFID technology and advanced recommender-systems algorithms. Museums invest human and financial resources to improve the learning experience that they offer to their visitors. However, with a large number of permanent exhibits and floor demonstrations, museums often more choices to the visitors than they can grasp in a single visit. Especially groups of visitors, like school students, tend to carefully observe only a small fraction of the exhibits, as younger visitors usually move fast from one exhibit to another[2]. Therefore, by rushing among the exhibits, visitors cannot fully explore the provided learning experience that the museum has designed for them.

By leveraging RFID technology and through the personalized Web application, REMIX allows a museum to deepen the visitors' learning experience, extend it beyond a single visit, and obviate the hurried visitor problem. Moreover, through the analysis of the data collected by the RFID monitoring system, the museum can study the nature of visits and the long-term preferences of the offered exhibits, and be in a position to provide better services to its visitors like, for example, recommendations for future visits. With all these means, the museum can increase the number of its visitors, the quality of its services, and to promote stronger relationships with its visitors, making them feel as members of the museum's community. Therefore, all the aforementioned results are expected to offer financial and cultural benefits to the museum, better exploitation of its resources. Another benefit is the possibility for additional exploitation of

[2] In such cases, the mean time of viewing an exhibit can be less than half a minute.

the Web personalized application within a business model that can promote advertising information at a regional and national level and e-commerce activities, such as the purchase of souvenirs, books, posters, etc.

The key-technology to attain the expected benefits of REMIX is personalization through the use of recommender systems. In this paper, we have described the new challenges resulting from the application of recommender systems in the context of a museum, and the main approaches we plan to develop for addressing these challenges.

The main point of our future work is the finalization of the software platform of REMIX, which will incorporate all the solutions described in this paper. Moreover, we plan to install REMIX in the Roemer Pelizaeus Museum (www.rpmuseum.de) in Hildesheim, Germany. This application of REMIX will provide the necessary benchmark for the evaluation of its usefulness.

Acknowledgement. This work is co-funded by the European Regional Development Fund project REMIX under the grant agreement no. 80115106.

References

1. Want, R.: An Introduction to RFID Technology. IEEE Pervasive Computing 5 (2006)
2. `http://Web.exploratorium.edu`
3. `http://Web.msichicago.org/`
4. `http://Web.tmw.at/`
5. `http://Web.naturhistoriskmuseum.dk/uk/info/infoUK.htm`
6. `http://Web.thetech.org/`
7. Srikant, R., Agrawal, R.: Mining Sequential Patterns: Generalizations and Performance Improvements. In: Apers, P.M.G., Bouzeghoub, M., Gardarin, G. (eds.) EDBT 1996. LNCS, vol. 1057, pp. 1–17. Springer, Heidelberg (1996)
8. Lin, M.-Y., Lee, S.-Y.: Fast Discovery of Sequential Patterns by Memory Indexing. In: Kambayashi, Y., Winiwarter, W., Arikawa, M. (eds.) DaWaK 2002. LNCS, vol. 2454, pp. 150–160. Springer, Heidelberg (2002)
9. Lee, A.J.-T., Chena, Y.-A.: Mining frequent trajectory patterns in spatial temporal databases. Information Sciences 179(13), 2218–2231 (2009)
10. Konstan, J.A.: Introduction to recommender systems: Algorithms and Evaluation. ACM Transactions on Information Systems 22(1) (2004)
11. Koren, Y., Bell, R.M., Volinsky, C.: Matrix Factorization Techniques for Recommender Systems. IEEE Computer 42(8), 30–37 (2009)
12. Konstan, J.A.: GeoDa: An Introduction to Spatial Data Analysis. Geographical Analysis 38(1), 5–22 (2006)
13. Bohnert, F., Schmidt, F.D., Zukerman, I.: Spatial Processes for Recommender Systems. In: International Joint Conference on Artificial Intelligence (IJCAI) (2009)
14. Lutkepoh, H.: Introduction to Multiple Time Series Analysis, 2nd sub edn. Springer, Telos (1993)
15. `http://Web.mymediaproject.org/`
16. Burke, R.: Hybrid recommender systems. User Modeling and User Adapted Interaction 12, 331–370 (2002)

17. What is RFID? RFID Journal (2005)
18. Weinstein, R.: RFID: A Technical Overview and Its Application to the Enterprise. IT Professional 7(3), 27–33 (2005)
19. Rao, K.V.S.: An overview of backscattered radio frequency identification system (RFID). In: Microwave Conference (1999)
20. Hofmann, T., Puzicha, J.: Latent class models for collaborative filtering. In: International Joint Conference on Artificial Intelligence (1999)
21. Hofmann, T.: Gaussian latent semantic models for collaborative filtering. In: 26th ACM SIGIR Conference on Research and Development in Information Retrieval (SIGIR) (2003)
22. Koren, Y., Bell, R., Volinsky, C.: Matrix Factorization Techniques for Recommender Systems, vol. 42, pp. 30–37. IEEE Computer Society (2009)
23. Sarwar, B., Karypis, G., et al: Item-Based Collaborative Filtering Recommendation Algorithms. World Wide Web (Web) (2001)
24. Diggle, P.J., Tawn, J.A., Moyeed, R.A.: Model-based geostatistics. Applied Statistics 47(3), 299–350 (1998)
25. Banerjee, S., Carlin, B.P., Gelfand, A.E.: Hierarchical Modeling and Analysis for Spatial Data. Chapman Hall/CRC (2004)
26. Schwaighofer, A., Tresp, V., Yu, K.: Learning Gaussian process kernels via hierarchical Bayes. In: NIPS (2004)

Multimedia for Cultural Heritage: Key Issues

Rita Cucchiara[1], Costantino Grana[1], Daniele Borghesani[1],
Maristella Agosti[2], and Andrew D. Bagdanov[3]

[1] Department of Information Engineering,
University of Modena,
Reggio Emilia, Via Vignolese 905/b, 41125, Modena, Italy
{rita.cucchiara,costantino.grana,daniele.borghesani}@unimore.it
[2] Department of Information Engineering,
University of Padua,
Via Gradenigo 6/a, 35131 Padova, Italy
maristella.agosti@unipd.it
[3] Media Integration and Communication Center,
University of Florence,
Via Santa Marta 3, 50139, Florence, Italy
bagdanov@dsi.unifi.it

Abstract. Multimedia technologies have recently created the conditions for a true revolution in the Cultural Heritage domain, particularly in reference to the study, exploitation, and fruition of artistic works. New opportunities are arising for researchers in the field of multimedia to share their research results with people coming from the field of art and culture, and viceversa. This paper gathers together opinions and ideas shared during the final discussion session at the 1st International Workshop on Multimedia for Cultural Heritage, as a summary of the problems and possible directions to solve to them.

1 Introduction

Cultural heritage preservation and exploitation have key importance to human culture, but at the same time, especially during periods of financial crisis, they are some of the most threatened activities. We strongly believe that, among all the fields in which modern multimedia research can yield a leap forward in data management and user experience, cultural heritage is undoubtedly one of the most promising and certainly one of the most important.

All the plurality of masterpieces (paintings, books, manuscripts, even photos of sculptures and architecture) can be effectively embedded into a unique "paradigm" through digitization. This allows a significant reduction in costs, an enormous expansion of public accessibility (and therefore income), and at the same time a tremendous freedom for data elaboration. In brief, digitization enhances pleasure for the public and usefulness to experts on cultural heritage assets. The use of multimedia technologies will allow the creation of new digital cultural experiences by means of personalized and engaging interaction. New

C. Grana and R. Cucchiara (Eds.): MM4CH 2011, CCIS 247, pp. 206–216, 2012.

multimedia technologies could be used also to design new approaches to the comprehension and fruition of artistic heritage, for example through smart, context-aware artifacts and enhanced interfaces that support features like story-telling, gaming and learning. To these aims, open and flexible platforms are needed to allow building services that support the use of cultural resources for research and education.

The informal working day, in which the 1st International Workshop on Multimedia for Cultural Heritage[1] was held, was a valuable opportunity to involve a wide range of users of cultural resources in diverse contexts. It was a profitable way to exchange ideas, opinions, experiences, and to share knowledge between participants. It also provided a fertile breeding ground for laying the foundations for future collaborations.

In the following sections we describe the outcome of the open discussion session of the workshop. The discussion topics, suggested by the organizers were the following:

1. Dealing with people/users
2. Deep archives
3. Technology that is useful
4. Funds and profit.

These suggestions originated from the third ICT Work Programme under FP7 of the EU, which defines the research priorities for 2011-12 in the fields of "Digital Preservation" (Objective 3 of Challenge 4: Technologies for Content and Languages) and "ICT for access to cultural resources" (Objective 2 of Challenge 8: ICT for Learning and Access to Cultural Resources) [1]. Many participants shared their ideas and insight on these topics, in order to further explore the future involvement of multimedia within cultural heritage.

2 Dealing with People/Users

Modern multimedia systems must be centered on user needs rather than on simply providing content and tailoring technical requirements of processing and storage systems [2]. As pioneered with the well known concepts of personalization, profiling and content adaptation in web contexts, we believe in the opportunity to apply the same kind of approach to the new generation of multimedia systems. The user's inclusion in the loop, leveraging on an engaging user-interaction design, allows systems to offer participation (thus interest) without boring the user with repetitive or irrelevant tasks, capitalizing on interaction as a primary source of knowledge with which to improve and personalize the multimedia experience. The analysis of user expectations is somehow fundamental to correctly designing the multimedia experience. In a general sense, we can highlight three aspects within the analysis:

[1] `http://imagelab.ing.unimore.it/MM4CH/MM4CH/Welcome/Welcome.html`

- the "utility of a multimedia system", defined as the level of satisfaction that a user can experience in front of it based on the raw list of functionalities;
- the "engagement", defined as the level of emotional satisfaction, which is not strictly related to the functionalities but also the quality of the interaction; and
- the "personalization", defined as the level of adaptation of the multimedia system to user habits, tastes and expectations.

These aspects do not have clear boundaries. The utility of a multimedia system is heavily influenced by the engagement they create through the user interface, the design of the application and the context in which it is proposed, the quality and the clarity of the interactive experience, and so on. Personalization can be seen by the user as a valuable and useful functionality (therefore influencing the perception of utility). Moreover some users could find engaging the possibility of personalizing the content and the interactive experience.

The utility of a multimedia system can be quite precisely evaluated in technical terms. In other words we can readily define, given the current literature background, which could be the most important functionalities to be included in the system, and we have metrics to evaluate the effectiveness of proposed results [3]. Nevertheless, academic research results sometimes are not (and typically do not have to be) instantly useful to the public. Most scientific research outcomes need time and effort to be engineered correctly, to become useful products and tools for users and not only for researchers. This could be a problem in the times of *instant experience*, i.e. the historical period in which the progress of technology and the interconnection of society boosted the demand of innovations, and add as a desired requisite the possibility of gathering in short times the benefits of innovations, in terms of great products and fulfilling experiences instantly available to customers.

The relation with users, in the design of the multimedia application for cultural heritage, should be profound: the user should be involved from the beginning of the innovation process itself, defining the functionalities, the boundaries and the interactions keeping the user constantly at the center of the design itself. Among all, interactions seems to be a key point to consider. The user interface and the user interaction paradigm is a fundamental aspect for every multimedia system, because it is the only part of the system which will actually link directly to the user's emotion. For this reason, if the proposed user interaction is good, the user will be pleased to come back and use the application again: good features with a bad interface are often rejected by users. This is also an highly desirable outcome especially if we want to pursue funding or self-funding in order to keep research and innovation alive.

We have to make technology work in the way users expect, employing natural interaction paradigms. The intuitiveness of a natural interface is therefore necessary even because most of these systems are oriented to public environments, with people passing through that begin interacting with the system moved by curiosity [4,5]. Consider, for example, the interactive navigation in the archaeological site of Shawbak proposed by Alisi *et al.* in [6], or the hand pointing

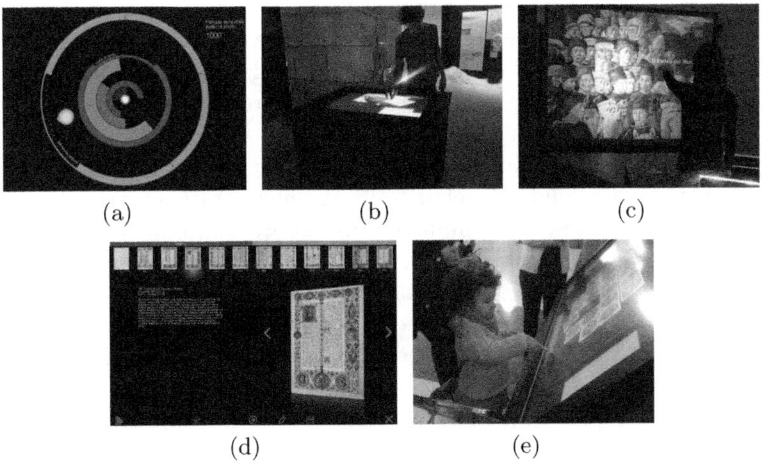

Fig. 1. Some example of innovative interactive installations for cultural heritage applications. In (a) and (b), a natural interaction based system designed to represent multimedia content related to the archaeological site of Shawbak (situated in the Petra region of Jordan) is presented. In (c) a nonintrusive system based on computer vision for human-computer interaction in 3D is exploited to augment the information recovery (of artists and artworks) while visiting a museum. In (d) and (e) Rerum Novarum, a multitouch installation for the interactive exploration of illuminated manuscripts.

understanding system in 3D environments proposed by Colombo *et al.* [7]. Grana *et al.* [8] showcased a multitouch media station for the interactive exploration of illuminated manuscripts, using classical image processing techniques, such as color features used in different contexts [9] and fast connected components labeling [10], combined with novel relevance feedback approaches. These are exemplars suitable for innovative interactive installations of interest for cultural heritage resources (Fig. 1).

People do not want to get bored learning how to interact: it should be a natural consequence of the interaction itself, with the system allowing the user to easily find out what is going on, maybe learning by imitation and thus encouraging the social aspects of the interaction.

Personalization can be considered another precious addition: the system can learn the needs, the expectations and even the artistic tastes of the user through logs and historical usage mining [11]. However we have to foresee how much this personalization is useful and, instead, the boundary beyond which personalization falls behind intuitiveness. In the same manner, we have to foresee the level of detail with which the functionalities must be implemented, evaluating correctly the user, his expertise and his expectations, and provide him with the right user interface. An example is "visual search" itself, one of the most attractive functionalities in such systems. This functionality is clear from the technical point of view of researchers in the field of multimedia retrieval but could be quite confusing from the users' perspective in some cases. Occasional users and visitors mainly interested in browsing an image collection could be frustrated, lost in the information sea without a specific goal. On the other side experts in the field of art and culture could find it far too rough, not sufficiently efficient for the specific searches they need.

This is the reason why, as multimedia researchers having by definition a very complex language, we have to change it. We must start adopting a more user-friendly and simple way of communicating innovation, both to art experts and people, learning for example from how Darwin's books (despite the fact that he was a scientist) were absolute bestsellers. We must improve our ability to explain to people how useful and fun the technologies we are able to produce are, and to experts the way in which they can be included in their research workflow and the positive impact they could have on it.

However, a complete and effective analysis, even from the marketing point of view, of this whole context is undoubtedly very complex. This is even more true considering that in some cases the general public might not be the main public we are referring to. Is it thus possible to achieve a single design able to fit the generally simple needs of normal people and at the same time the specific ones of experts, without sacrificing either the intuitiveness of the interaction and the power of advanced functionalities? Despite the fact that such a design could be considered a remarkable outcome, scientifically and economically and also in the eyes of users (interested, as mentioned before, in instant experiences), the risk is substantial. In fact we risk building a system which is inadequate for everyone. The alternative should be differentiation, but this opens up the dichotomy between general public models (cheaper but with a lower quality of experience) versus more costly and qualitatively better models but potentially segregated from most of the users and with negative impact on possible financial outcomes.

3 Deep Archives

An important category of recipients of such multimedia systems, within the class of experts, is the archivist. Probably this class of people is the most difficult to satisfy, basically for three important reasons:

- the level of detail for the required functionalities;
- the level of quality of results; and
- the amount of data they require to manage adequately.

Cultural archivists come from the cultural heritage community and they are used to particular *modus operandi* in their data management workflow. They require very specific functionalities and are used to a fine grained control over the database that manages data, rich metadata, and, sometimes, the documents in digital form. In Fig. 2 an example of user interaction with a specialised archive system, which manages both manuscript illustrations and rich metadata, is show [12].

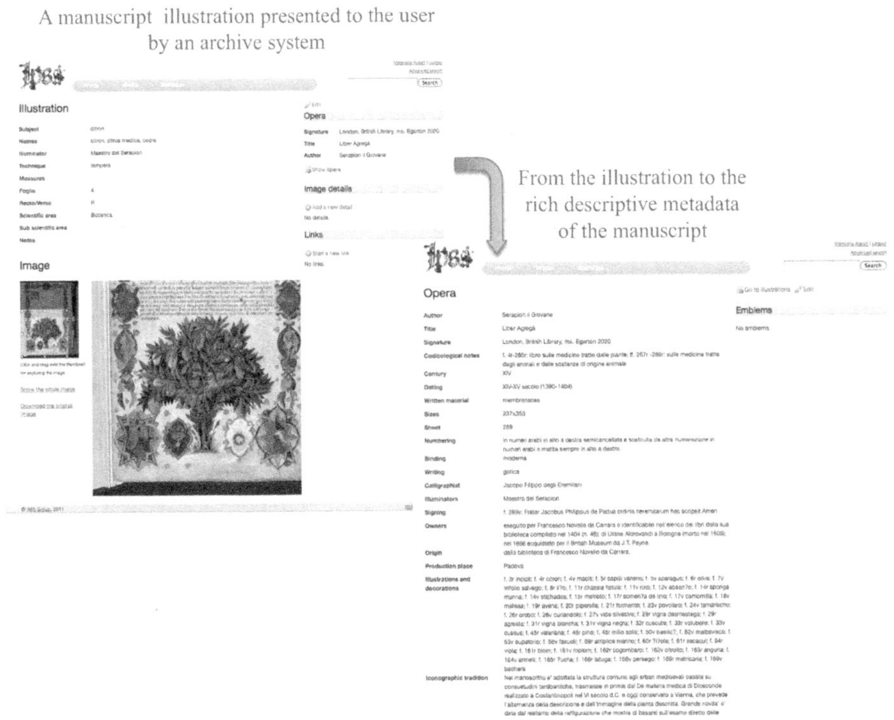

Fig. 2. User interaction/interface of an archive system specialised in the management of illuminated manuscripts

From a technical point of view, this may require a complication in the user interface and a major overhaul in the core logic of the multimedia system. This is a much more complex task considering the nature of the data we have to deal with – that is multimedia data like images, video and audio, in addition to text – and the amount of data. Efficient routines for the management of such sources are necessary. Moreover, people used to the quality of the results they can obtain in a controlled and structured context with SQL-based textual queries just expect the same quality of results moving to multimedia data. As researchers in this field, we should assure this level of quality.

To solve this problem the preferable choice should be the definition of content in a structured manner, using metadata and categorizations. Structured content leads us instantly to a situation in which interoperability is not just possible, but also easy to accomplish. Among the most used structured approaches, ontologies can be a good horse to bet on. Ontologies, and structured content in general, provide very good results, and a large volume of scientific literature has been produced to efficiently tackle the problem of management and querying. Nevertheless it is also known that the process of definition, design and building of the underlying architecture is long and costly, mainly due to the required standardization efforts. This problem can also become worse considering that different needs might demand different kinds of archives, in other words that the actual usage of an archive is somehow tailored to the design approaches. Is generalization possible in this situation? And how much time and money will it take?

An alternate solution is to rely on social metadata [13], very popular in recent years. The exploitation of the collaboration of a huge number of users, obtained by enticing them with appealing interaction paradigms, would allow the collection of a plethora of precious information that might benefit the level of engagement in the system and boost the possibility of personalization.

The other side of the coin is the social nature of such information. As covered by many works in the literature, especially in the field of social tagging and classification using social metadata as source of annotation, the information collected by users is noisy and unreliable. For this reason effective algorithms should be employed to filter them, maybe in collaboration with experts as "system administrators".

It finally must be noted that there are actually two kinds of perspectives in this situation: the people who build and populate these archives, and those who use them, i.e. the final users. It is therefore important to underline that, however complex the database architecture is, and however complex the routines to manage and query the database are, the final outcome of the interaction should be pleasant, both in terms of quality of retrieval and speed. In other words, the entire architectural complexity should be hidden from the user, and again appealing user interfaces should be provided to help the user to access the functionality of the system and the data it manages.

4 Technology That Is Useful

The last problem we need to tackle is purely an engineering one. In fact, by observing the situation from a birds-eye view and being aware of the aforementioned underlying problems, we need to provide solutions capable of covering these three aspects:

- the technological aspects, which is the set of technologies which are able to manage the data, accomplish the desired functionalities and present them to the user in an effective yet appealing way;
- the sociological aspects, being the set of policies required to deal with content; and
- the "philosophical" aspects, which deal with the amount of semantics, created and maintained by experts and researches in the field of the cultural heritage, which can be provided to the users as an immense added value to the artwork.

The technological, social and cultural substrata to sustain such aspects are indeed already available.

Modern technology, in terms of multimedia content analysis [14,15,16,17], large scale retrieval [18,19], multimodal aggregation of information sources and annotations [20] and finally database access and management approaches are available. These technologies offer quite generalizable solutions which can be easily adapted to work in very different contexts, and this is an important characteristic of a multimedia system for cultural heritage. In fact, the possibility of reusing the same system we developed for one museum with its particular focus and also for another museum or an exhibition, just because the underlying design has a structure that supports a number of different situations, is incredibly advantageous.

Standardization, even in this context, may be the best way to accomplish this outcome. Standardization, especially if derived from an international effort driven by important organizations and governments, allows a high level of interoperability between data and software components which will in turn represent a precious saving of money. Moreover, the use of platform independent software allows a great adaptivity, which gives the opportunity to apply the same solution to museums, exhibitions and libraries whichever information system they have. The openness of the platform and the software, even in this case, could result further savings in the long term.

The interoperability of data, partially included in the sociological aspects, means that the data should be open, not necessary in terms of ownership of the content but at least in terms of openness in the policies to access them, potentially encouraged and promoted by influential organization interested in the common good and aware of the importance of the spreading of culture. The content and the restrictions applied to it for copyrights, licenses and fees, in all these situations, is the weak ring of the chain. Some form of awareness campaigns, in the governments and in the public opinion, could be useful.

The inclusion of the world of the cultural heritage in the innovation process, so the participation of experts and researches in the fields of art, culture, history etc., should be extremely useful to bridge the "semantic gap" created by the community of engineers and researchers in multimedia retrieval. Collaboration could bring all these people to express directly to the actual developers what they like, and what they consider important in such applications. On the other hand, they should be the first beneficiaries of those innovations. This will provide to them advanced tools to make their research easier and more effective. In the end, the final user would have the possibility to enjoy in a more involving way the cultural content enriched by the use of advanced technologies and precious and detailed commentaries provided by experts.

5 Funds and Profit

Cultural heritage covers culture, art and education. Nevertheless all these activities can be supported only with a sufficient amount of funds to bootstrap, and a sufficient forecast of profit. The most common way of funding cultural heritage is pretty straightforward: regional, national and international funds to support culture are available, promoted by governments, organizations and foundations. The European Union itself appears particularly interested on this topic with the ICT Call 9 of the FP7, an opportunity to submit proposals in the field of "Digital Preservation" or of "ICT for access to cultural resources" [1]. These funds are however quite difficult to obtain, and sometimes may be not sufficient to satisfy the entire range of opportunities, especially in locations where the richness of history and culture is considerable. An ideal way to bootstrap these projects would be finding out a way to self funding the research and the activities. "City marketing" could be one possible way to do that.

City marketing consists in a strategic promotion of a city or a part of it, aimed at encouraging certain activities to take place there. The promotion of the overall image of the city can be a good means of promoting tourism, attracting new potential residents, and enabling business relocation. Therefore, it can also be used to attract inward investment and government funding to be devoted to cultural initiatives.

Self funding is the renewable energy of cultural heritage, but it supposes that some profit has to be achieved in order to make it possible. In the most common web-based business companies, the solution for this kind of problem is basically unique: advertising. The 98.7% of Google's turnover in 2010, for example, was obtained by advertising using the pay-per-click model. But does advertising fit with cultural heritage? Can we surround cultural content with advertising, however close to the users' interests, without sacrificing the importance of the work and the greatness of the artistic message, thus avoiding bothering him? Is there any kind of meaningful advertising content, maybe somehow related to other artistic content, that can be placed around artwork to generate significant revenue? The problem of profit is also related to who is actually supposed to make profit out of cultural heritage. The market in this context should be reserved to services and not content: in order to let the system work in the real world and to avoid that cultural content lose value and nobility (becoming a mere product), the content should be free, open and available everywhere. The services available with the content instead could be subjected to a fee or a payment. Instead, also the content could become a product: it is not so unusual to imagine selling cultural content in a way non dissimilar from what we are beginning to know in these years with the music and the movies (which are for all intents and purposes forms of art).

Nevertheless, in this situation, it is very important to analyze how people actually react to these proposals. The response of people is fundamental to create promising plans about how to make profit out of cultural heritage. Analyzing user expectations, as will be pointed out in the next section, could provide valuable information to prepare the content, to test the fruition methodologies, and to determine if a particular solution could lead to profit (because people will like it) or not. This kind of market study is necessary also because most of the people potentially interested in this kind of content (thus products and experiences) are not ready for the digital media/experience. Especially in the field of printing productions, including but not limited to cultural heritage ones, there is a significant problem regarding the transition from the physical format (i.e. the paper book) to the digital one (i.e. an e-book, or a multimedia application presenting in an augmented way his content). If the market is not ready, therefore if the potential customers are not really willing to change their perspective of usage and experience of such a content, there is a risk of proposing maybe very interesting prototypes from the scientific point of view but not sufficiently able to gather out profit.

6 Conclusions

As a concluding remark, we can state that the multimedia community has advanced technologies to apply to the field of cultural heritage, technology that can provide in an open and interoperable way software solutions and architectures. Intuitive interfaces will be able to capture both the public interest and the usefulness required by experts. From the other side of the river, the sense was that the community of art and cultural heritage is particularly interested on all these new possibilities. Listening to the participants of the workshop and their view of the situation, given their national or international experience, the overall perception was that, despite the economical difficulties, solutions are possible. The design of systems with a strong and long term strategy, including all protocols for the open exchange of information, will lead to impressive solutions that can radically change the way in which all people, at all level of expertise and expectations, interact with cultural heritage content.

Acknowledgements. The authors would like to thank all participants of MM4CH2011, and in particular Nicola Bernardini, Alberto Del Bimbo, Daniel Gatica-Perez, Joseph Llados, Luca Panini, Arnold Smeulders, Silvia Urbini.

The work of Maristella Agosti has been partially supported by the CULTURA project, as part of the Seventh Framework Programme of the European Commission, Area "Digital Libraries and Digital Preservation" (ICT-2009.4.1), grant agreement no. 269973. The work of Andrew D. Bagdanov has been supported by the MNEMOSYNE project (POR-FSE 2007-2013, A.IV-OB.2).

References

1. DigiCult: Expanding the use of Europe's cultural and scientific resources (2011), `http://cordis.europa.eu/fp7/ict/telearn-digicult/digicult_en.html`
2. Elgammal, A.: Human-centered multimedia: representations and challenges. In: ACM International Workshop on Human-Centered Multimedia, pp. 11–18 (2006)
3. Müller, H., Müller, W., Squire, D.M., Marchand-Maillet, S., Pun, T.: Performance evaluation in content-based image retrieval: overview and proposals. Pattern Recognition Letters 22(5), 593–601 (2001)
4. Jaimes, A., Gatica-Perez, D., Sebe, N., Huang, T.: Guest editors' introduction: Human-centered computing–toward a human revolution. Computer 40(5), 30–34 (2007)

5. Sebe, N.: Multimodal interfaces: Challenges and perspectives. Journal of Ambient Intelligence and Smart Environments 1, 23–30 (2009)
6. Alisi, T.M., D'Amico, G., Ferracani, A., Landucci, L., Torpei, N.: Natural interaction for cultural heritage: the archaeological site of shawbak. In: ACM Multimed. (2010)
7. Colombo, C., Del Bimbo, A., Valli, A.: Visual capture and understanding of hand pointing actions in a 3-d environment. IEEE Transactions on Systems Man and Cybernetics-B 33(4), 677–686 (2003)
8. Grana, C., Borghesani, D., Cucchiara, R.: Surfing on artistic documents with visually assisted tagging. In: Proceedings of the ACM International Conference on Multimedia, Florence, Italy, pp. 1343–1352 (October 2010)
9. Seidenari, S., Pellacani, G., Grana, C.: Computer description of colours in dermoscopic melanocytic lesion images reproducing clinical assessment. British Journal of Dermatology 149(3), 523–529 (2003)
10. Grana, C., Borghesani, D., Cucchiara, R.: Optimized block-based connected components labeling with decision trees. IEEE Transactions on Image Processing 19(6), 1596–1609 (2010)
11. Agosti, M., Crivellari, F., Di Nunzio, G.M.: Web log analysis: a review of a decade of studies about information acquisition, inspection and interpretation of user interaction. Data Mining and Knowledge Discovery, 1–34 (2011)
12. Agosti, M., Mariani Canova, G., Orio, N., Ponchia, C.: Methods of personalising a collection of images using linking annotations. In: Proceedings of the First Workshop on Personalised Multilingual Hypertext Retrieval (PMHR 2011), in conjunction with the ACM Hypertext 2011 Conference, pp. 10–17 (2011)
13. Agosti, M., Ferro, N., Frommholz, I., Thiel, U.: Annotations in Digital Libraries and Collaboratories Facets, Models and Usage. In: Heery, R., Lyon, L. (eds.) ECDL 2004. LNCS, vol. 3232, pp. 244–255. Springer, Heidelberg (2004)
14. Datta, R., Joshi, D., Li, J., Wang, J.Z.: Image retrieval: Ideas, influences, and trends of the new age. ACM Computer Surveys 40(2), 1–60 (2008)
15. Hurtut, T.: 2d artistic images analysis, a content-based survey. Technical report, Laboratoire d'Informatique PAris DEscartes - LIPADE - Université Paris Descartes (2011)
16. Uijlings, J.R.R., Smeulders, A.W.M., Scha, R.J.H.: Real-Time Bag of Words, Approximately. In: ACM International Conference on Image and Video Retrieval (2009)
17. van de Sande, K.E.A., Gevers, T., Snoek, C.G.M.: Evaluating color descriptors for object and scene recognition. IEEE T. Pattern Anal. 32(9), 1582–1596 (2010)
18. Torralba, A., Fergus, R., Weiss, Y.: Small codes and large image databases for recognition. In: IEEE International Conference on Computer Vision and Pattern Recognition, pp. 1–8 (August 2008)
19. Jégou, H., Douze, M., Schmid, C.: Product quantization for nearest neighbor search. IEEE T. Pattern Anal. 33(1), 117–128 (2011)
20. Datta, R., Ge, W., Li, J., Wang, J.Z.: Toward bridging the annotation-retrieval gap in image search by a generative modeling approach. In: ACM Multimedia, pp. 977–986 (2006)

Author Index